DEN OF LIONS

Memoirs of Seven Years

Terry Anderson

BALLANTINE BOOKS • NEW YORK

Library of Congress Catalog Card Number: 93-19802

ISBN 0-345-39054-7

This edition published by arrangement with Crown Publishers, Inc.

Cover photo of Terry Anderson at press conference in Wiesbaden, Germany 12/91, © Black Star/Peter Turnley.

Printed in Canada

First Ballantine Books Edition: December 1994

10 9 8 7 6 5 4

To my two daughters,
Gabrielle and Sulome,
equally beautiful,
equally loved.

ACKNOWLEDGMENTS

This book is our version of what happened to us over the past eight years or so. Other hostages have written their versions, some quite eloquently, and still other versions are yet to come. That there might be differences in facts and conclusions between this version and others should not surprise anyone. Each of us saw the same events from very different perspectives. Different things were important, and we understood the same things differently, often markedly differently. It is often difficult to figure out what's going on around you even when you're not blindfolded.

It should be apparent to all that the conversations in this book cannot be exact, despite the use of quotation marks. Neither Madeleine nor I had notes to refer to in writing it— only our memories. We are both satisfied that those memories are clear, despite the years that have passed, and that what we have quoted ourselves and others as saying is substantially accurate. Any errors are due to mistakes of memory.

There are a great many people who have had a hand in this book, and without whom it would not have been possible to finish it. Our families, of course, both the "official" ones—our brothers and sisters, Madeleine's mother, our many uncles, aunts, and cousins—and our AP family, most especially AP President Lou Boccardi and his wife, Joan, but including many others: Larry Heinzerling, who contributed much to the manuscript, Carolyn Turolla, Don Mell, and others.

By coincidence, it was Lou Boccardi's son Paul who as

assistant to the editor helped see the book through from its inception to its completion. Which brings us to the editor, James O'Shea Wade, vice president and senior editor of Crown. His wisdom, intelligence, and encyclopedic knowledge were both amazing and indispensable.

There were so many others. We are most grateful to the Freedom Forum Foundation for the generous fellowship at the Media Studies Center, Columbia University, that allowed us to write the book. The staff at the center has been efficient, friendly, and very patient with our haphazard way of working.

We're also grateful to the center's director, Ev Dennis, for his help and advice and for providing a first-class, top-drawer research assistant in Claudia Kalb. Claudia's ability, efficiency, and initiative has never flagged, nor has her cheerfulness in the face of the difficulties and complications we have caused her.

Finally, we want to acknowledge the efforts of all the people at Greater Talent Network, beginning with the boss, Don Epstein, and Holly Berger, who handles my schedule. It sounds simple, but she and I know how difficult it has been to keep track of where I was supposed to be at any one time, get me there on time and on to the next engagement, solve all the problems that seem to crop up at the worst moments, and still allow enough time to write.

There are others we have not named because they are too numerous. If this book is good, it is because of the help all of them gave us. If it is not, it is of course our responsibility alone.

PREFACE

This book is primarily a very personal account of my journey over the past eight years or so—an attempt to define who I was, and who I became under the pressure of the "fierce events" that overtook me. It is, as well, a small part of my fiancée's story—how she met the challenges that my kidnapping in the middle of her sixth month of pregnancy forced her to face, the loneliness and heartache of the next seven years, and the grace and courage she demonstrated so strongly. I have attempted to place these events in the context of what was going on in the outside world— Iran-Contra, the Gulf War, and so many other things that made the plight of the hostages in Lebanon so difficult and complicated—and to relate something of what I have since learned of the negotiations and dealings that ended this trying chapter in our nation's history.

The book should by right carry Madeleine's name on the title page, as well as mine. She wrote all of those sections under her name. I merely edited, and lightly at that.

It has been both easy and difficult to write this book. Easy, in that the events of those years remain vivid. Difficult, in trying to place myself back in those dark cells, to feel as I felt then, without allowing the powerful emotions of this past year of freedom get in the way.

It has also been useful in understanding what happened to me, personally and in the larger context of national and international events. More importantly, Madeleine and I have found that in writing each our own part of this book, we have been talking to each other, telling each other so much, and growing even closer together. Regardless of what others may find in it, that makes it for us a great success.

We have no lesson for anyone in mind, no message other than the events themselves relate. We do not know if there is anything here that others may make use of in their own lives. It is simply the story, as best we can tell it, of our time in the "Den of Lions."

Come away with me from Lebanon, my bride,
Come away with me from Lebanon;
Away from the peak of Amana,
Of Senir and of Hermon,
Away from the den of lions,
And the mountains of leopards.

Song of Solomon 4:8

ONE

STIGMATA I

Seven years in chains
while love lies barren,
while children grow;
one lost, one not known,
and others left unseeded
now will never be.
Grim, terrible years
in subterranean cells,
a pawn of evil hypocrites;
passed from hand to hand
across the Muslim archipelago,
taped and bagged like
some dead meat, despised,
inedible, but useful in a trade.
Harsh and painful years
of darkness, damp, and dirt,
humiliations heaped in myriads,
hatred and contempt received, returned.
Wasted, empty years? Not quite.
No years are empty in a life;
and wasted—that depends on
what is made of them, and after.

PROLOGUE

DAMASCUS, SYRIA.
DECEMBER 4, 1991.

Madeleine walked hesitantly into the large room. She was looking in the wrong direction, and didn't see me standing near the couch watching her.

It was after midnight of an incredibly long day. I hadn't slept the night before, waiting in that other, much smaller room, the last of so many prisons, for the end of our seven-year nightmare. It already seemed a thousand miles away, faded and dreamlike in my mind, drowned by the wave of emotion that had been building for weeks, ever since Tom Sutherland and Terry Waite had been taken out of our cell fifteen days ago, leaving me alone, the last of the American hostages.

I had been taken out of the cell, still blindfolded, just after dark. A short car ride, a last tirade from Ali about evil America, then the handover to Syrian intelligence—a colonel, who put his hand on my shoulder and told me, "You're free." I took off my blindfold and dropped it beside me, onto the road. Into the small sedan. No rush of joy, no real feeling at all for the first few minutes, just the strangeness of being able to look around freely. The night was clear, I recognized the road—Baalbek, as we had thought. Past the ancient Roman ruins. A sign, the road to Chtaura. Everything seemed new, especially the highway. Lots of new apartments, small office buildings. Last time I was there, seven years ago, the road was still narrow, potholed, and the years of war had left their mark everywhere. No sign of it now.

The beauty of the stars, unseen for so long, suddenly hit me. I leaned forward, peered up through the windshield awkwardly. After a minute or two, I heard the driver exchange a few words with the three agents in the backseat. Everyone laughed. I looked over, and he pointed up. There was a clear sunroof above me. I spent much of the forty-five-minute ride leaning back. The Big Dipper. Orion's Belt? Where is Cassiopeia? Then the lights of Damascus dimmed the stars.

A long, boring session at Syrian intelligence headquarters, as some general talked on and on about Saddam Hussein, his country's deadly enemy. He even showed a videotape of the Iraqi leader, as I shifted restlessly, looking pointedly at my watch. Patience. You should have learned that by now.

Then the short ride to the Foreign Ministry. I knew the drill, had listened so many times as my fellow hostages went through the dance. Into a small room where the American ambassador, Syrian deputy foreign minister, others are waiting. I'm introduced to the slim, handsome man standing quietly against the wall—Giandomenico Picco, the assistant UN secretary-general who had negotiated the series of releases over the last year, whom we had followed in his travels so intensely, hunching over the radio to catch each hint of progress, flinching at each setback.

"I've been wanting to meet you for a long time," I joked. He smiled, shaking my hand. "Me, too."

Short briefing, then down the hall into a small room jammed with reporters, cameras, glaring lights. All the carefully rehearsed speeches, the neat little phrases I'd been preparing disappeared. I was almost frightened, until I saw the enormous shaggy gray beard of Alex Efty, The AP's Cyprus correspondent. He grabbed me in a bear hug. There was Bill Foley, grinning at me over his camera. He looked as if he was crying! Others, old friends, colleagues, jammed shoulder to shoulder.

Speeches from the ambassador, the foreign minister, Giandomenico, mercifully brief. I made the obligatory gesture of thanks to the United Nations, Syria, Iran, answered a few questions, then begged to be excused. "I have an appointment with a couple of very beautiful ladies, and I'm late already." Laughter, a graceful exit.

The Syrians gone, I was in the hands of the Americans now, in the ambassador's car. My stomach felt hollow, the tension seemed to vibrate through my chest, almost audible. Not unpleasant, but building. A few minutes. Lord, thank you. Let it be all right.

Into the ambassador's residence. My minder, a pleasant young lady whose name I missed, guided me into a room.

"Do you want to see Madeleine now?"

"Yes. Of course I do."

Everyone left immediately. I stood in front of the couch, glanced around. Typical embassy, comfortable, expensively furnished.

Dear God, there she is. She looked so scared, even smaller than her five-one frame. Her hair was still long, hanging heavy and deep black. She glanced my way, spotted me, her eyes huge and dark. We walked slowly toward each other, and she was in my arms, her body slim and taut against mine. I stroked her hair, murmured, "It's all right. It's over. It's okay." She was crying, holding tight, reaching up to touch my face. I could feel the tears pressing against the back of my eyes. "It's over."

The feel of her, the smell of her, recalled so many times over the years until it was more imagination than memory, instantly seemed to erase the 2,454 days we had been apart, as if it had been only hours since I left her in bed, sleepy, six months pregnant, content. Almost seven years. March 16, 1985.

STIGMATA II

Pursuing idle pleasures,
abruptly snatched by wild
fantassins waving guns,
pushed and pulled down
from the sunny heights
into a darker world
where venomed voices
whisper menace and blows
erupt out of the night.
There's no appeal;
the laws and judges
of this court are ruthless,
mercy's alien and justice
twisted out of shape.
A man is just a thing
to be abused or not for
any whim or aim, or none.

BEIRUT. 8 A.M. MARCH 16, 1985.

The green Mercedes, sparkling clean in the weak morning
sunlight, drifted to a gentle halt in the narrow road, just a
few yards up the hill from the graffiti-covered monument to
Gamal Abdul Nasser. Don Mell, the young AP photographer I was dropping off at his apartment after our tennis
game, had noticed it earlier at the sports club but hadn't
mentioned it—it didn't seem important. Now, though, it
struck him as odd, especially the curtains drawn over the
rear window.

"A hamster-mobile," he remarked, using the nickname

6

given by journalists to all the armed young men swarming in and around Beirut.

The joke, already worn, seemed even less amusing when three unshaven young men threw open the doors and jumped out, each holding a 9mm pistol in his right hand, hanging loosely by his side.

My mind seemed to stall for a few seconds, and by the time I realized what was happening, one of the men was beside the driver's door of my car, yanking it open and pushing his pistol at my head. "Get out," he said fiercely. "I will shoot. I will shoot."

"Okay," I answered quickly. I pulled the keys from the ignition and dropped them between the seats. "Okay, no problem. No problem."

He reached in and pulled the glasses from my face. As I slid out of the seat, half crouched, he put his hand around my shoulders, forcing me to remain bent over.

"Come, come quickly."

I glanced up at Don, just a vague blur on the other side of the car, willing him to run, but not daring to shout the words. He just stood, frozen.

The young man, dark and very Arab-looking, perhaps twenty or twenty-five, pulled me along beside him toward the Mercedes, just four or five yards away, still forcing me to remain half bent.

"Get in. I will shoot," he hissed at me, pushing me into the backseat. "Get down. Get down."

I tried to crouch in the narrow space between the front and back seats. Another young man jumped in the other door and shoved me to the floor, throwing an old blanket over me, then shoving my head and body down with both his feet. I could feel a gun barrel pushing at my neck. "Get down. Get down."

The car lurched into gear and accelerated madly up the hill a few yards, almost slid around a corner, then another, and up a short hill.

The front-seat passenger leaned over the back of his seat. "Don't worry. It's political," he said in a normal tone as the car lurched back and forth, the driver cutting in and out of traffic.

The strange comment, apparently meant to be reassuring, wasn't. As my mind began to function again, it made me think of the other Americans kidnapped in Beirut for political reasons. William Buckley, missing twelve months. The Reverend Benjamin Weir, missing ten months. Father Lawrence Martin Jenco, missing two months.

There wasn't any real fear yet—it was drowned by adrenaline. Just a loud, repeating mental refrain: Anderson, you stupid shit, you're in deep, deep trouble.

The car rocked as it careened around corner after corner, left and right in apparent random. The left side of my face was pressed hard against the carpeted floor. The rough blanket made breathing difficult. Someone's foot was still resting on my head, skidding across my skull as its owner swayed with the car's motion. I could follow the route—I'd been through these streets so many times, in danger and for pleasure: through Basta, the slum area filled with Shiite refugees above the port, then up the hill into Hamra, down Bliss Street in front of the American University campus, tires screeching down the twisting, steep descent to the Corniche along the Mediterranean. Then a long, straight stretch in heavy traffic, the driver cutting into the oncoming lane and blasting the cars away with his horn. Down the coast to another slum—Ouzai, on the edge of the airport.

There was no conversation in the car, except for an occasional muttered "Down, down," and a shove with the foot, or a poke with a gun into my back. The gunmen said nothing to each other.

After fifteen or twenty minutes, the car turned off the main highway straight into what seemed to be a garage. A metal door clanged down, cutting off the street noise. The doors were yanked open, and hands grabbed at me, pulling me upright, but careful to keep the blanket over my head. There were mutterings in Arabic, short, guttural, incomprehensible.

Someone slipped the blanket away, slipping a dirty cloth

around my head at the same time, then wrapping plastic tape around and around. Other hands grabbed at my tennis shoes, yanking them off. Someone pulled at the gold chain around my neck, fumbled with the fastening until it opened. Then the gold bracelet on my right wrist, the watch on my left, also went.

"Don't," I said, involuntarily. "They're gifts. Don't take them."

"We are not thieves," one of the men said. He stuck my watch into my sock. Not the chain or bracelet. I never saw either again.

More tape, around my wrists and arms. I was pulled out of the car and guided clumsily to the side of the garage, pushed down onto a filthy blanket smelling of oil and gasoline.

My legs were taped tightly, around the ankles, knees, and thighs. I could no longer sit upright and slid sideways. One of the men lifted me up by my arm and shoulder and propped me against the wall.

The men talked among themselves for a few minutes, then several left. Only one seemed to be still with me, pacing back and forth.

After a while—twenty minutes? An hour? No way to tell—they came back. I was pulled upright, guided across the floor, and seated again.

"What is your name?" a voice asked, heavily accented.

"Terry Anderson. I am a journalist."

"Your company?"

"The Associated Press. A wire service."

The man seemed uninterested in my answers. Either he understood "wire service"—unlikely—or he didn't care.

"Why have you taken me? Who are you?"

Muttering in Arabic. "Quiet. We ask questions. Do you know where you are?"

"No." Explaining my deductions didn't seem wise.

"You are a spy."

"No. I am a journalist. I work for The Associated Press. What do you want from me?"

The interrogation went on, almost aimlessly, without heat. Accusations. Denials.

"Why do you have this?" A hand shoved something at me. Peering along my nose, through the small gap it made in the tape around my head, I saw the gold charm from my chain—an inscription from the Koran.

"It was a gift."

"You are Muslim?"

"No. Christian."

"Why do you wear this?"

"My wife gave it to me."

"She is Muslim?"

"No. Maronite. Catholic."

"You are not Muslim. Why do you wear words from the Koran?"

"They are beautiful. They are the words of God."

He was obviously unsatisfied, and muttered to his companions. Then more serious questions.

"What other Americans do you know? Who works at your office?"

"I can't tell you that."

"You must say. Give us the names of all the Americans you know."

"No. I can't do that."

"We can make you."

"I know you can try. You can hurt me. But I can't give you the names of my friends."

"We have electricity. You know?"

"Yes. I know. But I still won't give you names. They are my friends. I can't help you kidnap them." I decided to take a chance.

"Can you call my office? Tell them I am alive? My wife will be very, very worried."

"You want your wife here? We can go get her, bring her here."

"She is pregnant. You would not harm her. You cannot be so evil."

"We will take her, too. No one can stop us."

"God will stop you. No one has to stop you. You will not do this."

"Give us the names."

"No. I'm sorry. I can't. Do what you want to. I still can't."

More demands. Refusals. Strangely, the procedure was still without heat. It didn't seem as if they really meant the threats. It was hard to believe they might carry them out, though nothing I had ever seen in Lebanon gave me any confidence in their humanity or reluctance to inflict pain. They just didn't seem serious about it.

It ended after perhaps thirty or forty minutes. The men got up and left, except for one. He shoved me back against the wall, resumed pacing.

I could think of nothing except Madeleine, still in bed, sleepily kissing me good-bye at seven A.M. Six months pregnant, her belly making a mound of the blanket. She would know soon, probably knew already. Don would have gone straight to the office, alerted the AP people there. They would have gone to our apartment, just a few hundred yards from where I was kidnapped.

I began crying silently, rocking forward and back against the wall, my knees shoved tightly between my taped arms. Who would tell her? How? I twisted my wrists against the tape, struggling against it. The guard came, bent over and, surprisingly gently, put his hand on my arm. "No. No. No good."

I stopped struggling and tried to compose my mind. Breathe evenly, smoothly, gently. Calm. Don't think. Calm.

After a time, listening to traffic sounds outside, and people moving around inside the building, I realized several hours had passed. I needed to urinate. I groped mentally for the scraps of Arabic I had picked up in the past two years. "Hello. Excuse me. *Chebab*." Mister.

"Shu?" What?

"I need toilet. Toilet."

He pulled me upright, back against the wall, awkwardly balancing with my taped legs and arms. Then he picked up a tin can and held it near the front of my tennis shorts. I pulled them down in front with my thumbs, and tried to urinate, but couldn't, through embarrassment and awkwardness. "Sorry." Without replying, he put down the can, then lowered me to the floor.

A few minutes later, he brought half of a hamburger in a bun to me, and a can of Coke. *"Jowan?"* Hungry?

"Thank you." Taking a bite, I realized I hadn't eaten since the night before. I finished the half-can of Coke, which he held, then again told him, "Toilet." He helped me up, picked up the can, and held it. This time, success. Relief. Back to the floor.

It was probably around midnight before the others returned. They checked and renewed the tape, adding more around my mouth. Two of them picked me up by legs and shoulders and carried me back to the car, dumping me in the trunk. The lid closed.

2

PRIORITY:—URGENT—
THE ASSOCIATED PRESS
Copyright 1985 By The Associated Press.
All Rights Reserved.
DATE: Saturday, March 16, 1985
TIME-STAMP: 0414EST
SLUG: Reporter Kidnapped
DATELINE: BEIRUT, Lebanon

Terry A. Anderson, Chief Middle East Correspondent of The Associated Press, was kidnapped by armed men off a street in mostly Moslem west Beirut on Saturday morning.

Donald Mell, a photographer for the AP, witnessed the abduction and said three bearded men, two armed with pistols, forced Anderson into a green Mercedes and sped off.

The abduction took place in the Ein Mreisse section of west Beirut just after 8 a.m.

G.G. Labelle, Middle East news editor for The AP, said the agency was informing police, government and militia leaders and asking their assistance in gaining Anderson's release.

Nate Polowetzky, foreign editor of The Associated Press, said in New York: "We are deeply concerned about the events in Beirut, and are seeking all possible information regarding the welfare of Associated Press correspondent Terry Anderson. We will, of course, pursue all avenues for his release and safe return."

PRIORITY:—URGENT—END

BEIRUT. MARCH 16, 1985.

The apartment building we ended up in was only half finished. Peering through gaps in the tape around my eyes as I was hauled and bumped up flight after flight of stairs, I could see shoes and slippers in front of the apartment doors in the first few floors, then bare concrete, roughly finished, and empty door frames.

My guards huffed and cursed in Arabic at the 185 pounds of deadweight they were awkwardly hauling. Occasionally my head would hit the wall, or a stair corner.

Finally we arrived. I was dumped on a steel cot, with a thin mattress over the springs. A chain with two-inch links was attached to both my feet and fastened with a large padlock on each ankle. Another chain was wrapped around my left wrist and padlocked, and a fourth on my right.

The chains, apparently fastened to the walls, were not long enough to allow me to sit up, even if I had been allowed. It was quickly made apparent to me that I was not.

I have in my mind a mélange of images of those first few weeks: sharp, crystal-clear moments from which I can call up every detail—the creaking of the metal cot; the pebbly texture of the plastic bottle I used to pee in, rolling sideways and straining at the chains so as not to stain the mattress, and the slightly different shape of the nearly identical bottle containing my water; the sounds of my guards walking past the cot, or arguing among themselves; the noises of the street outside the building. These are surrounded by blurred hours and days, colors and emotions, rage and tears, frustration and remorse.

I remember waking up at dawn one morning, after a fitful hour or two dozing, to find my blindfold had slipped.

I'd been warned repeatedly and emphatically about that strip of filthy cloth. If I attempted to see anything, I would be killed immediately. Reaching up cautiously, I began to pull it straight. The guard lying on a mattress a few feet away stirred, and I felt the hard barrel of a gun touching my neck. "What you do?"

"It slipped. I was asleep."

"Careful."

"Yes."

Outside, the war continued. I could hear shelling and automatic rifle fire from time to time.

I was slowly being taught the rules of this new existence, with a combination of slaps and punches when I did something wrong, and short, nearly incomprehensible bursts of broken English. No noise, no speaking. Even rolling from side to side on the bed to relieve the painful muscle cramps brought on by lying still for hours would earn a slap or a poke with a gun. "Hssst. No move." The metal cot creaked with every small motion.

Occasionally, three or four young militiamen would burst into the room, fresh from the fighting outside. Chattering, laughing, cursing, they were high on adrenaline. When their attention turned to me, they'd curse or spit: "Death to America"—they were a cliché come alive. I'd felt their hatred before, in brief encounters with the bearded fanatics increasingly common in Lebanon. Now, though, I was helpless, a toy these young men were using to play out their power fantasies.

Twenty-four days. It must be about the eighth of April. I'd kept track by scratching a line in the wall next to my head each gray dawn, beginning with what I thought was the third day. My body was locked for hours each day in cramps from the effort of not moving. I was exhausted by the ceaselessly churning thoughts in my head, images of my family, friends, wrung by emotions so sharp and strong, my chest hurt.

Around and around, over and over, remorse, anger, pain.

Replaying endless scenarios in which I escaped, gunned the car, jumped out and dropped my kidnapper with a karate blow, grabbed his gun and shot him—useless, childish plays. Humiliation of trying to pee in a bottle while lying down. Humiliation of being poked and prodded and cursed at. I knew I was on the edge of madness, of losing control completely, breaking down.

Finally, as one of the guards walked past my cot, I called out softly. "*Chebab*. Hey."

"*Shu?*"

"*Tehki Inglisi?*" Speak English?

"*Lahsa.*" One moment.

He left, came back with another guard.

"What?"

"I can't do this anymore. I am not an animal. I am a human being. You can't treat me like this."

"What do you want?"

"A book. A Bible. And to move. You must loosen these chains. I will go crazy."

A grunt. The two guards exchanged a few words.

"I speak chef."

"Thank you."

The next day, late in the afternoon, the English-speaking guard came in and threw a heavy object on the bed. I reached for it, felt the smooth covers of a book.

The guard came around to the head of the bed.

"Good?"

"Yes, very good, thank you."

He began fiddling with the chain on my right hand. After some fumbling, he got the lock open, then replaced it, but allowing a foot or so more chain. Moving around the bed, he did the same on the other side.

"Sit up. But no look."

I sat up slowly, stiffly. He pulled the blanket off me and draped it over my head, leaving it hanging in front of my face. "Now look."

I cautiously pulled my blindfold up a bit, until I could

see the book. Red, new. A Bible, the Revised Standard Version. I caressed it gently.

"May I read now?"

"Thirty minutes. Be careful. No look."

"Thank you."

I leaned forward so the blanket would hang down over my face, but allow light from the bulb above me to fall on the book in my lap. Opening the cover gently, I sniffed at the pages, inhaling the new-book, paper-and-ink smell like perfume. My back started aching almost immediately, but I ignored it.

I read the title page, the publishing and copyright information, the notes of the editors, slowly, carefully. Then: Genesis.

"In the Beginning . . ."

TWO

Wait for me, and I'll return
Only wait very hard . . .
Wait. For I'll return, defying every death.
And let those who do not wait, say that I was
   lucky.
They never will understand that in the midst of
   death,
You with your waiting saved me.
Only you and I know how I survived.
It's because you waited, as no one else did.

Konstantin Simonov

3

MADELEINE

BEIRUT, LEBANON.
MARCH 16, 1985.

When I opened my eyes, I was looking straight at the clock on the wall: 8:30 A.M. Terry's not back from his tennis game yet. When he woke me with a kiss at seven, he said he'd be back by this time. We'd promised each other that no matter what happened, we would always be on time for our meetings. When someone you love is late in Beirut, you worry.

He'll be home any minute now, I thought. It's Saturday, my day off, and I can use another hour of sleep. I dozed off. It was about ten o'clock when our cleaning lady, Umm Mahmoud, opened the bedroom door, waking me. I was shocked at her coming into our bedroom. "What are you doing, Umm Mahmoud?"

"Oh, we thought you were sleeping at your mother's," she answered.

That's crazy. Why should she think I'm sleeping at my mother's? This is my home. I live here. What is she talking about? Why is she looking at me so strangely? And who are "we"?

"Where is Terry?"

She mumbled something I couldn't understand, but I realized something was wrong. For a second, I hoped she'd tell me he'd had an accident. Accidents are common in Lebanon, dangerous but seldom deadly.

21

"*Mustapha wants to talk to you,*" she said, still looking at me strangely.

Why would our landlord want to see me now?

"*What does he want?*"

"*I don't know.*"

Suddenly, I realized I was standing beside the bed naked, with my huge belly. Umm Mahmoud turned away, saying, "*Bismullah Al Rahman Al Rahim.*" In the name of God, the compassionate, the merciful. She left the room. I hurriedly dressed and ran out of the apartment and down the stairs to Mustapha's place on the ground floor. He was standing outside his door with his sister and her two daughters. They all looked upset, even angry. As they saw me, they fell silent and stared.

"*What's going on, Mustapha?*"

He began to mumble, just like Umm Mahmoud. Then he said more clearly that Bill Foley, a friend and former AP photographer who lived on the first floor, wanted to talk to me.

I knew something was badly wrong. I ran up the stairs again to Bill's flat. The door was open, and as he heard me coming, he came out. He looked sadly into my eyes and opened his arms to me. His girlfriend, Cary, was standing behind him. My mind was racing. I couldn't believe what I was beginning to think. It couldn't be true.

"*Did they take him, Bill? Did they take Terry?*"

He held me tightly, as if trying to protect me from something. He nodded his head. I could feel him crying.

The first thing I thought of was, I want to be with him, I want to be there, too, wherever he is. I felt terribly lost and confused.

Cary, who was crying also, took me into the apartment, tried to calm me down. I could hear her repeating, "*It will be all right. I'm sure he'll be freed soon.*"

I can't believe she's talking about Terry. I can't think anymore. Oh, my God, Terry kidnapped. It's not true. Please, God, it's not true. There must be a mistake. They, whoever they are, can't want Terry.

Bill talked to someone on the telephone, then came over to tell me what Don Mell had told him: A car followed them from the sports club, where they had played tennis, and as Terry stopped to let Don out at his apartment building, three men with pistols grabbed Terry, put him in their car, and drove off. Don tried to follow them with Terry's car, but lost them after a few blocks. He came to our place to tell me, knocked on the door several times, but when I didn't respond went on to the office.

"I want to see Don," I told Bill. My mind was numb. Everything seemed like a dream. I couldn't feel my body.

As we left the building, a CBS TV crew was waiting to talk to me. The cameraman asked if I would say something. I was crying. "What can I tell you? I have nothing to tell you."

I had worked on the story when the Reverend Ben Weir was kidnapped. I had seen his wife in our office, at NBC. I had watched her cry, and felt her pain. My mind rejected the thought of being one of those women whose man had been taken. This is not happening to us. I knew then I would never talk to the press.

When we arrived at the AP office, all our friends were busy working on the story. As I came in, they all stopped for a few seconds. One by one, they came to me, reassured me. Scheherazade, Eileen, Gerry, Farouk, Charles, Rima. They all looked devastated by the news, and seemed to be as lost as I was. The phones were ringing, some of our friends were writing, others were calling government officials, militia offices, party leaders. It was complete chaos.

Scheherazade took me into the back office. Muhieddine, the AP driver, asked me if I wanted coffee. Terry always said he made the best coffee. I had been in the office many times before, waiting for Terry to finish up a story. It was always pleasant to sit here at the end of our day. Now I'm sitting here watching them all working on Terry's story. This is only a dream. I will go home, go to sleep, and when I wake up in the morning, none of this will be true.

I knew I had to do something, but I didn't know what.

One thing kept running through my mind. Terry. Terry will come back tonight. He'll convince those people of the mistake they are making. Surely, it's the same people who took Steve Haguey a few weeks ago. They let him go after just a day. Terry called all sorts of people when Steve was taken, and it worked. It must be the same people. It can't be Islamic Jihad. It can't be. As long as we don't hear from them, we're okay. Terry is okay.

I wanted to call my family to reassure them. They must have heard the news on the radio. They're probably calling me at home. But I just sat there, without moving, watching the others as if they were on a screen. I can't even remember hearing their voices. There was only one voice in my mind.

Don arrived and repeated his story, as if he himself couldn't believe it. I could see he was still in shock. Robert Fisk, of the London Times, *was there at the AP office, trying to figure out what to do. Robert was Terry's close friend. They had encountered danger so many times together covering the war. His face was pale. I had rarely seen Robert scared. Today he was scared, and helpless. He wasn't just covering another kidnapping. This was Terry. It was Terry for all of them, and they were all helpless.*

I stayed in the office most of the day watching, waiting for something to happen, but nothing did. There was no news, no result for all the effort everyone was making.

Finally, Scheherazade asked me if I wanted her to come and stay with me that night. I was very grateful, and said yes. Later, Robert came to the apartment and spent the night on the couch.

Around two A.M., Terry's brother Rich called from Florida. I cried my heart out to him on the phone. He didn't know what to do, and asked me if there was anything I could think of. I had no answer. He told me if I wanted to come to the States to wait for Terry, his home was mine. I had no intention then of going anywhere. Terry might make it, might come home, and I was going to be here waiting for him.

Sunday morning, I asked Scheherazade to come along with me to visit a friend who had had a baby Saturday and was still in the hospital. If Terry were here, we would have gone together—they were his friends, as well.

We went from the hospital to the AP office. There had been no calls, no claims. We were as afraid of knowing Terry's whereabouts as we were of not knowing. As long as we didn't hear from the Jihad, Terry had a better chance to come home sooner rather than later. Scheherazade and I went home to the apartment.

It was around seven P.M. when a neighbor who lived below us came to tell me there was a call for me in her house. The AP had been trying to reach me, but couldn't get through on our phone. Telephone service in Beirut was often erratic, at best.

The neighbor, Gina, looked very pale. It scared me, especially when she tried to smile. My heart was beating very fast. I was afraid to pick up the phone. The voice on the line sounded deep and apologetic. Whoever it was said he was very sorry, but he had just had a call from Reuters News Agency saying a man claiming to be from the Islamic Jihad had called them to claim Terry's kidnapping. He continued talking, but I couldn't hear him. I could only hear my heart beating so fast, my voice screaming, "I don't want to know more. Oh, please God, why? Not the Jihad." Suddenly there were more people in the room, crying with me. They took me up to our flat and tried to calm me down.

I have never been as scared in my life as I was that moment. I felt helpless. Terry, in the hands of those people. What will they do to him? I tried to remember Jeremy Levin, and his accounts when he got out, of how the kidnappers treated him the day they took him. I thought about the baby I was carrying, of Terry and me.

Oh, God, have mercy on us.

I went to the office every day that first week, hoping for news, something, a word, from anyone. No one knew anything. None of the efforts everyone was making to trace Terry's whereabouts came up with anything. Pictures of him

*were distributed in Beirut by The AP, as well as in the
Bekaa Valley, eastern Lebanon, southern Lebanon. In Beirut, militia leaders and Shiite spiritual leaders were de-
nouncing the abduction, but did nothing further to try to
end it.*

*The silence was killing me. I knew that the longer they
kept silent, the longer it was likely he would stay there. If
anything was going to happen to get him out, it had to be
done now. They had already been holding three hostages
for many months: William Buckley, the Reverend Benjamin
Weir, and Father Martin Jenco. Levin managed to get away
in February—whether he'd escaped or been released was
still a mystery. Now Terry had joined the list. Islamic Jihad
didn't seem to be getting anywhere with the U.S. government. They needed more hostages. The Shiite fundamentalists' hatred of America and the West had made them blind
to any human rights. They couldn't tell their enemies from
their friends anymore. And their power had been growing
rapidly in the last year.*

*Lebanon was being ruled by the weakest government
since the war began, divided among parties from all sects.
The Christians who had dominated the country since its
birth in 1943 were split, with even the powerful Maronite
Catholic sect divided among feudal families. The Maronites
were locked in deadly enmity with the Druse, a much
smaller but fierce sect dominating a large section of Lebanon's central mountains.*

*The Muslims were split between Sunnis, careful business-
men and old families in large part, and Shiites, mostly poor
and originally laborers from southern Lebanon and the
Bekaa Valley. But the once-quiescent Shiites, oppressed and
exploited by the other sects, had become angry and radical-
ized. They were inspired by the Islamic Revolution of their
fellow Shiites in Iran, and by the unofficial but undoubted
fact that they outnumbered all the other sects, and probably
made up more than half of Lebanon's population of three or
four million. The fundamentalists in Iran were sending
money and mullahs to preach revolution and hatred of the*

West to the Shiites. Israel, now ruling their home territory in the south with a very heavy hand, only fueled the fire.

All of these factions were locked into a struggle over the rigid and now outdated unwritten agreement, called the National Covenant, dictated by the French before they left: the Maronites would provide a president, the Sunnis a prime minister, the Shia a speaker of parliament, and the Druse some senior military men. Every government office and job in the country was allotted by that formula.

That already terribly complicated situation was further enflamed by an influx of Palestinians who had been kicked out of Jordan in 1970, and insisted on waging their war against Israel from Lebanese soil, and the meddling of everyone in the Middle East, including Israel and Syria, the next-door giant from which all that was now Lebanon had been taken just fifty years before, and which refused to really acknowledge that independence.

The mixture had erupted into civil war in 1975—a war that had still not ended and would continue for sixteen years.

Among the most fearsome of the many radical groups that plagued Lebanon was the one that called itself Islamic Jihad—Islamic Holy War. It was believed to be a cell of Hezbollah, the Iranian-founded Party of God, and was creating an atmosphere of terror that enveloped Westerners and Lebanese.

Tens of thousands of Shiites had been driven out of their homes in the south by the fighting between Palestinians and Israelis in the first Israeli invasion, in 1978, then by the 1982 Israeli invasion and continuing occupation. They took refuge in Beirut's suburbs—a matter both inconvenient and unpleasant for the Lebanese who originally lived there.

I am a Maronite Catholic, but was still living in the old West Beirut neighborhood, now largely Muslim, where I was brought up. It had changed greatly over the years. Once a pleasant area near the yacht club and harbor, Minet El-Hosn was now filled with refugees, mostly Shiites. A block away, the nineteen-story Holiday Inn, com-

pleted in 1975, was a shell-pocked artillery observation and sniping post, as well as a militia headquarters.

All of my family's longtime neighbors and friends had left during the first few years of the war. Their homes had been ransacked by whatever party or militia group happened to hold the area after each period of fighting. There were still many non-Shiites there, both Christians and Sunni Muslims, but the fundamentalists among the refugees had managed to take control.

My family consisted almost entirely of women—my mother, two sisters, two nieces. We also had a brother, but he had left the country. As the number of Shiites there grew, and the power of the fundamentalists became established, it became harder and harder to lead our own lives. We were obliged to take account of Shiite sensibilities in dress, behavior, even in practicing our religion. We could not wear short skirts, or be seen with any man not known to be a fiancé or husband. We did not even dare to make the sign of the cross, or go to midnight mass at Christmas.

Whether it was the new sense of power the fundamentalists were gaining after years of oppression or the ambition they had for themselves and for their cause, some kind of a monster was being born, and could not be stopped. It was interfering in our private lives.

The fundamentalists seemed to hate everything and everyone who was not of their religion. They believed the West and Satan America were behind every evil that occurred in Lebanon, and Israel was America's instrument for bringing that evil about. They believed they had to fight back with the only weapon they had—kidnapping of Westerners.

By no means did all Shiites think that way. Most were just ordinary Lebanese, trying to live their lives. But those who disagreed could not express their opinion. It was not practical to oppose the power that protected them, and fed their children when they could not do it themselves.

When the civil war had started in 1975, I had gone ahead with plans I had to travel to England. Like many

Lebanese, I thought the war would last only a few months. As the Americans had in 1958, some country or other would interfere and stop it quickly. I was wrong. This war was fiercer than anything the Lebanese had ever witnessed. The hatred that had accumulated between the Christians on one side and the Palestinians and their Lebanese Muslim allies on the other was beyond comprehension.

I had left Lebanon at the beginning of the civil war. I spent about a year in England, visiting my sister and her family, then four years in Sweden after I married a Swedish man. The marriage didn't work, and after our divorce, I finally returned to my country. My family had told me of the changes, but still I was shocked to see what had happened in those five years. The destruction caused by the civil war was truly shameful.

I went to work for an American television network, ABC. Covering the Israeli invasion in 1982 and the war taught me a lot about my people. I saw the effect of the war on them, and how it turned them from their usual kind and loving nature to hatred and murder. I saw the destruction they inflicted on themselves and how they allowed neighboring countries to use them, turning Lebanon into a killing field.

It was during that time that I met Terry, at a party given by a CNN cameraman. Such parties were frequent—we had little else to do, since going out at night was too dangerous most of the time. Terry offered me a drink, and sat next to me. I had never seen him before, and didn't know who he was. He was wearing a suit, which was unusual at that kind of a casual party, and was very fat, with a beard that made his face look big and round. After talking to me for a few minutes, he moved on. I thought, I wonder if I will ever go out with this man. The idea seemed almost sarcastic—he wasn't my type at all.

At the beginning of 1984, I started working with NBC News. The war had taken a different shape. Violence brought more violence. Lebanon was exporting terrorism, and the Lebanese had learned a new trade—kidnapping Westerners, mainly Americans.

NBC and AP worked together a lot, and helped each other. We used AP's wire reports, and I had seen Terry's copy frequently. I admired his accuracy and writing style. Bonnie Anderson (no relation), the NBC correspondent, gave a party at her flat, and Terry came.

It was the first time we had said more than a few casual words to each other. A few weeks later, Terry called to ask me out for dinner. I declined, but left the possibility open for another time. I wasn't sure I wanted to go out with him. Terry called again, and again my answer was, "Maybe another time." I knew I should have told him the first time I wasn't interested, and I still don't know what made me hesitant to do that.

Finally, after several invitations, I accepted. During the evening, he told me he was married. I had seen him a couple of times before then, but never with a woman. He was always alone. He told me his wife had returned to Japan and would not be rejoining him. He was to be reposted to Mexico at the end of the year, but she didn't want to go.

The marriage had not been going well for a long time, he told me. But his respect for Mickey and love for his daughter, Gabrielle, showed me something I had not seen in other men. I wasn't at all sure I wanted to continue to see him, but it was difficult to decide to end it. Nevertheless, he was leaving in a few months, and I was preparing for a long vacation trip to Jamaica to meet an old friend I hadn't seen in ten years.

Terry liked to surprise me, and often did as we continued to see each other. But his biggest surprise came after a few months, when he said he had told AP headquarters in New York he wanted to stay in Lebanon, and they had agreed. Two days later, he told me he had asked his wife for a divorce.

I knew, of course, what he was trying to tell me. I was overwhelmed. This man was changing his life for me. He was proposing. When I said yes this time, I decided I would give him nothing but love and happiness.

It wasn't long before I became pregnant. We didn't expect

it. I thought I couldn't—though I had been married before, I had never gotten pregnant.

Destiny is something you don't choose or plan. It is chosen for you. Meeting Terry, falling in love with him, and carrying his baby were things that God had chosen for us. We felt we were made for each other. Planning our lives and our family was the most normal thing to do, as though we had been together for years. We traveled to the States in January 1985 to visit Terry's father, who was critically ill. Terry wanted him to meet me before anything happened to him. I met his sisters and brothers, and felt immediately as one of the family.

Then March 16, 1985, came and ended the wonderful dream we were living. The traders decided to knock at our door, but they weren't buying or selling. They just robbed us of our happiness. They took everything in a blink of an eye, and planted hate instead of love in my heart. Hate that only Terry's return could eliminate. But Terry didn't come back.

Hoping that he would show up any minute, I stayed home constantly for days. I refused to go to my family, and they were afraid to come to stay with me in case the kidnappers decided to return. My mother insisted that I go to her place and wait there, but I couldn't. I knew Terry would want me to be home waiting for him if he was set free. Those first days were very painful, and endless. For the first time in my life, I knew what losing someone I loved meant. That kind of fear was unknown to me. I had faced danger before on several occasions, and faced death once or twice. It scared me, but it also made me stronger. I had always won out. Now, losing Terry, I was weak, and had lost terribly.

I could not let myself think of how Terry was feeling, how scared he must be. I felt ashamed. These are my people who are doing this to us. And it was because of me that Terry was still in Lebanon. Many times I wished I had not known him, so he would not be where he was. I often wondered if he was thinking the same thing. But no matter what, I knew that he knew I loved him very much. The *thought of our love gave me comfort in the most terrible times, and those times came quickly. More people were kidnapped. On March 22, two Frenchmen were abducted. Other abductions followed. It was obvious nothing was going to stop the kidnappers unless their demands were met. But no one seemed to know what the demands were.*

It was at this point that I realized I had to leave Lebanon. It had been three weeks since Terry's abduction, and I was entering my eighth month of pregnancy. AP had arranged with Terry's sister Peggy for me to fly to Batavia, New York, his hometown, and stay with her. I had refused earlier when they suggested it, but as the time grew nearer when I would be unable to fly because of my pregnancy, I was afraid that Terry might get released and I would be stuck, not able to join him. The thought of being in Lebanon while Terry was somewhere in the States was unbearable. So I left.

THREE

HIGH WIRE

The high-wire artist risks his life
to please the crowd, for fame,
the thrill of danger, and the pleasure
of performing feats that few can do.
We risk our lives, and souls,
for motives much the same, plus
the heady feel of being next to power,
even wielding some ourselves.
We take as many casualties, maybe more.
The names of those who die,
in gold and silver, are posted on the
press club wall. Others we carry
quietly, or just ignore until
they are encountered in the bar—
burned-out relics of too many wars.
You see, you cannot go on bathing
in the world's violence unscathed,
touch so many people's pain and grief
and not be burned. Tell me you could
look into a hundred children's eyes,
dark, huge with uncomprehending
pain and hunger, and purge yourself
of all you feel in a thousand words or so.
So we grow our shells. Those who can't
don't last. Some grow them all too well—
the cynical, abrasive ones who
cannot feel. Perhaps they never could.
They count their coups in front-page
headlines, and pay in other ways.
Most of us just try to keep our balance,
like the man up on the wire,
eyes fixed straight ahead,
never daring to look down.

4

BEIRUT, 1982.

When Israel invaded southern Lebanon on June 6, 1982, southern Africa was quiet, and I was restless. I'd been covering the region out of Johannesburg for nearly a year, and while the country was beautiful and the people interesting, it had failed to take hold of me the way Asia once had. The stench of apartheid overwhelmed everything. The Afrikaners were right about one thing, distasteful as it was to admit it—few white foreigners were able to deal with South African black people on any real basis of trust or understanding. Blacks in South Africa didn't understand us, and we certainly didn't understand them. South Africans of all races might hate each other. But they understood each other. It was enormously painful to try to talk to a black man or woman, and watch his or her discomfort grow, see the bowed head, hear the instinctive "Yes, master. No, master." Not all, certainly, reacted that way. Black leaders had already lost their deference, were proud and defiant. But they were as scornful of foreign liberal meddling as the Afrikaners.

We had little to offer these people in their struggle. And there seemed little hope then that they could help themselves. I was tired of South Africa after only a year, and deeply uncomfortable there. As soon as the news of the Israeli invasion broke on the AP wire, I was on the phone to my foreign editor, Nate Polowetzky: "Do you need help? Can I go?"

Nate urged caution, told me to wait a few days. Finally, though, he called back. Yes, go to Israel.

Twenty-four hours later, I landed in Tel Aviv, dropped my bags at the Sheraton, and went down to the AP office. Bureau Chief Larry Thorson gave me a short briefing, then handed me the keys to a rental car.

I had little knowledge of the Middle East, other than what I had read on the wire and in the newspapers. I'd spent all my time overseas in Asia, and my only foreign language was Japanese—hardly likely to be useful in Lebanon. Still, I was excited. It was a war, it was the world's biggest story, and I was a journalist.

Buoyed by the high that was still drowning out the effects of a twenty-four-hour airplane flight, I drove to the very northern tip of Israel, a kibbutz called Qiryat Shmona that pressed against the now-breached chain-link fence marking the border. I met up with an AP photographer, obtained some credentials from the Israeli Army, and crossed into Lebanon escorted, as all foreign journalists had to be, by an Israeli press officer.

Those first few days were a disaster. I battled constantly with the Israeli press handlers and censors. My press credentials were yanked the first day when I left my escort. He wanted to visit historic Beaufort Castle, on its beautiful mountain ridge overlooking Israel. I wanted to get to the war. "I'm not a tourist. They took Beaufort days ago."

My credentials were eventually returned. But my relations with the Israelis did not improve. After a week of this, I decided to part company, and arranged private transportation up to East Beirut, where The AP was setting up a separate office as the situation in the western, Muslim half of the capital grew daily more chaotic and dangerous.

My departure did not please the Israeli Army, which was intent on keeping as much of the press as possible under its control. Independent coverage of the war, especially from the Lebanese side, was not what they were interested in. They couldn't stop me, but one press officer made it clear: "Don't come back. You're not welcome."

East Beirut was held by the Christians, who had encouraged the Israelis to invade their country to drive out the hated Palestinians and shore up Christian domination of the Muslims. It was fairly safe, with the increasing number of Israeli forces ringing the western half of the city concentrating their fury on the Muslims and Palestinians trapped there, along with a few Syrian troops.

It was a peculiar war, where we could sit in lawn chairs on top of our hotel, the Alexandre, just a few dozen yards from the "Green Line," the no-man's-land of destruction dividing the city, and watch Israeli tanks and planes destroying the western half. We could even, at one point, see the Palestinian and Muslim snipers in a building a few dozen yards across the way. They never fired at us as we lounged in plain sight, until some Israeli Army officers discovered our vantage point and began using it as an observation post.

During the day, AP Middle East News Editor Tom Baldwin and I would range up and down the front line, gathering material for our daily stories. One day, Tom even accidentally wandered across the line, suddenly discovering himself among fierce-looking Syrian commandos, with combat knives stuck upright in their chest packs.

At night, we would go out to one of the several fine French or Lebanese restaurants that remained open just three or four blocks away from the hotel.

Lebanon fascinated me with its endless complications, its cross-currents, and subwars within larger wars, and feuds within subwars. The Maronites, the Sunnis, the Shia, the Druse, the Palestinians—each with their factions and their temporary alliances and shifting goals. The Syrians, the Israelis, the Iranians and Libyans and Iraqis, each with a part, large or small, to play—not to mention the Americans and French and Italians and British.

The culture was an incredible mix of the superficially European and deep Arabic substance. The more I learned, under the pressure of war, the more I saw parallels with Asia. This "Middle Eastern" country was more eastern than middle. Its subtleties were almost easy to grasp after the much more difficult psychology and sociology of Japan. And somehow, it had already taken hold of me, captured me. I had found again the deep fascination I had once felt for Asia, and had never been able to sense in Africa. I was hooked, both as a newsman and as an individual.

Then there was the incredible violence. I'd seen violence before, many times in my six years as a foreign correspondent, as a reporter in the States, and before that as a Marine in Vietnam. But the scale and intensity and sheer ferocity of these people appalled me.

Lebanese factions murdered each other, and each others' families, with sickening regularity. Christians, whom the West could not help associating with the tenets of Christianity, would drag live Palestinians at high speed behind their cars. The Syrians wiped out the entire town of Hama, one of their own, in a few days to quash a small rebellion. No one would even have known what happened had not one Western reporter, Robert Fisk, managed to get into the town and record the destruction. The town became a phrase in reporters' vocabulary. Showing special viciousness was afterward known as "playing by Hama rules."

Israel played by Hama rules, also. The clichéd "David" I'd watched from afar fending off the Arab "Goliath" smashed Beirut with Old Testament viciousness, without regard for the half million Lebanese caught there, without even a small attempt to distinguish among combatants and noncombatants, men, women, or children.

After a few days in East Beirut, I crossed over the front line, moving into the AP office in besieged West Beirut with AP Middle East Correspondent Nick Tatro; his wife, Earleen, a first-class AP correspondent herself; and the dozen or so Lebanese reporters and photographers who stubbornly remained, defying the danger.

Through the fiercely hot Mediterranean summer days, I wandered through the city and talked to refugees camped in parks and half-destroyed buildings. I climbed office and apartment buildings, stair after weary stair, to gain a vantage point to watch Israeli F-14s and Kfirs swoop down and lay their terrible cargoes almost gently on the homes and businesses below them, invulnerable, untouched by the Korean War–vintage antiaircraft guns of the Palestinian and Muslim militias defending the city. Then I would take to the streets again, trying to get to the bombed areas, check on the destruction, watch the bodies and pieces of bodies being loaded into whatever emergency vehicles could get to the scene.

I traveled through front lines that were nearly invisible, eyes twitching nervously across empty intersections, peering into the blank windows surrounding us, muttering to my Lebanese driver or the other journalists riding with me, "I don't like this. Why are we doing this? This is shit."

Despite the horrors, the bodies, the blood and despair that surrounded us, the fascination never faded. And mixed with it was the awful, heady rush of danger. "Nothing in life is so exhilarating as to be shot at without result," the young Winston Churchill wrote (*The Malakand Field Force*, 1898). We covered that war almost as if it were a horror movie, feeling ourselves exempt from death, our eyes and ears wide, hearts thumping wildly, careening from sporadic encounters with wild-eyed gunmen to terrifying, stretched-out minutes huddling under shells and bombs or cowering from snipers, only to return to the Commodore Hotel, climb on a bar stool, and blandly trade the day's war stories with our colleagues over a giant gin and tonic.

The pose of observer, the veteran immune to the pain of others, was just that, though—a pose, and a protection. No one, not the most cynical, blasé correspondent, got through that summer in Beirut without pain of his or her own.

For me, it was the dark, deep eyes of Palestinian and Lebanese children, the sight of doctors operating on grievously wounded people, hunched over the table to keep the plaster dust shaken from the ceiling by shells from drifting into the gaping, bloody holes—the "Begin Syndrome," they called it, after the Israeli prime minister. "We get few lightly wounded people," one doctor told me. "They're either very bad or dead. We get a lot of autoamputations."

Shrapnel from a 155mm shell takes off a leg or an arm (or a head) just like a giant scalpel.

Beirut in the summer of 1982 was summed up to me by the pitted body of three-year-old Ahmed Baitam, lying on an intensive-care bed in Barbir Hospital, on the Green Line, while doctors tried to bring him out of shock. The pits covering his skinny frame were from phosphorus. The doctors failed, and he died while I watched. The bodies of his five-day-old twin sisters were in a morgue drawer down the hall. An intense, chain-smoking woman doctor, appearing on the edge of a nervous breakdown, showed them to me. She said they had smoldered for hours after they had been brought in, and had to be left in a tub of water to smother the chemical. Fourteen members of that single family died when two shells hit the basement they were hiding in.

But Beirut was also an incredibly stubborn, brave, independent people: Elias, my Christian driver whose family lived on the Green Line, and whose baby cried constantly because of the shelling and sniping he'd heard since birth; his cousin, Tony, dubbed by the AP staff "The Wonder Driver" because of his willingness to go anywhere, anytime; Muhieddin, a Sunni, unflappable, calm, courteous, and humorous, even after he and three other AP staff were kidnapped by Shia and held overnight; and day after day, the thousands of Lebanese who just kept trying to live their lives, go to work, raise their kids, while their country went mad.

On one very bad day, Don Mell and I decided that despite the intense fighting in the city, we had to go out to find out what was happening. We pulled out a pair of flak jackets, covered in white cloth with "Press—Don't Shoot" emblazoned in red Arabic, French, and English letters across the back, and dodged down Hamra's narrow streets. Dashing across Bliss Street, literally under the trajectory of shells from a Lebanese Army tank firing down the street, we ran around a corner and crashed into a group of perhaps a dozen Lebanese men and women. They were calmly lined up in front of a tiny bread shop, buying the day's bread—

vital to both them and the shop owner who had come in to fire up his ovens at dawn.

In August, as the tortured negotiations among the United States, the Lebanese government, the Palestinians, and the Israelis approached an end, Nick Tatro called me into his office. Tom Baldwin would have to leave. His wife, Toni, was seven months pregnant. Even if the war ended, conditions in Beirut would remain rough, and they would not be able to stay. Would I exchange jobs with Tom?

I barely hesitated. Of course, given the expectation that the war would be ending soon, and my wife and six-year-old daughter, Gabrielle, could join me, I'd love to have the post. We agreed that I would return to Johannesburg and close up my house, take a short vacation, and return to Beirut by the beginning of October. The only thing left was to get a temporary replacement for me, and AP Rome correspondent Sam Koo was available.

Sam entered West Beirut a day or two before I was to leave. A gentle, handsome Korean-American who had covered the Vatican for a number of years, Sam was stunned by the violence and destruction he was seeing. I showed him around the city, pointing out front lines and vantage points to watch the fighting and bombing, which continued despite the peace talks. At one point, sitting on the roof of a high apartment building overlooking the Corniche Mazraa and the southern suburbs, Sam lowered the binoculars we were using to watch yet another Israeli bombing raid, and said, "Terry. I don't know if I can do this."

"Well, we'll see," I said. "Give it a try."

The next day, our office and most of the city was shaken by an enormous explosion. An Israeli "smart bomb" had been dropped on an apartment building used by Palestinian families a few blocks away. (We learned later that the Israelis had hoped to catch a Palestine Liberation Organization leader at his home. He had already left.)

Sam and I hurtled down the four flights of stairs from the AP office to the street and ran toward the site. The building had completely collapsed, killing most of the people in it, and sealing an unknown number in the basement. A bull-dozer was already maneuvering into the wreckage, trying to open a hole. Bodies were being pulled out and loaded into cars or ambulances as they arrived. Palestinian militiamen shouted and waved their guns, firing into the air to try to keep the crowd back.

One woman, perhaps thirty-five or forty, visibly preg-nant, waved her arms and shrieked in grief. Sam ap-proached her and tried to talk to her. Her husband and children were in the building. He looked at me, a few yards away, and called for the tape recorder I was carrying. I waved him off—another body was coming out of the build-ing.

Abruptly, a shattering blast knocked us all to the ground. I rolled over and over, and scrambled for the doorway of a building behind me. I remember stepping on someone—alive? a body?—as I threw myself into the building. Hud-dling against a wall, we waited for the next blast. Nothing. Carefully, I edged out the door. "Sam? Sam!"

There were burned, torn bodies everywhere, it seemed. The woman Sam had been talking to lay on the ground, the bodice of her flowered print dress soaked in blood.

Many of the bodies were completely unrecognizable. I walked among them, peering closely, gagging. None looked like Sam. Walking quickly away as rescue workers once more rushed forward, I flagged down a passing car, and asked the Lebanese man driving it to take me back to the Commodore. Neither of us said a word during the short trip. I stood in the street and shouted up at the open AP of-fice windows.

"I can't find Sam. I don't know where he is."

Tatro leaned over the balcony. "He's here. What hap-pened?"

Filthy and shaking, but unhurt, Sam sat at a desk. "She's dead. What was it?" He had been picked up by a couple of Palestinian militiamen and brought back to the office. In one of Lebanon's cruelest tactics, someone had driven a car full of explosives to the site of the bombing, knowing a crowd would gather, and carefully set it off where it could do the most damage.

Sam wrote the story, then left for East Beirut the next day. Despite his horror and revulsion, he continued to work there, surviving another car bomb at the hotel he was staying at, and a car crash under shell fire, before returning to Rome.

A few days later, I told Nick I had to leave. My nerves had begun to go. After so many weeks, I had to believe my luck was running out. He agreed. I packed my bags and, early one morning, left in a taxi for East Beirut. As we drove away from the Commodore, I could hear the shelling a few blocks away. I held tightly to the door handle. Just a few more minutes. Just a couple of miles. Then one shell hit a building to our left. Another landed down the road, blowing a hole in an apartment. A third, a fourth. But we were through, speeding frantically toward the only open crossing through the Green Line.

> The child is dying of his wounds
> and others' hatred.
> His body, stretched by growth
> and pain and malnutrition,
> lies bare before us,
> tubes like hungry snakes
> invading every orifice.
> There's no affront in this indignity;
> our shame lies in the pits
> left in his flesh by burning phosphorus.
> This is the vile, unpardonable
> result of all our follies;
> the last, unnamed, and mortal sin
> that even God cannot forgive.
> We'll write of this in bitter,
> burning words, and be convinced
> they'll have effect because
> the paper's dotted with our tears.
> We must believe; it's why we do this.

The only point can be if we prevent
or somehow ease the next child's dying.
There will be one—there always is.
We'll watch it, and we'll write again in rage,
and cry our helpless tears.

I arrived back in Beirut in early October of 1982, Japanese wife, daughter, two Siamese cats, and a sprawling,
friendly Rhodesian Ridgeback bitch in tow. Mickey was
understandably nervous, and the first view of the southern
suburbs of Beirut from the airplane did little to reinforce
my assurances that "it will be all right. It's all over." But
after nearly fourteen years of marriage, I was accustomed to
dismissing Mickey's concerns.

A sweet, quiet, and very traditional lady from Hiroshima,
she had been trailing along behind me ever since I talked
her into ignoring her parents' fierce objections and marrying me while I was serving with the Marine Corps in Japan.
I had just turned twenty-one, and she was a young twenty-
two.

The marriage had not gone well. We "married in a fever," as the song goes, and that carried us for a while, but I
was too young and bullish to use any sensitivity in our relationship, and the gaps in temperament and culture were
too great to allow any real communication. Journalism puts
great strain on a marriage anyway, and I had often left her
to cope alone while I was off covering something or other
I thought more important. She never complained—a Japanese woman from a conservative family has limited expectations of marriage.

As we lived our parallel lives, though, my expectations
had changed, and I had often fulfilled them elsewhere, with
a series of other women. I even used that pathetic cliché on
myself: I'm careful. If she doesn't know, it can't hurt her.
Of course, she knew, and was hurt, but never spoke of it.

So far, the level of unhappiness had not reached the critical point. I knew the break would never come from her,
and I had never had the nerve or necessity to face the pain

it would inflict on our daughter, Gabrielle, a beautiful, incredibly bright and cheerful sprite of seven, let alone on Mickey herself.

This tour in Beirut was exciting to me, and important to my career. For Mickey, who had found South Africa comfortable, it was just another strange place, and a frightening one at that. It would prove, finally, just too much for our marriage to survive.

Much had changed in the city. The fighting was over. During my vacation, the PLO had left, and the Israelis, flagrantly ignoring the agreement they'd just signed, had used the assassination of President-elect Bashir Gemayel in September 1982 as an excuse to move into West Beirut, just days after the three-nation truce force brought in to oversee the evacuation had itself pulled out. Lebanese Phalangist militiamen, with at least the tacit permission of the Israeli Army, had massacred hundreds of men, women, and children in the Sabra and Chatilla refugee camps, prompting the immediate return of the Multinational Force—the units of American, French, and Italian troops sent into Beirut to oversee the evacuation of the PLO. A 100-man British unit would join the force in 1983.

The Lebanese, with their incredible spirit, were busily rebuilding. The city resounded with the crash of hammers, the roar of trucks carrying concrete and sand and glass. The rubble of the hundreds of destroyed buildings was being dumped in the bay a few hundred yards from my new apartment, forming a landfill that was supposed to allow the seafront Corniche to be extended through to East Beirut.

At the airport, the U.S. Marines were settling in, sending out patrols in jeeps and on foot. On my first visit to the Marine headquarters, I met an old friend—Capt. Dale Dye. A Mustang (former enlisted man), Dale had been my boss in Vietnam, in the Marine Combat Correspondents' detachment in Da Nang. Now, he was the spokesman for the Marine Amphibious Force. Forceful, confident, a good Marine, he reflected the spirit of the whole two-thousand-man unit, and the pleasure they felt in this job: peacekeeping.

As I settled into my new job during the late fall of 1982, the optimism flooding Beirut was infectious. I followed the Marines as they patrolled on their "peacekeeping"—entirely a show, to build confidence. They drove through the city in jeeps, and walked through the southern suburbs, home to a million or more poor Shia. I watched children toss oranges and flowers to them. I wrote about the Italians with their new field hospital and dental clinic. I wrote a short series titled "Lebanon Rebuilds" about the problems the people and government faced now that the war was over.

I learned a great deal about the various religious/ethnic groups and their subdivisions: the Christians, dominated politically by the Maronites, who had run the country for decades, but including Greek Orthodox, Russian Orthodox, Syriac Christians, and more, each a tiny independent community; the Sunnis, old families, urbane, businessmen mostly, who shared power with the Maronites; the Shiites, historically left out of both political and economic spoils, even though everyone else knew—and denied—they were a majority (that's why no census had been held since the 1930s); the Druse, a mountain tribe with a religion so secret they didn't even tell their own men about it until they were forty or so, but with a reputation for ruthlessness won during their deep and seemingly permanent blood feud with the Christians. Each group had its own militia, of varying strength, and it was really the number of guns that counted.

I learned about the outside influences: the Syrians, who believed Lebanon was still a part of Greater Syria (a feeling not at all shared by the Lebanese), and whose army had been in the country as an "Arab peacekeeping force" since 1976 with no sign of leaving; the Palestinians, much hated by most Lebanese for their arrogance and power before the 1982 wars, and who had countless subdivisions of their own; the Israelis, who had been wooing the Maronites for more than a decade, with varying degrees of success; the other countries, like Libya, Iraq, Iran, even France, Britain, and the United States, all of which had their own protégés in the awesomely devious and complicated pavane of Lebanese power politics.

I mastered it all, as best I could, at least well enough to function. Then I tried to get a handle on the larger responsibilities of being Middle East news editor. I traveled to Syria and Iraq and Jordan and Bahrain and Cyprus, at least getting acquainted with the different problems and power structures of each.

But it was still Lebanon that gripped me, as it had taken hold of so many Westerners before me. Despite the ravages of the war, it retained an atmosphere, that mélange of the Orient and Europe, sophistication and wealth, and simplicity and poverty, that so many had tasted and never forgotten. And it seemed to be in a renaissance. Even the Lebanese, so long deceived, believed or made everyone believe they believed that the good days were returning.

The pessimism of veterans like Farouk Nassar, who had watched thirty years of Middle East crises for the AP, or Robert Fisk, the London *Times* correspondent who was rapidly becoming my best friend with his brilliant analytical mind and cold, critical look at everything that passed before him, seemed excessive, cynical.

I had quickly grown to like and admire Robert after I met him in the first weeks of the war. He had little of the clichéd British reserve, he seemed to like me, and we had traveled together a good deal. He was not afraid to say "I don't want to do this," and never failed to pay heed when instinct told me on little or even no evidence that we should get the hell out of some place or other. I paid him the same compliment, without reservation.

He was a faintly weird character who had been here since 1976, following six years covering the equally vicious war in Northern Ireland. Short (my five-seven almost exactly, perhaps a bit more), most often disheveled, hair wild and shirttail sticking out, glasses covered with finger marks and dust, he was inexhaustibly enthusiastic, fairly bubbling with the joy of a "good story, Uncle Terry, good story, this." And his *were* always good stories. He saw things at a different angle, fifteen or twenty degrees at variation from the rest of the world. That and his penetrating intelligence threw a light on events that couldn't be found anywhere else but on the pages of the *Times* of London.

Mickey, Gabrielle, and I had ended up moving into an apartment in the same building "Fisky" lived in, and that deepened the friendship. I shared his love for good wine, especially champagne, good food, and first-class conversation. My daughter loved him because he spoke to her as an equal, treated her with dignity, and shared her sense of humor.

We spent many days in the field together, and many evenings on my balcony, popping champagne corks at the Marine in the armored personnel carrier parked below us, and arguing about Lebanon and the world. Above all, he tried to keep me alive. He drilled the fundamentals into me each time we ventured into that dangerous world that was Lebanon, among the militias and armies and snipers and car bombs: "There are no good guys. The gunmen are all little furry creatures with yellow teeth and small brains and guns. All of them, Israelis, Lebanese, Syrians, Palestinians. Yes, Uncle Terry, even the British and French and Americans. Sooner or later, they all behave like hamsters. And we must report on all their mistakes and wickedness equally. All the same."

I often wondered where Fisky put the pain. I know he felt it, had seen him wince, seen the anger in his eyes as we watched the bodies pile up at the scene of some bombing or pointless firefight. He had done it for so long. That's where his profound neutrality came from. He had seen them all do it, counted the bodies on everyone's side, until there could be no sides for him. What was left was just rage at everybody who misused power, low or high.

He told me once that he was searching for "the roots of violence." He didn't explain, and didn't need to. He desperately needed to find a reason, a logic, a justification for all this. Without religion, without a deep faith that I could detect, except in the power of the truth, he just had to keep on looking.

I respected him greatly, but everything I saw and heard during that late fall of 1982 and early 1983 belied his caution and pessimism. The Lebanese, the Americans at the embassy, everyone saw an end to the war, an end finally to the bad times.

Even the Israeli occupation of much of Lebanon, harsh as it was, as many mistakes as the Israelis seemed to be making, seemed less serious because of the obvious fact that it couldn't last. There was no way the Israelis could hold on to that territory. They would have to leave, and fairly soon.

That didn't mean there wasn't bad news to report. Lebanon and the Middle East always provided plenty of that. Car bombs; shootings; vicious and labyrinthine political maneuverings, domestic and regional; unrest among the Shia as the Christian-dominated government tried to maintain its hegemony over the nation; a growing number of fanatical and radical splinter movements with strange names. But it was still possible, at least for a few months, to be optimistic. The divided city suddenly was, at least nominally, open. Traffic moved from east to west and back again relatively freely. Schools opened, the nightlife, which never totally disappeared even during the siege, grew brighter, more frantic, with discos open until dawn and restaurants packed.

Through the spring and summer, I worked frantically. I paid little attention to what I saw as an increasingly fruitless marriage, neglected my growing daughter, drank and smoked heavily. But I was fascinated by this new world and determined to master it. My boss, Nick Tatro, was due to leave, was expecting a transfer any week, and I wanted his job badly. It was one of the top foreign service positions in The AP, and would represent a major jump in my career. Chief Middle East correspondent for The Associated Press. To become an expert on this horribly complicated, violent region in a year? I *would* do it.

I became even more determined as the optimism following the end of the fighting faded to unease, and the unease
to fear, in Beirut. The new Christian-dominated government, under Amin Gemayel, was heavyhanded and stupid
in its dealings with all the other sects. Fighting broke out in
downtown Beirut when the government evicted Shia refugees from a school they had occupied, with no provision
made to house them elsewhere. Bulldozers began plowing
under the shacks of thousands of other refugees along the
coast so rich Christians could reclaim their formerly occupied land for new apartment buildings.

In south Lebanon, resistance to the Israelis grew, despite
severe reprisals and random sweeps of the villages by
Israeli-led militiamen. Renegade Army Maj. Saad Haddad,
an Israeli puppet with a couple of thousand men—Lebanese
mercenaries really—tried to expand his enclave along the
border of Israel to take in nearly half the country, but
couldn't exert enough influence to hold so much, even with
Israel's sponsorship.

In the beautiful mountains above Beirut, Christian Phalangists, who had encouraged the Israeli invasion, felt confident in their Israeli backing, and began "arresting" Druse
men at random checkpoints. Those arrested usually just disappeared. Fighting broke out in villages where the two sects
had lived in relative peace through the first years of the
civil war. Innocent villagers and travelers were murdered
out of hand because they carried the wrong identity card.

In Washington, the goal of the Multinational Force
seemed to become blurred. Over strong protests from both
the U.S. embassy and the Marine command, the Reagan administration shifted from peacekeeping to "support of the
legitimate government." The problem with that was the
Gemayel government had little claim to legitimacy and less
to governing.

Western reporters had become accustomed to wandering
freely around Lebanon, subject perhaps to a little verbal
abuse or an occasional roughing-up, but accepted by even
the most radical of factions as journalists, separate from and

independent of the U.S. and British governments. The PLO knew the value of treating the press well. Even the creepy-crawlies we ran across on the Green Line or in the Bekaa Valley seemed eager to tell their story.

Riding from Baalbek to Chtaura in the Bekaa one day with Fisk, we passed through checkpoint after checkpoint manned by armed men in hoods—formal fancy hoods, hastily stitched hunks of cloth, even a few paper bags with holes cut out for eyes. *"Wain rayeh?"* Where are you going?

"Sahafi." Reporter. "We go to Chtaura."

"American?"

"Yes."

"Okay. *Yaatik el aafiyeh."* God give you strength. *"Allah Issalmak."* God keep you safe.

Now, though, in 1983, the atmosphere was changing. With the victory of Ayatollah Khomeini in Iran, Iranian money poured into Lebanon to influence the Shia, many of them disaffected from their own native leadership. Conflicts between the Christians and Muslims, Christians and Druse, Palestinians and everyone, sharpened. The shift of position in Washington was noted quickly by all the other players in the Lebanese war, and sharply changed the view they held of the Multinational Force, and even of Western reporters. The radicals got more radical, the contempt and hatred for America and the West a little more personal, the encounters with bitter gunmen a little harder to get out of gracefully.

Ten Italians and five U.S. Marines were wounded on March 16, 1983, in separate attacks. The Marines had been walking patrols through the Shia-inhabited area daily, with unloaded weapons. Supplies for isolated outposts had been carried casually on unescorted trucks through the crowded, narrow streets and alleys. No longer. "Hooterville," as they called the slum area, was getting unfriendly.

Later in the day, the Agence France Presse office in Beirut received a call from a Lebanese man. He said he was from an organization called Islamic Jihad, which no one had heard of, and wanted to claim responsibility for the attacks on the Italians and Marines. Such claims were common. With no basis on which to judge, we usually ignored them.

On a sunny April day, as I lingered in my apartment on the Corniche Manara, facing the Mediterranean, the building shuddered from a massive explosion. By now, I had enough experience to note the two most important things—it was big, very big; and it was close, very close. I ran down the stairs, into the street. Nothing, except a few stunned people looking east. The U.S. embassy was that way, just seven hundred meters down the road. I began to run toward it, but the fat, cigarettes, and booze took their toll almost immediately. By the time I got near the embassy, I had slowed to a dogtrot, heaving for breath and sweating.

As I rounded the small bend, though, my exhaustion vanished. The embassy, a large, three-sectioned building, was blanketed in black smoke. Two men were carrying a body down the small driveway to the street. "Oh, Jesus," I muttered. The smoke lifted momentarily. The building's entire center section was collapsed on itself.

More mutilated bodies, unrecognizable as either Lebanese or American, were being pulled out as Beirut's emergency crews arrived, as always within one or two minutes. One body, in a white shirt, was hanging head down from the fifth or sixth floor, its lower part trapped in the wreckage, blood staining the concrete.

I turned away and began running again, this time looking around frantically for a telephone. I darted into the doorway of an apartment half a block away, shouting at the first person I saw in the street Arabic I'd picked up. *"Telefon! Ween telefon?"* Where's the telephone? Then I realized the person, an older woman, was crying, and I looked about me. The apartment was a mess. All the windows had been blown in. Everything was covered with glass and rubble. I turned around and ran out.

Finally, I flagged down a Lebanese policeman, jumped in his car, and mentally searched for a few more words of Arabic. *"Yallah, minfadlak. Hamra. Commodore. Ana Sahafi."* Let's go, please. To Hamra. Commodore Hotel. I am a reporter.

He looked blankly at me, then put the car in gear and stepped on the gas. A few blocks later, as we ran into a traffic jam, I jumped out. *"Shukran,"* I called. Thanks. I ran on to the AP office.

Swarms of journalists and investigators pieced together the story. A man in a black pickup truck had driven through the light wooden gate at the embassy, slamming into the building just beside the front door and detonating his cargo of explosives. Sixty-three people died, including a line of Lebanese waiting for visas, passersby on the Corniche promenade, and seventeen Americans in the embassy itself. The American victims included a half dozen men meeting in a conference room on one of the upper floors—virtually the entire Middle East section of the Central Intelligence Agency.

The explosion eliminated the embassy for all practical purposes. It also destroyed the confidence of both Lebanese and Americans in what we were doing there. In what would turn out to be as serious later, it also wiped out American intelligence-gathering capability in the country during a crucial period.

5

BEIRUT, LEBANON. APRIL 1983.

Beirut and Lebanon were disintegrating, and so was my life. I'd gotten the job I wanted. I was now the chief Middle East correspondent, and wholly wrapped up in trying to keep track of the increasingly weird events in Lebanon; handle a spirited, feuding staff of journalists; administer a million-dollar budget; and coordinate coverage for a dozen other countries, from Cyprus to the Gulf. Overwork, too much alcohol, and the emotional and psychological toll of unending violence left me with little room for anyone else, and little interest in my marriage. My wife and I had almost nothing to say to each other. There was no hostility—indeed, on the surface, things seemed as calm and friendly as they ever did. There was simply nothing in the relationship. We were too different, and I had outgrown my youthful need for a submissive, unchallenging woman who would run my household and inflate my ego. I had nothing particular against Mickey, but our life together was flat and uninteresting, in bed and out. My guilt at needing to search constantly elsewhere for stimulation made me seem ugly even to myself. It was not a situation, I knew, that could go on forever without destroying both of us. Yet guilt also kept me from doing anything about my feelings. I had tried several times over the years to discuss them with her, but had met only incomprehension and hurt.

My daughter was beautiful, intelligent, alive as only a

seven-year-old can be. But a child cannot cement together two adults who do not fit.

Events continued to pile up around us. The U.S.-brokered "May 17 agreement" of 1983 that was supposed to be a peace treaty between the Gemayel government and Israel turned out to be a joke, repudiated before it was even signed when Syria, which still occupied the Bekaa Valley and northern Lebanon, made clear its displeasure. In August, the Lebanese Army and Syrian-backed Druse militiamen began a fierce battle over positions in the mountains overlooking the capital. The Army took a major drubbing and broke up. Half its men took their weapons over to the various Shia and Druse militia in West Beirut and the southern suburbs. The other half fell effectively under the sway of rightist Christian Phalange leaders in the eastern half of the capital. In September, a short-lived rebellion in West Beirut drove the Army completely out of that part of the city for several days, until Christian-dominated units could be pulled out of the mountains and sent in to restore a tenuous control.

The Marines at the airport were being left deeper in shit. Their positions were laid out on the flat coastal plain, lined on one side by a warren of concrete buildings inhabited solely by Shia, many of them radical fundamentalists, and directly under the guns of the Druse in the mountains ringing the plain. They were in a militarily untenable position, as their commander pointed out bluntly to his superiors. Politically, they were in worse trouble, as U.S. support for the Gemayel government increased, alienating all the other factions.

The Israelis still occupied nearly one-third of the country, from the Israel-Lebanon border up to Beirut, plus part of the mountains surrounding the city. Syria occupied the Bekaa Valley, to the east, and part of the north. The right-wing Christian militias held more power in East and Central Beirut than did the government they were allegedly serving. The government controlled almost nothing, except the presidential palace.

In the midst of all this, the Israeli government suddenly decided to pull its troops out of the Chouf Mountains, where they had at least kept a damper on the fighting between Christians and Druse. The Druse, a tightly knit mountain group, made up only ten percent of Lebanon's population. But their fierce love of land and delight in fighting their Christian enemy, and Israeli meddling with both sides, had fanned the conflict to the absolute edge of war.

The Israelis cheerfully announced they would not disarm the militias they were leaving in control—militias they had armed freely throughout their occupation. As the Israeli units pulled out, they—and we—watched village after village explode into battle almost over the heads of the last departing Israeli soldiers.

The Marines had been receiving sporadic sniper fire for some time. Now, they were being shelled. Lebanese Army units stationed within yards of Marine outposts were firing up at the Druse in the hills, and of course, the return fire fell around the Marines' posts. Eight Marines were killed by a single shell in one such incident.

Inevitably, given its perplexing assumption that President Gemayel represented the "legitimate government" of Lebanon, the Reagan administration stepped up its support for the Christian-dominated Army. First resupply, sending truckload after truckload of shells and other gear up to Lebanese Army units fighting the Druse. Finally, sucked in by a panicky call from the Lebanese high command for help during a major battle in the mountains, the U.S. Navy ships in the bay started firing in support of the Lebanese Army. The Marines thus became, effectively, just one more faction in a civil war. They, and the other members of the Multinational Force, would pay a terrible price for that mistake in policy, or lack of understanding.

The two explosions on October 23, 1983, came within seconds of each other, at 6:20 A.M. The closest was heavy enough to make the walls of my apartment house shudder. As I headed downstairs, AP photographer Bill Foley was emerging from the front door of his apartment, two floors down. Scrambling for the car, we were joined by Fisk, racing down from his sixth-floor flat. We tuned in the radio for the first flashes.

"Where was it?"

"Rauche. French headquarters, they said. And another one out by the Marines."

Traffic was light. In three or four minutes, we came up the hill and turned left into the narrow street where the French paratroopers had their headquarters. *Had* was the operative word. The building had almost disappeared, collapsing into a pile of broken, smoking concrete perhaps ten or fifteen feet high. French soldiers and officers were stumbling around in shock. Lebanese rescue workers poured onto the site. Several were gathered halfway up the pile, pulling and heaving at the pieces. One man—French? Lebanese?—was gently holding a hand that stuck up out of the mess, the man who owned it completely buried, but still alive.

Shouting questions, interrogating men who could barely speak, we quickly learned that dozens of the soldiers were buried in the rubble. Foley was scurrying about, snapping picture after picture. Then someone shouted at me: "They've hit the Marines, too."

I grabbed Foley, yelled at Fisk, practically dragged them to the car. "If they've done this here, what have they done to the Marines?"

Another frantic five miles to the airport. Another pall of smoke, screaming sirens. Something was terribly wrong. "Where's the BLT?" I asked, referring to the battalion landing team headquarters.

"What do you mean?" Fisk sounded puzzled. "It's just up there."

"No, it isn't. It's gone."

Two stunned Marines, smoke-smudged faces streaked with tears, manned a large gap in the chain-link fence of the airport. They said nothing as we climbed through. The bodies were already being laid in rows a few yards from the pile of smoking, broken concrete that had been the main barracks for the 1,200-man Marine and Navy unit.

Five minutes trying to count the torn bodies, talk to crying Marines, get some kind of account of what happened from men too horrified to even think about what they were saying. A truck bomber, a suicidal man who smiled as he ran his truck directly into the building's entrance.

"Fisky, cover for me. I've got to get to a phone. I'll be back."

The horror was overcoming me, as well. There were bound to be men I knew in that smoking rubble. I'd been a Marine for six years. These were *my* people.

U.S. intelligence was quick to assign a name to their attackers—Hussein Mussawi, an almost-unknown Shia Muslim who had split from Amal, the main Shia political and militia group, to form something called Islamic Amal. Closely linked with the Iranian Revolutionary Guard detachment sent to the Bekaa during the Israeli invasion by Iran, he also seemed to be providing the muscle for a new, ultrafundamentalist coalition of mullahs that called itself Hezbollah—the Party of God.*

---

* While we had heard the name before, it seemed to involve only a small group of Iranian-inspired mullahs in the Bekaa Valley. But even that fragmentary "knowledge" was far less than the truth. Hezbollah was already becoming a well-organized terrorist group. Many of its operatives were trained by Yasir Arafat's Palestine Liberation Organization. One, a senior official named Imad Mugniyeh, had been a member of the PLO's feared Squad 17, known as Arafat's personal elite bodyguard unit and enforcer squad.

As later information from intelligence sources and sources within Lebanon and Iran would show, Hezbollah had without question planned and carried out the attack on the embassy. More importantly, it had set up as early as 1982 a special operations center, known as "Ali's Center," to gather information on Westerners in Beirut. With nearly four hundred people working out of a computer-equipped building in West Beirut, the center began compiling lists of names. Operatives, including many women, were assigned to follow Westerners. Others were to try to develop informers in the offices where the foreigners worked. All the information gathered went into the data bank.

William Buckley, a political officer at the American embassy and known to be the station chief for the Central Intelligence Agency, was a top target. At some point, my name was linked with his in the data bank at Ali's

Fisk and I took off for Baalbek, the ancient temple city and former tourist goal in the Bekaa. Mussawi's headquarters was just up the street from the ruins of the Temple of Apollo—a small, plain building with several bearded young men lounging on its porch, AK-47 rifles slung carelessly over their shoulders or propped next to them. We were greeted with suspicion, but not hostility. Mussawi was a slim, somewhat feminine man in an outdated dark suit. A former schoolteacher, he looked like a caricature of a Muslim fanatic—small, dark beard, flashing dark eyes. His hatred of America was expressed with fervor, his militancy overt. He denied having anything to do with the attack on the French and Americans, but said plainly he wished he had.

"This deed is a good deed which God loves and which his Prophet, may God praise his name, loves. I bow before the souls of the martyrs who carried out this operation.

"Definitely there will be new operations against them," he added, referring to the Western forces. "I hope to participate in future operations."

Mussawi was one of the few men I have ever met that I felt absolutely repelled by, of whom I felt I could fairly say, "This man is evil." Not because of his enmity toward my country, or endorsement of violence, but because of the almost palpable force of intolerance and fanaticism he projected.

As Fisk and I were leaving, one of the militiamen demanded my passport. Not Fisk's, just mine. He took it, produced a round tin of Danish cookies, and left. A few

Center—probably because I had developed a friendship with another embassy official, whom I often talked with and occasionally invited for dinner at my home. Another bit was added to my file after Buckley's kidnapping when I refused to buy pictures of him and another hostage, the Reverend Ben Weir, from a couple whom I believed to be linked closely to the kidnappers, then reported the attempted sale to the embassy. Eventually, Ali's Center would list me as the "second man" in the CIA in Beirut. Needless to say, I was never a witting or unwitting "asset" of the CIA or any other intelligence agency.

minutes later, he came back with the passport and a photocopy. "We know where you live," he told me.

After the Marine bombing, October 23, 1983, Lebanon just seemed to fall apart. Any faint optimism, any discussion of a future for the country seemed fatuous. The wars proliferated: Christian East vs. Muslim West, Druse vs. Christian, everybody vs. Israel, Muslim fundamentalists in Tripoli vs. anyone, even Palestinian vs. Palestinian as Arafat's PLO broke under the pressure. At one point we had to travel through two battles—at the Green Line and in the mountains—to get to the one we wanted to cover in the Bekaa, where the Syrians were backing Palestinian rebels in an attempt to destroy Yasir Arafat's leadership, as they had always wanted to do. The "Old Man" and his loyalists were driven out of the valley and decided to make a last stand in the northern Lebanese port of Tripoli, which Syria proceeded to bring down about his ears. Once again, the road to Palestine had taken a strange turn, in which it was necessary to destroy a Lebanese city in a battle with other Arabs to further Arafat's hopeless war against Israel, and proving once again that the Palestinians' worst enemy was not Israel, but themselves and their fellow Arabs.

In Beirut, more and more bearded men appeared on the street, carrying more and more signs echoing Iran's revolutionary fervor and anti-Western propaganda. The Marines had hunkered down in bunkers at the airport and behind a massive concrete-and-earth wall and rolls of barbed wire at the British embassy, now shared with U.S. diplomats. A Marine amphibious armored vehicle and machine gun post were both just below the window of my apartment, next to the embassy. An antiaircraft missile unit perched on top of the building next door.

Shells fell sporadically and randomly on the city and suburbs, automatic rifle fire could be heard nearly every night; and the battles in the mountains continued throughout the year.

* * *

In December 1983, a group of Iranian-inspired Shia launched an attempt to destabilize Kuwait with attacks on the U.S. and French embassies, power stations, and other installations. Though people were killed, the attempt failed miserably. Hundreds of Shia were rounded up, and seventeen convicted and jailed. A number were given death sentences, others long prison terms. The event, far off in the Gulf, got wide coverage, but was soon forgotten, at least in the West. There was no immediate connection with events in Lebanon, no hint that the repercussions would involve half a dozen countries and leave dozens of Westerners, including me, in chains for months or years.

The climax came on February, 5, 1984. Scheherazade Faramarzi, an Iranian and the best reporter in the AP bureau, Don Mell, and I had to renew the press passes we had received from Amal. Their headquarters was in the southern slum of Bourj Al-Barajneh. As we sat chatting with Amal's press officer, we could hear some gunfire. Driving back into the central city, we noticed hooded gunmen in a vacant lot, huddled around a rocket launcher. Then more on a street corner. The sound of shelling and rifle fire increased. Driving rapidly down the Corniche, around the Rauche curve, we suddenly came on a gray Lebanese Internal Security armored car—Squad 16, the semimilitary, semipolice unit nearly everyone despised. Its machine gun was firing steadily at a forty-five-degree angle into an apartment house above it. AK-47 fire was pouring from the building, and others around it.

I jammed on the brakes. Don leaped out and ran, crouching, toward the armored car, shooting pictures awkwardly all the way. I called to him, but he didn't hear or ignored me. "He'll make it back," I told Faramarzi, then stepped on the gas, hurtled past the firefight, and turned up the hill toward Hamra. Other cars, horns blasting in panic, had jammed the side roads. I pulled to the side of the street and we jumped out, running the short distance to the AP office.

Within hours, Druse and Shia militias had taken over all of West Beirut, driving the Lebanese Army out of the city in a complete rout. The next morning, along with dozens of other Americans and Westerners, my wife and daughter boarded a Marine helicopter in front of our apartment building and left for Cyprus. That "temporary" separation from them became permanent. It was the end of hope for Lebanon for the next eight years, and the effective end of my sixteen-year marriage.

The U.S. Marines at the airport were now isolated, totally cut off and surrounded by Shia and Druse militiamen who held the southern suburbs and all of West Beirut. Washington capitulated. The Marines would be pulled out immediately. The U.S. ships would remain in the bay, uselessly. American influence on events in Lebanon had evaporated.

As the last Marines boarded boats and amphibious vehicles at Long Beach, next to the airport, bearded militiamen wandered through their deep bunkers, stepping carelessly over barbed wire. A jeepful of Amal gunmen drove onto the beach and hoisted the green flag of Islam on the same pole that had, minutes before, carried the Stars and Stripes.

In Beirut, the warnings were there, as early as the beginning of 1984. But they went nearly unnoticed in the general chaos of Lebanon. In January 1983, Malcolm Kerr, president of the American University of Beirut, was murdered in his office by two young men. As always, the list of possible motives was long. Palestinians? Muslim fundamentalists? Christian militiamen? Syria? No clues.*

Frank Regier, an American academic, and Christian Joubert, a French engineer, were kidnapped in February,

* The assassination of Kerr was a carefully planned operation of Hezbollah. Kerr was labeled a "dangerous spy" by Ali's Center, the central data bank on foreigners in Beirut. A woman agent was sent to smuggle a gun in her purse into the American University campus. The gun was buried beside a tree near College Hall. It remained until an official *fatwa,* or religious ruling, was issued by Hezbollah's central council condemning Kerr to death. On January 18, 1984, two male agents were sent to carry out the sentence, shooting Kerr twice in the head at close range. He died immediately. The two assassins fled without hindrance.

then rescued two months later by Amal. Their kidnappers—
the Islamic Jihad, referred to reflexively as "shadowy" and
"almost unknown."

In March, Jeremy Levin, bureau chief for CNN, went
missing. A week later, William Buckley, described as a
counselor at the U.S. embassy but generally known as the
station chief for the CIA in Lebanon, was taken almost
from his front door, despite a professional's security precautions.*

Each kidnapping was dutifully reported, then virtually
forgotten by the Beirut press corps, struggling to keep up
with the never-ending violence, the enormous complications
and permutations in Lebanon's rat's nest of a war.

In the south, the Israeli occupation became increasingly
harsh. Units of Israeli intelligence operatives and Israeli-led
militiamen raided Shia village after village. Stories of brutal
interrogations, inhuman conditions at Ansar prison in the
south, and even executions abounded. Relations between
the Israeli Army and the press were worse than ever.

Sporadic fighting continued in the mountains, on the
Green Line. Some days were worse than others; none was
good. Arriving at the AP office early one morning, I found
no reports of deaths overnight, no reports of fighting. I pre-

---

* The Hezbollah operation against Buckley was almost a model of counterespionage. Buckley had developed a woman Shiite agent named
Zeynoub, sister of the woman involved in the assassination of American
University President Kerr. Unknown to him, she was a double, a "responsible," or official in Hezbollah, whose true loyalty was with the fundamentalist
party. According to one usually reliable source, Buckley grew enamored of
the woman and began an affair with her. Later, however, the professional
CIA man began to grow suspicious. Before he decided to act on those suspicions, the woman became aware of them. With the information she now had,
and access to his apartment, the kidnapping was easy. The decision to take
him was made on Friday, March 15, 1984. On March 16, in an operation involving twelve cars full of Hezbollah agents, he was snatched.

Buckley was tortured repeatedly and severely for the next ten months,
under the supervision of Imad Mugniyeh, one of Hezbollah's senior officials, and a Lebanese doctor. He resisted bravely, refusing to give any information, but as was inevitable eventually broke. The intensity and length of
his interrogations broke his health, and led directly to his death.

pared a lead for the daily story based on the idea that, for at least one night, it was quiet in this bedeviled country. The current cease-fire, one in a series of dozens, seemed to be holding. Farouk Nassar, out of his thirty years' experience, shook his head. "Never put a cease-fire in the lead," he said. "Just wait a bit." Sure enough, less than an hour later, the late reports of overnight battles began coming in.

Foreigners were becoming more and more nervous about going out at night, though many restaurants remained open. We found our amusements in parties at each others' flats, drinking and dancing almost frenetically. NBC rented a closed disco next to the AP office for one going-away party. Amid the blasting rock music, I was paged. Shells were falling along the Corniche Manara. Don Mell was calling from the Riviera Hotel, where UN officials and soldiers often stayed. He was trapped, huddling behind the front desk. Waiting for the shelling to die down, I drove the five minutes to the hotel, ran in, got Don, and we left. The rest of my colleagues, in the basement disco, hadn't even heard the shelling.

At another party, I chatted up a slim, stunning Lebanese woman with long, black hair and beautiful eyes. Her name was Madeleine Bassil, and she worked as a researcher and production assistant at NBC, next door to The AP. A couple of weeks later, I asked her if she'd like to have dinner, but got turned down. I tried again after a few days. No luck. Again. Finally, she agreed.

On May 8, the Reverend Benjamin Weir, a Presbyterian missionary who had lived in Lebanon thirty years, mostly among the Shia in the south, was snatched from the sidewalk near his Beirut apartment.

At the end of July, the last U.S. Marines, still guarding the combined British/U.S. embassy, were pulled out. A relief—the armored vehicle and machine guns were gone from under my window, the barbed wire pulled down, and the concrete-earth barrier blocking the Corniche taken away. The seaside promenade was again filled with evening strollers and the tiny trucks that sold the bitterly strong Lebanese coffee.

As always, the summer was bright, hot, the Mediterranean sun never letting up as I drove from one end of the country to the other, usually with Fisk, sometimes with Mell or Faramarzi or a couple of colleagues from other news organizations. Southern Lebanon, hundred-year-old olive orchards, scores of bright green orange trees, bulldozed by the Israeli Army after a sniper attack; the bare, gray-green mountains, thousand-foot drops off winding, one-lane roads; massacres in this Druse or that Christian village; the Bekaa, with its ever-larger number of tiny fanatical groups.

September 20, 1984. "They've bombed the embassy." What embassy? "Ours. The annex, in East Beirut." Classic déjà vu. A lone suicide bomber in a truck, penetrating what was supposed to be incredibly tight security, and this time in Christian East Beirut. Fanatics there might be on that side in plenty, but not the kind that bomb embassies, especially not ours. Only this one didn't succeed entirely. At least fourteen dead, including two Americans, and heavy damage. But thanks to an alert British bodyguard, the bomber didn't succeed in getting close enough to completely destroy the building.

The story, heard several days later from the bodyguards themselves, who happened to be close friends, was bizarre, entirely fitting for this war.

The half dozen bodyguards of British Ambassador David Miers were standing around idly outside the U.S. embassy annex in East Beirut while Miers met with the U.S. ambassador, Reginald Bartholomew, upstairs in Bartholomew's office. Large, efficient, deadly men, at times they could play like puppies, and inside the embassy's security ring, this was one of those times. One of the men slapped a large dragonfly, knocking it to the ground and earning immediate sarcastic criticism from the others. He picked it up, carefully placed it in a small discarded cardboard box. The bodyguards lined up for a mock funeral. The biggest, a heavy man assigned to carry the largest machine gun available, reached in the car and pulled it out, to fire a make-believe salute.

But a real shot echoed from the gate, and an engine roared. Before anyone could turn or pull a gun, a van hurtled down the driveway toward the building's entrance. The machine gunner dropped his weapon's muzzle the few inches he needed, clicked the safety, and snapped off two shots, one into the door, the other through the driver's head. The vehicle crashed into a stone wall just feet from the entrance and exploded. Most of the blast was diverted.

Picking themselves up and startled to find they were mostly unhurt, the British bodyguards rushed into the building, up stairs littered with debris and wounded men, and into the ambassador's office. There they found British Ambassador Miers, standing stunned but also unhurt. U.S. Ambassador Bartholomew was trapped under part of the ceiling that had fallen. They pulled him out, carried him downstairs, tugging their own charge along, and flagged down a car on the street outside. Within minutes, both ambassadors were in the American University Hospital, being treated for minor injuries and shock.

Once again, the attack was claimed in a telephone call to a Western news agency on behalf of Islamic Jihad.

Despite the frantic pace—or perhaps because of it, because of the things I'd seen over the past two years—I began to do some heavy thinking. I'd never been introspective, never stopped pushing long enough to think about where I was going, what I was becoming. I was a mess, physically, morally. It couldn't go on. I began cutting down on my drinking, trying to get some exercise, running on the Corniche along the sea in the early mornings.

I asked my wife for a divorce—painful, so painful, especially trying to explain why to an eight-year-old daughter who loved both her parents blindly. Madeleine and I had by now begun dating steadily, quietly. I proposed, and asked her to move into my apartment. She agreed. Both of us were working twelve-, fourteen-hour days. The peace of that small third-floor flat, with its lovely expanse of sea just across the road, was the antidote to each day's craziness.

I also began once again to read the Bible. I was raised a Roman Catholic, but had left the church as a teenager. I called myself an agnostic—just a lazy man's way of avoiding the question, avoiding the commitment called for. But I'd remained interested in religion, almost as an intellectual exercise, I thought, and had read widely—Buddhism, Islam, Judaism, Christianity. This time, though, I knew I was looking for something more than intellectual stimulation. I just didn't know what.

Madeleine was getting increasingly nervous about my safety. She wouldn't let me speak English as we wandered through the street markets; she speculated aloud about the unshaven young men sitting idly in cars along the Corniche near the apartment. I paid little attention. I'd wandered freely through the country for two years. Sure, it was dangerous. I could handle it.

Some of my colleagues were also nervous. Several asked me privately: "What should I do? Leave? Stay?" I refused to give advice, refused to take responsibility for anyone else's life. "If you're uncomfortable, if you think it's too dangerous, you should certainly leave. I'm staying. I have to."

The Spanish ambassador was kidnapped in October of 1984, but was released a short time later. More significantly, the librarian of the American University of Beirut, Peter Kilbourne, an elderly, ill man, disappeared in December.

Madeleine became pregnant. She wasn't supposed to be able to, had never conceived in her first marriage. There was never any question of what to do. It was inconvenient, but to give up a child she'd always longed to have, and one I welcomed, was unthinkable. We rejoiced, and thanked God.

We took a couple of weeks off in December 1984, after I had spent a few frantic days in India helping cover the riotous, deadly aftermath of Indira Gandhi's assassination. We stayed with Madeleine's sister and brother-in-law in Sunderland, England. I ran in the bitter cold dawn along the sea, and wandered through the streets of the small industrial town, just trying to come down from the tension and excitement.

As we walked around Sunderland and Newcastle, I kept catching sight of the tall, sharply pointed traditional steeple of the local Catholic church. Every time I turned around, it was there. Finally, during lunch at a nearby restaurant with Madeleine and her sister, I excused myself, walked around the corner, and entered the church, trailed by the two puzzled women. I sat down in a pew and just looked at the altar, at the cross with its crucified figure. I didn't pray, not really. But I felt a perfect sense of being at home, where I belonged. After so many years of avoiding it, I recognized myself: I'm a Catholic, a Christian. Whatever I've done in the past, that's what I am. The sense of relief, of some unrecognized strain being loosened, was powerful and immediate. I didn't know what I was going to do with my new knowledge, whether I could live up to the obligations and duties it would impose. I would have to work that out later. For now, just knowing was enough.

> I'm not Catholic by conviction,
> or through belief that this one
> road is better than the rest.
> I cannot even say that I've accepted
> all the teachings, and certainly
> I've failed to keep this narrow path.
> If I could choose, I think I'd be a Quaker,
> or a Buddhist, even Hindu—reincarnation's
> such an elegant and reassuring thought.
> But I can't—my parents chose before me.
> And though I've spent a large part
> of my life trying to choose otherwise,
> one still half hour in an

empty church defies all logic. I am what both my fathers made me,
and I'm content to find myself at home again.

Madeleine and I returned to Beirut in time for Christmas, 1984, and resumed the frantic pace of our jobs, taking refuge each night in the peace of our apartment, and in each other. By the end of 1984, the city had settled into a kind of permanent chaos. Armed men wandered the streets freely, and car thefts were common. A German man was shot to death, apparently when he refused to give up his car to some thug.

Fundamentalist Shiites went on a rampage, smashing up restaurants and bars throughout West Beirut. One group even raided the Commodore Hotel, whose bar had been for years the major hangout for Western correspondents. As always, though, the staff was well informed. By the time the hamsters stormed in the door, waving AK-47s and shouting, most of the bottles at the long bar were hidden away, leaving little to be smashed. In days, nearly all restaurants were officially dry, in conformity with Muslim law.

Fuad, the ever-resourceful manager of the Commodore, had set up a "private" bar in a top-floor suite, and in most of the places frequented by reporters, the coffee cups were filled with anything but coffee. But the fundamentalists had managed to cow virtually the entire city.

On January 8, 1985, Father Lawrence Martin Jenco was forced from his car in Beirut. The priest was head of Catholic Charities in Lebanon, charged with distributing millions of dollars to the needy, Christian or Muslim. The usual anonymous caller to a Western news agency (most often it was Agence France Presse) said he and the other missing Americans would go free "if all Americans leave Lebanon." Anti-American and anti-Western feeling among the fundamentalists had been growing, and was freely expressed, often in the Friday sermons at the city's mosques.

* * *

Late in January, a Lebanese man and woman showed up at the AP office. They had a tape of Benjamin Weir, William Buckley, and Father Jenco, they said.

"Where did you get it?"

"From the kidnappers. We have good contacts."

They said they wanted money for the tape, but didn't name a price. After some discussion, I said, "No, thanks." Despite the obvious news interest of the tape, I felt uncomfortable with the whole thing. The couple were too mysterious, too well connected. I suspected that they were, if not a part of the group holding the men, at least very close, and the money was quite likely to be paid directly to the kidnappers. I wanted no part of it. Later, I called Nate Polowetzky to tell him of the incident and explain my feeling. He made no objection. "If you don't like it, don't do it." I quietly told the U.S. embassy about it, so they could inform the families of the hostages of this indication that the men were still alive.

The couple immediately went next door, to NBC, and sold the tape to them.

On February 14, Jerry Levin, the CNN bureau chief who had been taken in 1984, escaped from his kidnappers. The story was broken by Agence France Presse, whose stringer in the Bekaa happened to be sitting in Syrian intelligence headquarters there when Levin was brought in. He told officials his guards had forgotten to fix his chains properly and he had climbed out a third-story window, using sheets and blankets to lower himself to the ground. He seemed shaken and distraught, but in reasonable health. I joked to a couple of friends: "They had a priest, a minister, an embassy official, and a journalist. They've lost the journalist. I suppose they'll be looking for a replacement."

At the beginning of March, I went to Cairo for a regional bureau chiefs meeting. Lou Boccardi, the newly appointed president of The AP, was there for an International Press Institute meeting, along with several other top AP executives. He asked me several times about Beirut, expressing concern for my safety, but did not press the question when

I assured him I didn't want to leave, and that with reasonable caution, it was still possible to work and live. We spent most of our private discussion on the question of salaries for the AP local staff—Lebanon's economy was disintegrating, and the value of the Lebanese pound, one of the most stable currencies in the Middle East, was rapidly being destroyed by hyperinflation.

Just two days after I returned to Beirut, a car bomb went off outside the office of Sheikh Mohammed Hussein Fadlallah, a fundamentalist mullah considered the most radical Shiite leader and identified by Western intelligence as the "spiritual adviser" to Hezbollah—the Party of God. Hezbollah's influence had been spreading to West Beirut from its base in Shiite-dominated Baalbek, in the Bekaa Valley. It was closely tied to Iran, and virulently anti-American. Apparently very well funded, the group paid its militiamen well, and also doled out allowances in some of the Shiite neighborhoods to women who would wear the *chadoor*, the all-enveloping black cloak of Iran. More a loose coalition than a unified group, Hezbollah was engaged in a power struggle with the more moderate Amal, for long the primary political and military force of the Shiites. At first a great deal weaker than its rival, Hezbollah was using its Iranian-supplied money well, and had grown into a powerful force.

Mell, Scheherazade Faramarzi, and I went to talk to Fadlallah the morning after the explosion. The scene was all too familiar—buildings torn, piles of rubble in the street, gunmen everywhere. The blast had killed nearly eighty people, but missed Fadlallah. Most of the victims were civilians, many women and children.

The hostility we encountered was incredible, hatred blasting from the eyes of the militiamen and civilians all around us. On top of one ten-foot-high pile of rubble was a makeshift sign: "Made in America." Fadlallah was not available. Other Hezbollah officials spoke briefly to us, and we left quickly.

The U.S. embassy had been quietly warning Americans to leave Beirut—a warning that most of the newspeople just ignored, though several took the advice or moved to East Beirut, considered a much safer place. After the United States vetoed a UN resolution condemning the Israeli occupation of southern Lebanon on March 12, the UN ordered out all Americans working for its international agencies. Many diplomats were also leaving. I talked with Polowetzky, the AP foreign editor, by telex. He pressed me about the danger. I reassured him. "Frankly, I think the danger is greater from thugs just after money or a car."

On March 14, a British metallurgist, Geoffrey Nash, was kidnapped, and a Dutch Jesuit priest named Kluiters disappeared.*

On March 15, I went home for lunch, as had become my habit. As I drove along the Corniche on my way back, a new Mercedes pulled up beside me, then cut in sharply. I downshifted and stepped on the gas, swerving to the right and then back, ahead of the Mercedes. A minute later, as I turned up the hill toward Hamra, they tried again, on the smaller side road. This time, as I shifted down and rammed my foot to the floor, I glanced at the car. Four bearded young men, but no guns in sight. I swerved sharply down an even smaller road, catching the driver of the Mercedes by surprise. By the time he stopped and backed up to make the turn, I was fifty yards ahead. The other car chased me for a few hundred yards, but dropped off when we approached a Lebanese Army checkpoint.

In the office, I called my news editor, Gerry Labelle, and Fisk into the back office and told them what happened. "Were they trying to kidnap you?" Labelle asked.

"I'm not sure. I think so, but I didn't see any guns."

Fisk offered the use of his car for a few days. I declined,

---

* Many years later, after my release, I learned that Nash had been set free in just three weeks. Kluiters's body was found April 1, two weeks after I was taken. Catholic church sources said he had been severely tortured. Some reports said the killing was a personal matter, not political.

and asked them both not to say anything. "Madeleine would get upset."

That evening, I worked late, then stopped in the Commodore for a moment. My upstairs neighbor, Tom Aspell, was sitting at the bar. His wife was in the hospital, in labor. We chatted, I wished him luck, then left. Fisk dropped in later, and we talked about the danger of kidnapping, carefully avoiding mention of the day's incident. Fisk was adamant—he'd never let them take him. He'd fight. "Don't be a fool, Fisky. They've got guns. If you fight, you'll just get killed. Go along. At least you'll be alive."

He left, and Maddy and I went to bed early, since I had to be up at six A.M. for my tennis date with Don Mell.

FOUR

STIGMATA III

Early endless weeks,
chained, blindfolded.
Each small movement brings
a curse, a threat, a blow.
Sometimes the vultures
gather round to poke and
prod with talon, stick, or gun,
mutter maledictions and
predict an early, painful end.
The don't impress; no thief
throws away his booty.
More frightening are the
vultures of the mind.
Remorse, regret circle
through the night, alighting
each in turn to tear
a tasty morsel from the soul.
There's much that vultures love—
noisome, rank, and nasty.
Petty vices, packets full of lies,
soft, overripe indulgences,
and rankest, juiciest of all,
selfish pain inflicted
on an open, trusting heart.
The leavings of this carrion feast
are meager, unimpressive:
some kindnesses, bits of charity,
a few small acts of real love,
and heaps of good intentions;
all strung together by
the only thing of value here—
a steel determination to survive.

6

I've had the Bible two days now. It's what—April 9? 10? Hard to keep track. The guards haul in several large sheets of plywood and some two-by-fours, dumping them noisily on the floor next to my cot. Stepping over my chains and bumping against me, they begin hammering. Late in the afternoon, they unfasten my chains. "Get up." Pulling my elbows behind me and holding tight, one guard pushes me forward and into a narrow closetlike space they had made with the plywood, just wide enough to hold a cot, with a plastic shower curtain hanging at one end.

I lie down on the cot, and they refasten my legs and one arm with the chains and padlock. I can sit up and even lean back against the wall. "When closed, you can lift *couvrez-yeux*," one of the guards say in bastard English-French, rattling the curtain. "We come, you close eyes. You see me, you dead. Okay?"

"Yes, okay."

The curtain closes. I cautiously lift the blindfold—the first time in nearly four weeks. Cot, blanket, water bottle, pee bottle. Bible. Curtain. Nothing else. I lie back. The plywood partition ends a foot or so from the high ceiling. The chains run underneath, perhaps to a bolt in the wall or floor. The guards' movements and chatter, just the other side of the plywood, are plain.

The curtain is suddenly yanked aside. I grab at the blindfold, lying on the bed. Too late.

"Couvrez-yeux," he shouts. "No look. No look."

"Okay. Okay." Fumbling the cloth back in place.

"No good. You no good." A slap on the head. "Keep here. No put down. Keep here."

"Yes, I understand. Sorry."

"You see, you dead."

Silly. I'd already seen, and he knew it. Typical militiaman—small, thin, scruffy beard, sharp Arab nose, black hair. Completely inseparable from a thousand, ten thousand others.

Dim, gray light. Blank ceiling, bare electric light bulb just visible over the top of the partition, but giving no light, since the electricity was off again. Snoring of guards. Tired. Just tired. Hours, long nights, praying. "Dear God. What have I done? I'm not good, I know that. I've cheated and lied. I've strayed so far from you. Self-indulgence. Stupidity. I'm sorry. But do something. Anything. I just can't do this. I can't."

It's surprising what you can remember when you have nothing to do but remember. At first, the mind is a blank. Jesus, I always thought I was smart. Where are all the things I learned, the books I read, the poems I memorized? There's nothing there, just a formless, gray-black misery. My mind's gone dead. God, help me.

Start with the memories. Forget the stupidity of not paying attention, of walking out into the street after one kidnap attempt, the very next morning, to give them your open, stupid self. That's done. You're paying. Think about Madeleine—so beautiful, all dark and flashing and loving. You're so lucky, to win this woman now, after all these years. What is she doing? What is she feeling? Stop. It hurts too much.

What about Mickey, and Gabrielle? I've hurt them both, greatly. Especially Gabrielle. She sounded so sad, had so much pain in her voice the last time I talked to her on the phone. She's eight. How can she understand? Thou shalt not commit adultery. So many times, in so many places. No excuses. No "but if only she'd . . ." No. You did it. Accept it. Be sorry.

But I'm not sorry about Madeleine. No matter what. We didn't plan this child. Maddy wasn't supposed to be able to conceive. But so much joy when it happened. Inconvenient, sure. But never regretted. Is that wrong, God? To be thankful for this joy? So short a time together—what, ten, eleven months? Worth all this, if I die today, worth it.

I'll not apologize for this, God. Never.

All the other memories. The people. The mistakes, offenses. How arrogant I was! It must have been hard to like me. Did they all? Or was I just tolerated? I don't like me much. How can anyone else?

Hours, days, nights, weeks. Blank nights. Gray dawn after gray dawn.

An English-speaking man came in today and dictated a short letter to me. At least I know why I've been kidnapped, or at least what the "official" reason is. He was abrupt, but not threatening. Simply gave me a pen and a piece of paper, then told me what to write:

"I am fine. I received your message. You should know that I am a victim of the American policy that favors Israel and which forced the detained persons in Kuwait to do what they did. My freedom is tied to the freedom of the detained over there. The American government still does not care about us. I ask you to do your best to pressure the American government to release the detained people over there because we are very close to being hanged in the case that this term is not met. The American government takes all responsibility and the American president, Mr. Reagan. Please do your best and move very swiftly to end my detention because I cannot take it anymore."

No discussion allowed. I asked about the "message" I was supposed to have received, but got no answer. After he left, I thought about those people who had been arrested in Kuwait, after the bombings there in 1984. A straight swap, it looks like. Unfortunately, I can't believe the United States will allow itself to be pressured into in turn putting pressure on Kuwait to release convicted terrorists. It's going to be a long time.

The days begin to settle into a kind of routine: Sleepless nights, watching the dawn light grow slowly on the ceiling, shifting and turning, trying to ease the stiffness and pain of lying on a bed twenty-four hours a day. Listen to the roaches, occasionally watch one or two or three, two inches long, crawl slowly up the wall. Hear the stirring and muttering in Arabic as the guards awaken. Food—usually a sandwich of Arabic bread and dry, yellow cheese. Brief trip down the hall to the filthy bathroom. One guard unlocks the chains. Another stands against the wall holding a small automatic pistol with a silencer. Back to the cot. Read the Bible for a while. Lunch—perhaps a bowl of soup, or cold rice with canned vegetables dumped on top. The evenings are sometimes enlivened by short visits from one or two of the young men, sometimes to ask questions in broken English, sometimes just to amuse themselves. Occasionally, one or two will kneel or sit on my chest, poke their guns in my ear or neck, and hiss threats: "You dead. I kill you." "Sure. *Tfaddal.* Go ahead. You kill me, my problems are over."

One guard in particular seems determined to get a list of American names from me, even though his superiors have apparently given up for the time being. Threats, curses. He takes away my water, refuses to give me food for a day, two days. Then another guard, arguing fiercely, brings back my water bottle, throws a sandwich on the bed.

Late afternoon. The guards begin hammering again, on the other side of the room. A few hours later, well after dark—midnight? no way to tell—there's a subdued stir and bustle. Apparently two or three guards, but very quiet. Clank of chains, the snap of padlocks. A few words in English: "Sit. No speak." Another hostage? Who?

The next morning, my trip to the bathroom is delayed. Someone else is being taken, perhaps two people. As the second returns past the door of my room, a guard stops him. *"Riyada. Sportif. Yallah."*

I hear the sound of someone jogging in place, doing jumping jacks, for five or ten minutes, then he's taken into another room.

My turn. Before getting onto the cot afterward, I speak to a guard. *"Riyada?* Exercise? Sport?"

He slaps my face, hard. Again, and again. "Sport? You want sport?" Slap, slap. "No sport here. *Yallah."*

Brief shock, then an explosion of burning, blinding rage. Almost physically, I clamp down on it. Don't move. Don't show *anything*. Do not fight back. Do not show any emotion.

Back on the cot. Chains pulled tight, painfully tight, and padlocks snapped. My feet begin to swell almost instantly, quickly start to ache. Four, five hours. Another guard brings lunch. "My feet, the chains. No good."

He pulls on the chain, then hisses. "Sssst. Who do?"

"The other guard."

'He *majnoon*." Crazy. He goes for the key, kept somewhere in another room, opens the locks, eases the chains.

My brief undershorts, tennis shorts, and T-shirt are filthy—unchanged since my kidnapping. My hair feels stiff from dirt. I smell of sweat and urine. My teeth are starting to hurt, and feel as if they're covered with rough plastic. No chance to wash during the brief trips to the toilet each day, no toothbrush. The dirt offends me. I'd been taught thoroughly in the Marine Corps, in Vietnam—no matter what, jungle, mud, rain, the enemy: stay clean. Stay healthy, and you might stay alive. The next morning, in the bathroom, I strip off clothes and begin to wash myself with the hose connected to a tap on the wall. The door slams open.

"What you do?"

Crouching, naked on the floor, back to the guard, blindfold lying on the bathtub. "I'm washing. Very dirty."

"Come. *Yallah*. Finish."

I wipe myself off with my T-shirt, get dressed, put the

blindfold back. In the hall, the guards push close. "Why you wash?" Fist hitting my chest. "I say no wash. Why you wash?"

"I'm dirty. Not good."

"No wash. I say when." Another blow, not hard, on the breast.

"Okay. But not good dirty. Get sick."

Two or three days later, the guards bring in white cotton shorts and T-shirt, and a pair of cheap, Chinese-made briefs. This time, I'm allowed to use the tub, take a real shower, not just a quick hose-down.

The weather has shifted fully now. May in the Mediterranean, and even the nights are hot. I have a rash in my crotch from the sweat—showers once a week now, but I still can't stay as clean as I need to. From time to time, I can hear a guard speaking to others in the room, and the one next door, in broken English—the same kinds of things he says to me: "Stand up." "Sit." *"Couvrez-yeux."* Once, he uses a name—William. Buckley? Probably. There are now, I think, three other hostages in the apartment, all in chains. I ask about them. "No speak. Not your business. Quiet." Who are the other two? Levin escaped before I was taken. That leaves Jenco, a Catholic priest. I can't think of any others.

Despite the severe, repeated warning—"If you see us, you are dead"—I sometimes take peeks through the curtains, or under my blindfold as I'm going to and from the bathroom. No matter how tight the strip of cloth is, it's always possible to see along my nose, and the guards know it. If I tilt my head back gently, I can sometimes see down the hall, or into the room, as I walk. The images are blurry—I'm very nearsighted, and they took my glasses—so it's practically useless, but I can't resist the urge once in a while.

I'm beginning to sort out the guards, mainly by voice, and by the way they act. One, who gives his name as Sayeed, speaks reasonably good English and seems friendlier than the others. Sometimes he comes for a talk, usually about "evil America." I try to explain to him that, yes, Americans have done bad things, but we're not evil. What about Vietnam? Okay, I was there, I didn't like it. But I was a Marine, and did what I was told. The discussions are fruitless, just going around and around, but they help pass the time. And every time we talk, it might help them to see me as an individual, a human being.

Sayeed seems the most religious of the guards, praying five times a day in a loud voice. He never sits directly on my cot, always bringing a small board to put on top of the blanket. He won't touch me after I've been to the toilet, explaining once that he must remain "clean" to pray.

My Marine years fascinate one of the other guards, named Badr. A small, thin, frenetic young man, perhaps twenty-two or twenty-three. He's a gun nut, and comes from time to time to show me his latest weapon—a 9mm automatic pistol, or a .357 revolver. Removing the bullets, he hands it to me, saying, "Good, good?" I peer carefully under the bottom of my blindfold. The .357 Magnum he loves. "Boom!" he shouts, waving it around. A child, without any sense that what he's doing is serious.

I ask Sayeed, "How can you do this? Doesn't the Koran say you may not punish someone for another's sins? I'm innocent. You know that."

The question bothers him. He goes to the chief, an older man held in great respect by all the guards. A little later, he comes back. "The chef says I must not talk with you about this. He says you think like a snake," weaving his hand back and forth, held low enough for me to see under the blindfold, through the small gap next to my nose.

Another of the guards is simply evil. Calling himself Michel, he claims to be a Christian from East Beirut—an obvious lie. He prays the same as all of them. He delights in sneaking up to the curtain at the end of my cot and snatching it suddenly open, then screaming at me, "No look. You look. I kill." Sometimes he creeps up and just sticks the barrel of the silenced pistol through the curtain. "Bam. Bam," he says quietly.

Michel throws the little fruit we get—a banana, an orange—over the top of the partition. Often it just falls between the side of the bed and the wall, onto the floor where my chains prevent me from reaching it. The two or three bananas there already smell, bringing dozens of huge cockroaches. Once Michel sets a bowl of soup on the end of the bed, just out of my reach. Knorr's dried chicken noodle, I can tell by the smell. Stretching painfully for it, chained arm stretched out straight behind me, I knock it over, spilling soup and noodles onto the bed. He laughs and walks away, leaving the mess. It stays overnight, until another guard helps me clean up.

It's difficult to talk to these men, to bring myself to be polite, to act as if I care what they think. Their minds are alien to me. They seem to think that what they're doing is some kind of small but necessary unpleasantness. Only the loneliness, the hours and days without speaking a word bring me to talk to them. That, and the devouring desire to find out what the hell is going on, what they want, what the chances are of getting out of here. But on that subject, they have little to say. "Soon, and very soon, *Inshallah*"—God willing—is the unvarying response.

The fighting outside the building is becoming worse, and seems to be closer. Sporadic shelling gradually gets heavier. One evening, a guard pulls aside the plastic curtain and tosses something heavy on the bed. He climbs onto the end of the cot and unlocks my wrist chain, then pulls the object over and pushes it at me. "Put on."

It's a heavy flak jacket—green canvas, apparently U.S. Marine issue, with thick plastic inserts in the chest pockets. I pull it on awkwardly, and he snaps the chain back on my wrist.

On the next trip to the toilet, I stumble against something in the hallway. Peeking down under the blindfold, I see a twenty-five-gallon steel drum, filled nearly to the brim with sand. There seem to be a dozen or more strung along the side of the hall.

A day or so later, Sayeed and another guard come in and

release the chains on my hand and feet. "You go home now," Sayeed says. I don't believe him, but my stomach tightens, and my heart begins racing. I can't help it. Amid much bustle, I'm taken into the hallway and pushed down on a mattress on the floor. A chain is again fastened to my leg, and Sayeed laughs.

There are sand-filled steel drums all along the side of the hall, and several on one side of my new bed, but the mattress still sticks into the middle of the hall. The position is uncomfortable—every time a guard goes by or a hostage is taken to the toilet, he has to walk across the bottom of my mattress. Already I'm becoming possessive, almost neurotic, about my "space." The constant procession of feet tromping on my bed drives me to distraction. I try pulling up the end of the mattress every time I hear someone coming, but quickly tire of it. Several times I snap at the guards: "Don't walk on the bed. It's dirty." They pay no attention.

There had been no explanation for the move into the hall, and there is none a few days later when they again unchain me and move me back into the large room I had come from, though this time on the other side.

I lie on the cot, listening to the sound of airplanes taking off, loud, close. We must be right at the end of the runway, in Hay El-sellum, or Bourj Al-Barajneh. I can remember the slum neighborhoods well, the one- and two-story concrete homes, the narrow, shell-pitted roads, the many ruins from the civil war and the Israeli invasion. Each time a plane takes off, I picture the rows of men and women, sitting tensely, the lift of the huge machine. I imagine a stack of passenger manifests sitting on a desk in the airport, three, four feet high. Somewhere in that stack is one with my name on it. Every plane brings it closer to the top.

I'm allowed to wash more often, perhaps twice a week, but still am filthy most of the time. The room is a mess, with bits of rotting food and dirt underfoot. The rough army blanket I've been given has obviously never been washed. I'm moved from the cot against one wall to another plywood-partitioned space against another wall. As they release the locks on my chains, Sayeed again says, "You go home now." Again, I don't believe him, but again, involuntarily, my stomach tightens, my heart races. I can't help it. Five minutes later, I'm chained again a few feet away, and again Sayeed laughs.

I can hear the guards talking to Buckley. He's put in my former place, perhaps six feet away from me. He's ill. All of us have had colds for the past week or so, filling the small apartment with coughing and sneezing. Buckley is the only one not recovering. Instead, he develops a fever, mutters to himself. One phrase is clear, "Oh, God. I've lasted a year, and now my body is going." He goes delirious, moaning in the night, and can't keep down food. They give him a bucket, but he vomits little. I ask about him, but am rebuffed.

A new hostage is brought in late in the evening. He speaks loudly. When asked, he gives his name to one of the guards—David Jacobsen, administrator at the teaching hospital of the American University of Beirut. He is placed on a mattress just outside the plastic curtain of my cubicle, and chained to the wall. I peek cautiously during a quiet moment in the apartment. Tall. Long, thin pale legs. Blindfold like mine. White shorts, T-shirt. I don't dare whisper to him—the guards are lying on their mattresses just two or three feet away.

One or two days later, in the evening, the chief comes in. He's always referred to as "the Hajj," a title of honor given to those who have made the pilgrimage to Mecca, and the guards show much deference to him. He talks with his men, then walks over to Buckley's cot. In Arabic, he mutters, *"Mareed. Ktir, ktir mareed."* Sick, very sick. Then he goes out.

The guards won't give Buckley water or juice. "No good. You sick." They believe that anyone with a fever should not be given liquids—exactly the opposite of proper treatment, like many such "remedies." He pleads for an orange. Finally, in the night, there is the sound of him gasping, floundering about on his cot. The guards come in. A thump, like Buckley kicked the wall. Then silence. After a few minutes, the guards unlock his chains and carry him out of the room. The conviction leaps to my mind—he has died. I begin praying for him, as I had many times before.

The next day, I ask Sayeed about him. "Where's Buckley? Is he okay?"

"Oh, yes, he is in a very good place," Sayeed replies lightly.

There is a patch on the wall just above my bed—a hole in the cement, filled with soft plaster. Someone has scratched in it "Jesus Lives." Not one of the guards, for sure. It must have been whichever hostage was here before me. I begin again to keep track of the days as best I can, casting my mind back to try to figure out how long I've been here—seventy, seventy-five days? It's hard to remember. They're all the same, and I've been moved from bed to bed several times, losing my scratch marks in the wall. I begin marking off each day in the plaster, using Roman numerals in the hope the guards won't notice or understand. But during one of his visits, Sayeed sees the scratches. "Who write this? You?"

"No. I don't know."

He goes out, into the next room, and I hear him asking someone there. "You write on wall before?"

"No."

He comes back, rubs at the scratches, smoothing out the plaster, "Don't write."

"Okay."

From now on, I'll try to count the days in my head. But when I wake up each morning, I can't seem to recall what the previous day's number was.

Since Sayeed seems the friendliest of the guards, I ask for books every time he comes. "I'm not a dog. I can't just sit here day after day. I have to have something for my mind. I need books. Please get me books."

One morning Sayeed drops several hardbound books on the bed: Nikki Kedde on Iran; a collection of essays about

Iran; one on the origins of Shiism; a book about the Druse I'd heard about but never read; and a 1950s political science textbook, *The State*, by a British communist.

I devour them all in two days, reading all night. Then I read them again, and ask for more. "You finish already?"

"Yes, I read very fast, and I have nothing to do. Can you get me more?"

He laughs. No more books arrive.

The nights are still horrible. Filled with half dreams. No real sleep—just dozing, jerking awake. I decide to begin examining myself—every moment I can remember, back as far as I can. My first memory—a blackboard, chalk, my aunt teaching me to read. I was about three. Lorain, Ohio. Albion, New York, where we moved when I was six. Batavia, high school.

Many memories fill me with shame. I was not a good husband. Drinking, womanizing. I examine my marriage, moment by moment—how it failed, why. The sense of anger at my own stupidity grows. I pray, often. Bargains, pleas. God, I'll do better. I'll go to church. I'll give to the poor, spend my life on good causes. I read the Bible, try to understand what's being asked of me. I can't do some of these things. How far do I have to go? Give away everything? Renounce Madeleine, our child? Not possible. Even if I die here. Besides, how does it help to cause more pain and heartache? Would that make up for the pain I brought on my first family? How could God ask that?

What about the anger, the hatred that fills me toward these people? How can I pray for them? Love thy enemy. I can't. That's too much. How do you love evil? How is it right to feel anything but revulsion toward your kidnappers, your tormenters? Hate the sin, love the sinner. What does that mean? How can you separate a person from his actions?

I almost chuckle sometimes—this punishment, if punishment it is, seems perfectly designed for my sins and weaknesses, as only God could. I drank too much—no alcohol here. I chased women—no women here. I'm arrogant—

what better than to put me in the hands of these so-arrogant, uncaring young men. I've been careless of others' feelings—these people give not one tiny thought to mine. I've been an agnostic most of my life—my only comfort here is a Bible, and my prayers.

I reach so hard to touch God, concentrating, waiting for something, some acknowledgment from Him that I exist, that He's listening. I get back only blankness. I know I'm not evil—these people are evil. I'm not like that. But I *feel* sinful, unworthy. If I were God, I wouldn't talk to me, either.

My memories of Madeleine keep me from condemning myself completely. She's such a lovely person, strong, knowing herself, happy with who she is. Intelligent. What does she see in me, beyond all these weaknesses? There must be something there for her. But I can't build pictures of her in my mind, can't think about the months together in any detail. It still hurts too much, far too much.

Long nights, squirrel-in-a-cage nights. Mind spinning, thoughts, emotions whirling. Anger. Frustration. Pain. Guilt.

I can't do this, God. I'm finished. I surrender. There's nothing I can do to change anything, nothing anyone can do. And it's just going to go on, and I can't do it. Help me. There's no reason why you should. Don't we always turn to you when we're in trouble, and away from you when things are good? I'm doing the same. But you say you love me. So help me.

So far down. My mind so tired, my spirit so sore. And more to come, more and more. I just can't do it.

But at the bottom, in surrender so complete there is no coherent thought, no real pain, no feeling, just exhaustion, just waiting, there is something else. Warmth/light/softness. Acceptance, by me, of me. Rest. After a while, some strength. Enough, for now.

It happens once, twice. A few hours later, it fades, and the anger and frustration and longing are back. But the memory is there, the sense of presence. And sometimes the place is reached again, briefly. Not often, but sometimes.

Meanwhile, the hours are endured, the days gotten through. And the nights are spent in prayer, and thought, and the effort to get back to that place.

7

STIGMATA IV

Prayers in the night hurled
fiercely at an absent God;
pleas, promises, bargains offered,
but no answers. Not until
each act in life's examined
and acknowledged; remorse, regret
put in their proper places—
commendable but useless.
Then, after hours of cold
and bitter honesty, into
exhausted calm comes a presence,
softly, almost timorously,
of warmth and light and love.
It will not stay; recoils
from each new blast of anger;
flees absolutely from
hatred's demon glare,
but leaves behind a longing,
comfort, and all anguish
smaller than before.
No flawed man, beset by passion
can hope to hold it long,
though some rare souls
bathe often in its glow.
For most, a light,
infrequent touch, perhaps
just once a life,
must be enough.

A few days after Buckley's disappearance, late at night, the guards bring in the Hajj and a strange man who speaks a little English. He says he is a doctor, takes my pulse and blood pressure, asks me about my health. "I'm okay," I tell him, "but I need exercise, and I need to be able to wash more."

The next day, the guards begin bustling about early in the morning. They sweep and scrub the floor, move the cots, give me clean clothes—shorts and T-shirt—and blankets. For the next few days, I'm allowed to use the small hose found in all Middle Eastern bathrooms to shower, and I get maybe ten minutes to do stretches and push-ups before I'm chained up again.

Two weeks later—mid-June? I'm not really sure of the dates because I have no way to check my calculations. I keep forgetting the numbers in the morning; was yesterday eighty-one or eighty-two? I know the guards lies when I ask. Don't know why, perhaps just for fun. Sayeed and the Hajj come in about midafternoon. Sayeed puts his board on the end of the bed and sits cross-legged. The Hajj stands at the end. A newspaper is shoved under my nose—Arabic, with a large picture of an airplane on the front page. I look immediately for the date. It's in Arabic, but I learned in my first few months to read the numbers. June 14.

The Hajj speaks while Sayeed translates. "You know?"

"No, I can't read Arabic. What is it?"

"Our friends. They take this airplane. You go home soon."

"How? What does this mean?"

"They take an American plane—TWA. Here in Beirut. Many Americans, fifty, sixty."

"What do they want?"

"They want people in Atlit free. Our people. We want people in Kuwait free. Americans say yes. You go home, maybe few days."

I remember Atlit, the grim prison in southern Lebanon, run officially by the South Lebanese Army, the Israeli proxy militia, but actually by Israeli intelligence. It's mostly a holding pen for Israeli "stock"—the Lebanese picked up in sweeps to be used as trading material.

"I don't think that will work. They won't trade me for those people in Kuwait, you know that."

"Yes, they will. American government says yes."

"I hope so. But I don't think it will work. Hajj, you know the U.S. government is not going to make Kuwait give up your friends. They've already said so, haven't they?"

"Yes, but that is just for the public, the newspapers. They will do it."

"I hope so. I really do. But I don't think so. If that's really what you want, I'm going to be here for a long, long time."

Over the next few days, I keep asking Sayeed what's going on with the airplane, but get little information. "They are negotiating," he says at first, then the answers get even shorter. Finally he just ignores my questions. I know it's over, and it didn't work. My depression grows. What now?

The new routines don't last long. A week later, around midnight, several guards and the Hajj come in the room. I can hear them unchaining the others, then they come to unlock my padlocks. "Quiet. No speak," one says to me. I'm led out of the apartment and down the stairs, a guard on each side, one draping his arm over my shoulders. Out the door and down a dirt road for 100 or 150 yards, then into another building. This time, we stay on the first floor. Into a room—clean, tiled floor. Mattress. A chain is wrapped around my left ankle and padlocked. Another hostage is chained across the room. The guards go out, and the door closes.

Cautiously, I raise my blindfold slightly. I can see the blurred image of a man leaning against the wall, peeking back at me from under the rag wrapped around his eyes. Jacobsen? I think so, but it doesn't matter at all. After all these weeks, at least I have a companion. The relief is immediate, immense. Can we talk? Don't know—no instructions. Better not try right now. He grins through a thick, brown beard. I wave, smile at him.

FIVE

My Lady of Kedar,
I wonder at your certainties,
your sense of self.
Where are the fears I feel
despite my manly masks;
hesitations, tremblings I hide?
Do you hide, too?
Or are you, as I believe,
all one throughout,
your beauty just a mirror
of your soul?

8

MADELEINE

It was Easter Sunday when I arrived at John F. Kennedy Airport, in New York City. Terry's cousin Tom, a policeman, was waiting for me and helped me through immigration. His wife, Sue, and Peggy, who had just moved up to New York from Florida, were waiting outside. Peg and I hugged each other and started crying. We caught another plane for Rochester, New York. Peg, her husband, David, and I stayed with David's mother in nearby Batavia for a week before we found a house.

It's difficult to explain how I felt in those times. Far away from home and family, waiting for Terry to come back, expecting a child without a father around—this was not the way we had planned it. Terry and I had decided after long discussions that I would stay in Lebanon for the birth so we could be together, instead of my going on to the States alone and having him join me later. We were so pleased that we were going to be able to stay together all the time.

I don't remember going to bed one night without crying. Terry was so far away now. Many times I thought of going back to Lebanon just to be near him, although I knew the longer he stayed, the more he would want me to be out of there.

Terry's father, his brothers, and his sister Judy were also in Batavia for a while. It felt good to be with his family. They were all trying to find out what they could do for him. His younger sister, Judy, Peggy, and I went to Wash-

ington, D.C., ten days after I arrived in the States. With the help of the AP people there, we managed to meet with some State Department officials. They didn't seem to have a clue what was going on in Lebanon, and promised nothing, saying only they were doing their best to get the hostages released.

I was very disappointed to discover the Americans really had no idea where the hostages were, or how to end the problem. Like all Lebanese, I believed the American government had the power to find out anything it wanted to, and do anything. I learned quickly that we were dealing not only with Lebanese terrorists who were ignorant of the Western world, but with Americans who were equally ignorant of Lebanon, and Terry and I and our families were suffering the consequences.

One day at the beginning of May, a State Department official called to say a letter from Terry had been found in an envelope on the steps of the State Department. After making some forensic tests to make sure it was actually written by him, the official was sending the letter to us. We received it a few days later.

We never knew how long they had had it, and I was puzzled why they hadn't notified us immediately. We were his family, and wanted to know about him. I thought it was rude and not very intelligent of them to treat us in this way. While I understood their need for secrecy in some things, I resented their lack of humanity. Somehow they didn't think we needed or had a right to the information as much as they did.

Everyone in the family agreed to keep the letter away from the press.

On May 15, pictures of several hostages were released by Islamic Jihad, with a warning and a demand for the release of their friends being held in Kuwait. One of the pictures was Terry's. It's absurd to say I was happy, but I was. A picture of Terry meant he was alive. He looked angry in the picture, which meant he was feeling something, he was not giving up. Of course, I was very sad, as well. Just to have his picture taken this way, to be treated like a common criminal by criminals must be very humiliating for him. I used to imagine how he must be fighting to keep his dignity intact. He also did not have his glasses on in the picture. I knew Terry was unable to see much without them. Just the thought of him practically blind in the hands of those people was unbearable to me. I would have given my life to prevent what was happening to him.

Unfortunately, my life was not what these people wanted. And what they wanted no one seemed to be able to give. The Kuwaitis were not going to release anybody who was a danger to their country. The seventeen prisoners in Kuwait had committed terrorist acts. Islamic Jihad was never able to understand that even America could not solve this problem for them.

Two more Frenchman were kidnapped three days after the statement, then an Englishman and another American, David Jacobsen.

On June 6, I went into labor. David Junior, Peggy's stepson who lived with us, started taking pictures of me and cracking jokes. Peg also made me laugh, saying it was a false alarm (we later called the baby a false baby). We were all very nervous.

They drove me to the hospital, and called the family. But at midnight, I was still walking around the hospital without any contractions.

I couldn't sleep all night thinking of Terry and the baby I was about to have with him. All the plans we had made for this day—Terry had wanted to be in the delivery room with me. I wasn't sure I wanted him to see me delivering. Now, though, I didn't care what position he might see me in, so long as he was there.

It wasn't until noon the next day that I started getting contractions. I was nervous, and trying to breathe as I had been taught in the prepartum classes. The doctors put me on a monitor to check on how the baby was doing, then Peg came into the room. She told me I had to decide in the next ten minutes whether to give them permission for a ce-

sarean delivery. Apparently the baby was under stress every time I contracted, and I still wasn't dilating, as I should seventeen hours after my water broke.

I couldn't believe it. All through my pregnancy, I felt well. I had exercised with Terry every day. Now I felt like I had failed him and my motherhood. Nothing had gone right since he was kidnapped.

Ten minutes later, I was in the operating room, listening to the doctors talk about what they were doing. My whole body was numb from anesthesia, except for my head. I could hear, and feel the tears in my eyes. As I looked at the ceiling, my thoughts wandered to when I had met Terry, and then how he was the first to decide I was pregnant. I had laughed at him—at the age of thirty-four, I had given up on the idea of ever getting pregnant. How happy he was, how proud he made me feel to be a woman when it was confirmed. How he held me and kissed me in the elevator at the hospital when we got the test results. For six and a half months, I saw nothing but admiration and love in his eyes whenever he looked at me, at my growing belly.

It was all a miracle—a miracle that came to life at 12:51 P.M., Friday, June 7, 1985. I heard a baby crying from a distance, and then heard it again, only to realize it was my baby, Terry's baby. The pediatrician held the baby to my face and said, "Here is your daughter, Madeleine." I looked at her tiny face, her black hair and fair skin. "She is beautiful," I said. I wanted to hold her, but it wasn't possible. They took her away. I cried and cried. This was not what we planned for. I wanted to see her and Terry together. Why, God, why? Why did you choose us for this? I felt no comfort from God. It was as if he did not exist.

Terry had wanted the name Danielle or Daniel for our child. But one day I dreamed a strange dream about the name Sulome. We were in England, and I was about three months pregnant. In the dream, I was in the middle of a desert—a Western desert, not Arabian. Then a grave appeared. As I approached the headstone, I saw in very large letters the name Sulome—*the u was very clear*—and in much small letters underneath Anderson. I got the strong feeling this woman was somehow very important in American government and history. Then I saw a house with a large brown door, very old, and a small Latin sign. The only thing I could understand was the word Jesuit. I tried to look back at the grave to see when this woman lived and died, but everything became blurry. I woke to find Terry shaking me gently to tell me it was six A.M., and he was going out jogging.

"We're going to have a girl, and her name will be Sulome," I told him sleepily. "What are you talking about?" he asked. "I have to go." I explained the dream to him later, and from then on always knew we would have a daughter, and that would be her name. Terry often laughed, and warned me to think about a boy, as well, in order not to be disappointed.

Two days after Sulome Theresa was born, I heard on television about the abduction of another American, Tom Sutherland. It was obvious that whatever effort the Americans were making to free the hostages, they were not working. The kidnappers needed more hostages. I held Sulome tight, and wondered when she would see her father. How long, and what is it going to take, before we become a family?

Our hopes were raised a short time later when the news broke of the hijacking of a TWA plane to Labanon. A State Department official called to say they were trying to negotiate for Terry and the others, as well as the plane's passengers, and that we should expect news soon.

I knew the Lebanese Shiites, and how they operate, and I found it difficult to believe. They were not going to mix the two cases together. To them, they are completely different. But they couldn't hurt us any more than they have, so we just waited. The TWA plane's passengers were released August 30, without Terry. I had been doubtful, but I had hoped to be wrong. I found that they could still hurt us more, after all.

9

DATE: June 29, 1985
TIME-STAMP: 07:38EDT
DATELINE: Washington

The Reagan administration said American hostages from the TWA hijacking left Beirut in buses early today, headed for Damascus, Syria, and freedom after more than two weeks in captivity.

"We hope and pray that this is the beginning of the journey to freedom," White House spokesman Larry Speakes said in an early morning briefing for reporters. "We have seen reports from various sources that a group (of hostages) has been loaded on buses and the buses are moving."

WASHINGTON, D.C. JUNE 1985.

The TWA hijacking that summer shattered a lot of people's hopes, and illusions. To begin with, the press coverage was abominable. From the first few minutes, it turned into a shameful circus, with one television network buying the "rights" to the "story" from the Shiite militia Amal, and thereafter taking over the Summerland Hotel, where the

102

hostages were trotted out for press conferences. The amount of money involved is unknown, except to those who paid and received it, but rumors had it in the tens to hundreds of thousands of dollars, cash. The fact that one American, Navy diver Robert Stethem, had already been murdered by the hijackers and dozens of lives were in the balance became only a reason for more hype, not one for caution and prudence. It was really a *big* story.

The families of the hostages taken earlier simply assumed that, when it became clear that the United States was negotiating for the release of the TWA hostages, their brothers and husbands and sons would be included in the deal. After all, it was the same people holding all of them, for the same demands, wasn't it? The Reagan administration did nothing, at first, to disabuse them.

In fact, while the plane was originally taken by members of Hezbollah, the same "Party of God" whose leadership also comprised the "shadowy, underground" Islamic Jihad, which held the seven Americans and others, the more "moderate" Shiite militia Amal had quickly taken control. Slipping their own gunmen aboard the plane in the guise of providing security for their "brothers" of Hezbollah, they congratulated the real hijackers for their wonderful effort, then sent them quietly home. After the first few days, it was Amal's demands that were important, not Hezbollah's. The Islamic Jihad hostages were out of play.

In the end, despite his loudly repeated pledges never to negotiate with terrorists, Ronald Reagan extracted Israel's agreement to release several hundred of the Lebanese Shiites it was holding without charges in a prison in southern Lebanon, and Amal agreed to free the TWA hostages. The crisis was over.

Peggy Say got a call from her contact at the State Department, Jackie Ratner. "We have reason to believe that when the hostages reach Damascus, Terry and the others will be with them," Ratner told her.

Reagan himself told members of the Jenco family in Chicago that "all" the hostages were being released.

But when the bus got to Damascus, only forty Americans were on it—the forty from the TWA jet. The seven original hostages were still missing.

"We've been had," was Say's immediate reaction. "I can't believe my own government did this to me."

Her anger grew over the next few years as her campaign led her into meetings with hundreds of top U.S. officials, diplomats, and politicians, as well as the leaders of a dozen other countries. But somehow, she would never lose that sense of disbelief.

"I've met so many important people, and I just stop and wonder," she wrote later in her book, *Forgotten*.

"They make deals in private, deny them in public, and then renege on the whole thing; they sit there in their suits or caftans and lie to your face. These are the people who are running the world. Where do you go to find somebody you can believe, someone you can trust?"

July 3, 1986: David Kimche, director general of the Israeli Foreign Ministry, visited Robert "Bud" McFarlane, President Reagan's national security adviser, at the White House.

Kimche informed McFarlane that top Israelis had been meeting for some time with an Iranian who claimed to represent certain "elements" in the government and army of Iran who were interested in changing that country's policies. They were clearly hinting at some sort of coup. Kimche said only three or four people in the Israeli government knew of the meetings, and asked specifically that the American CIA not be informed.

In fact, the United States already knew of the talks, and even knew that Israel had been shipping arms to the Iranians as early as 1981, less than two years after the revolution and the subsequent taking of the U.S. embassy hostages. In all their testimony in the later hearings and trials concerning Iran-Contra, U.S. officials insisted that they had never approved of such weapons transfers. Again in fact, Secretary of State Alexander Haig had given the go-ahead to Prime Minister Yitzhak Shamir.

The weapons shipments stopped in the fall of 1981, apparently because Haig withdrew his approval. In the succeeding several years, the idea of trying to woo Iranian factions in this particular way never gained any support again, in either Washington or Israel. But in early 1985, the CIA produced, at McFarlane's direction, a new analysis of U.S. policies and options on Iran. Based wholly on speculation, not very well founded, the new analysis suggested that there was likely to be opposition to the Khomeini regime in Iran because of the economic failure of the new government. In order to encourage such opposition, "evidence" of "bona fides" would have to be produced. In the Middle East, that meant only one thing—weapons.

"It was all theory. It was all CIA [gaming]," McFarlane said in an interview in 1993. "I did agree with it, and I said let's at least ask the question."

A "study memorandum" was circulated to all cabinet officers, and drew sharp reaction. "Cap Weinberger [the Secretary of Defense] was quite sharp in saying that this was out of the question. We cannot do this. There are no pragmatists in Iran. George Shultz [the Secretary of State] was less vitriolic, but agreed, 'Yeah, I don't see any evidence that this holds water.'"

McFarlane was primarily interested in overall U.S. policy on Iran and grand strategies that might change the situation there. His boss, Ronald Reagan, was interested almost to the point of obsession in gaining the release of American hostages in Lebanon. Everything the United States had tried so far had failed.

"It was clear that Reagan's concern was the release of the hostages, come what may," McFarlane said. "Come what may being the Iran-Contra affair. And I think that while he may not have realized something of that scale and political enormity [would happen] ... he believed that at the end of the day, his commitment to releasing the hostages was not only right but ... politically sound. That Americans would find it defensible to do damn near anything in the world if you could release those hostages. It broke the law, it went against policy, it offended allies, it [angered] the Congress. And he really did think about those things. That was not a high price to pay."

At that first meeting in July of 1985, Kimche made no suggestion of any weapons-for-hostages deal. He was simply informing his country's ally and sponsor that he was in touch with an Iranian named Ghorbanifar, who claimed to represent Iranian officials interested in a rapprochement. He also did not mention that Ghorbanifar, a well-known arms merchant, had a reputation for lying and exaggeration. Was the United States open to such a dialogue? McFarlane briefed the president. "He said, 'Well, if there's a basis for believing that these people are genuine and represent elements that really want to change, then of course we're open to a dialogue. Tell them that.' And I did. And he [Kimche] went back home."

This was the Middle East. It was not, of course, that simple.

Ten days later came another message from Kimche, via an Israeli arms dealer named Al Shwimmer. The Iranian "dissidents" had decided they were too vulnerable. They would arrange the release of the hostages, but just as the CIA study had predicted, they needed some evidence of their "clout"—specifically, weapons. More specifically, 100 antitank missiles (TOWs).

Once again, McFarlane says, he briefed the president. "[Reagan] said, 'Well, no, we can't do that. We cannot ship American weapons to Iran until we know a little more about just who it is we're dealing with, and their bona fides.' "

He wasn't shocked at the idea, McFarlane recalled. He just wanted to make sure the United States would be giving missiles to the right people.

A few days later, Kimche was back with another, slightly altered proposal. Would the United States approve of Israel's giving its own (U.S.-supplied) weapons to the Iranians and, by the way, promise immediate replacement of whatever the Israelis gave away?

"So, we had another meeting with the president and the same cast—Cap, George, Casey, Regan, Bush*—and I went through this all with them," McFarlane related. As in all the previous discussions of the subject, Weinberger and Shultz objected. Casey and Regan were generally in favor. "Bush said, yeah, it's worth a try," according to McFarlane. Reagan, of course, was all for it. "No reservations."

Thus, in July of 1985, arms-for-hostages was born.

---

* William Casey, the director of the CIA; Donald Regan, the White House Chief of Staff; and George Bush, the Vice President, respectively.

SIX

STIGMATA V

Isolation ends; other denizens
of this mad gulag bring relief
and aid in staving off
the savages without, within.
Self-flagellation can be purifying,
but carried on too long becomes
indulgence, a twisted kind of pride.
New minds bring fresh air;
new shoulders can be leaned on;
new regards provide a scale,
a balance that makes it easier
to maintain both faith and hope.
Personalities and politics
are different; five egos
in a room must clash and rub.
But differences are unimportant
next to shared laughter and shared pain.
Each takes from each;
each gives of what he has.

10

BEIRUT. JULY 1985.

Jacobsen is a tall man, with thin, long legs, a quick smile, and a penchant for monologues. The administrator for American University Hospital, he'd been in Beirut only about six months, spending most of that period on the hospital or university grounds because of the danger.

The morning after our arrival in the new quarters, we're given permission from the guards to talk quietly, and we quickly exchange stories. David had been snatched as he walked the short distance from the university to the hospital, without a guard. The Lebanese doctor walking with him was unable to stop the young men from taking him, though David said he and the doctor fought hard. One of the kidnappers walloped David over the head with his gun, stunning him long enough to get him in the car. He'd been brought directly to the apartment where I was being kept. He'd also heard Buckley in delirium, and was as convinced as I was that he died. The only difference was he thought that last loud thump was the guards knocking Buckley on the head. I don't agree, but there's no way, of course, to know. Jacobsen had been brought over to this apartment/cell at the same time the previous evening, walking down the dirt road, but he said he had been allowed to look up briefly at the stars.

He seems fairly cheerful and unafraid. His biggest immediate problem is his eyes—he's very farsighted, and his glasses were lost in the kidnapping. When the guards bring

111

my Bible, David says he is a committed Christian. I begin reading to him, a few minutes in the morning and afternoon—mostly psalms, or Paul's letters.

At first, the guards don't bother us much, and the room is a great deal cleaner than our previous one. The building is obviously fairly new, someone's house, not a regular prison. There are no windows in the room, just two small fans high on the outside wall. The inside doorknob has been removed from the door, and a steel plate covers the hole.

We're also able to get a little more exercise, with only one three-foot-long chain on an ankle. I learn to pace one step in each direction, keeping my turns precise to avoid tripping on the chain. I do sit-ups and push-ups in sets of twenty and twenty-five throughout the day, using the physical exertion as a kind of tranquilizer, whenever my spirits drop too low or my mind spins too fast.

One evening not long after the move, the Hajj stops by. Already I have learned to recognize his voice, a light tenor, soft but authoritative. In an uncharacteristic move, he sits down on the floor and starts a conversation, with Sayeed next to him translating. First, he apologizes for the chains. It's necessary, he says, for security. Besides, the seventeen Shia jailed in Kuwait are suffering much worse conditions.

"When are we going home?"—the first and obvious question for both David and me.

"Soon, *Inshallah*," the Hajj replies, but it's quickly apparent that he's just making reassuring noises. In fact, according to him, the U.S. government is refusing to negotiate. "They say we are terrorists." The word angers him. "We are not terrorists. We only do this because it's the only way."

"Hajj, look in the dictionary. That's what *terrorist* means—someone who uses violence for political purposes. You may not like the word, but that's what it means."

The reply is quick, almost practiced. "What can we do? We don't like this, but your government will not pay attention to us."

"Talk to the Kuwaitis. If you want your people out of Kuwait, you should be talking to them."

"They won't do anything." He is scornful. "They are just puppets of the Americans. If your government tells them to let our brothers go, they will do it. But your government has told them not to."

"It's not that simple, Hajj. The Kuwaitis are not puppets, like you think. The American government can't interfere in these cases, where a legal trial has been held."

"It was not legal. They just took many hundreds of Shia off the streets. It was not a trial." He is oblivious to the irony.

"I don't know anything about that. Only that they were sentenced for trying to kill many people. Some people were killed. The American government isn't going to ask Kuwait to let them go."

"They must. Or you will not go home. How can we make the government talk to us?"

"If you don't like being called a terrorist, do something to convince them that you're reasonable. Let at least one of us go."

"And then what do we do? Will they give us what we want?"

"Maybe at least they'll talk to you."

He doesn't sound convinced, of course. It's difficult to tell if he's serious, or just playing with us. It's also very strange to be talking like this with my kidnapper, pretending that it's all perfectly normal, rational, and that reasoned argument will make any difference at all. Pretending that I'm not enraged, frustrated, and terribly, terribly lonely.

I'm blindfolded—I can't see his face, can't look into his eyes. Does he see any of this? Does he really believe I'm a human being, like himself? Does he feel any of my pain? If he does, how can he do this?

He asks if we need anything. Books, a radio, newspapers. Why do we want news, he asks, half jokingly. Everything in the newspaper is lies, anyway. We need it to keep sane, we reply. To fill the hours. To stay in touch with the world, and not feel so alone. He promises to get us something, then leaves.

After the door is closed, David and I raise our blindfolds and look at each other. "Do you really think he'll do anything?"

"Probably not. But it can't hurt to argue with him. Maybe something will happen. Maybe we'll get a few books, anyway. It can't hurt."

The two small fans keep the room reasonably cool—when they operate. But, as always in Beirut, electricity is erratic. When it goes out, the room quickly becomes stifling. It is full summer now—the beginning of July. Three and a half months.

After some argument, the guards agree to open the door when the power is out. They do so early one morning. We've been aware of the prisoners in the next room, listened to them going back and forth to the toilet in the morning, and tried to count them. We've had several long discussions, trying to figure out who they are. But David was always too busy to pay much attention to the news reports while he was free, and after one hundred days, I figure my information is probably out of date. Today, eagerly but carefully, we sit back against the wall and slowly tilt our heads to peek through the gaps in the blindfolds as our neighbors are escorted past our door, one by one.

David recognizes a colleague at the university, Dr. Tom Sutherland, among the three. "He looks like a ghost," he says later. "He's so pale, and walks like a zombie."

Later in the day, I ask Sayeed about them. Surprisingly, he tells me. "They are Americans. A priest—Jenco. Ben Weir. And a professor at the American University—Sutherland."

"Can we speak to them?"

"I will ask."

The next morning, Sayeed tells us we can say good morning, but nothing more as the men go by our door.

First, Ben Weir. "Good morning, Reverend Weir," David and I both call out gently. "Good morning," he answers.

Next. "Good morning, Father. How are you?" "Good morning, okay."

"Good morning, Tom." "Good morning."

That's it. But the lift is immediate. I talk to Sayeed again later. "Can we meet them, talk with them?"

"I don't know. I must speak to the Hajj."

David tells Sayeed he knows Tom Sutherland, had worked with him at the university, and would like to talk to him.

"Tell the Hajj I am a Catholic," I add. "I want to talk to the priest, Father Jenco. I want to say confession."

"Confession? What do you mean?"

"It is part of my religion. To talk with a priest, to talk about my sins."

"You can tell me your sins." He laughs.

"No, I have to do this if I can. It's part of my religion."

"Okay, I will ask."

A day later, after our morning trip to the toilet, Sayeed and two other guards bring Father Martin into our room, seating him on David's bed, back against the wall. He takes David into their room, where Ben Weir and Tom Sutherland remained.

We all, of course, remain blindfolded, and two guards stay in the room. Half lying on the floor, chained leg stretched out behind me, I grope toward the priest with my right hand, saying softly, "How are you, Father?" I find his hand and squeeze it gently. "How are you doing?"

Turning toward Sayeed, I say, "I want to say confession now. Can you close the door?"

"No, go ahead. We will stay here."

"That's not right. We have to be alone. This is private."

"I can't close the door."

"Why not? This is part of my religion, too. We have to be alone."

The two guards exchange a few words in Arabic, then Sayeed says, "You have ten minutes." The two go out the door and close it behind them.

Cautiously, I raise my blindfold. Father Jenco, a white-haired man with a full beard and a gentle smile, is sitting cross-legged on David's mattress. We clasp hands. "I'm Lawrence Jenco." "Hi, Father. I'm Terry Anderson. I don't know where to start. It's been a very long time since I said confession."

"It doesn't matter. Just go ahead." He nods in encouragement.

"I left the church when I was young. For a long time, I was an agnostic, or at least I said I was. I don't know what I meant by that. Just laziness, I guess. Didn't want to deal with it. I came back just a few months ago. Haven't gone to confession, or taken communion yet, though. But I'm a Catholic.

"I was in the process of getting a divorce when I was kidnapped. Mostly my fault, I know. I was not a good man—chasing women, drinking. Seems like I just kind of lost my way for a while."

The discussion goes on for twenty minutes or more, twice the time the guards had agreed to. Father Martin's responses are always quiet, gentle. Mostly, he just listens. A few times he offers brief assurances on points I do not understand, such as how difficult it might be to get an annulment of my first marriage.

For a Catholic, ritual confession, or the sacrament of reconciliation, as it is called now, is an emotional ceremony, no matter how informal the setting. This was my first confession in twenty-five years, my first formal step back to the church. I'd spent months wrestling with myself; months trying to understand where that moment in an English church six months ago was taking me; more months lying chained on a cot with nothing to do but examine myself, study the Bible and try to deal, alone, with my anger, frustration, remorse. This smiling, soft-spoken priest, also a hostage, dressed like me in white cotton shorts and T-shirt, frightened, in his own pain and anger received the full flood of my emotions, guilts, and concerns, returning warmth, love, and understanding.

By the end of our session, the bare floor around us is littered with crumpled tissues. Both he and I are crying. Finally, I kneel beside him. "Father, forgive me, for I have sinned, in word and in thought, in what I have done and what I have not done."

He rests his right hand lightly on my head. "In the name of a gentle, loving God, you are forgiven." He pulls my head gently to his shoulder and hugs me. We sit back and look at each other. In a few moments, we hear a guard turning the lock on the door, and we pull our blindfolds down over our eyes.

FAITH

Where is faith found?
Not in a book,
or in a church,
not often or
for everyone.
In childish times
it's easier;
a child believes
just what it's told.
But children grow
and soon begin
to see too much
that doesn't match
the simple tales,
and not enough
of what's behind
their parents' words.
There is no God,
the cynics say;
we made Him up
out of our need
and fear of death.
And happily
they offer up

their test-tube proofs.
A mystery,
the priests all say,
and point to saints
who prove their faith
in acts of love
and sacrifice.
But what of us
who are not saints,
only common
human sinners?
And what of those
who in their need
and pain cry out
to God and go
on suffering?
I do not know—
I wish I did.
Sometimes I feel
all the world's pain
I only say
that once in my
own need I felt
a light and warm
and loving touch
that eased my soul
and banished doubt
and let me go
on to the end.
It is not proof—
there can be none.
Faith's what you find
when you're alone
and find you're not

11

David and I broke into amazed laughter the other night. We were sitting in the room, with Michel just outside the open door, when we heard a bell outside in the street. David asked, "What is that? It sounds like an ice-cream truck."

"Yes, *bouza*," Michel said.

"Well, why don't you go get some? It's hot."

"Okay." And he did. The only guard there (that we knew of), and we sent him out for ice cream! Weird, but delicious.

The Hajj also finally came through. He delivered a stack of old *Herald Tribune*s and a few magazines—*Time* and *Newsweek*. Mostly a couple of weeks old, but better than nothing. In one, there was a short piece on Buckley—Islamic Jihad announcing they had killed him. No surprise. We both were sure he died that night. And IJ would certainly try to turn his death to its advantage. Means nothing much, though it's an indication the negotiations, if there are any, are not going well. Also no surprise.

David and I both have suffered a bad attack of gastroenteritis. We were fed *kibbeh naiya* for dinner one night—a mixture of raw meat and cracked wheat. The three in the other room wouldn't eat it, so we were given their portions, as well. They were right. We were sick for three days, shouting for the guards to take us to the bathroom five or ten times a day. They usually did, though we often had to wait for a while—sheer torture when your gut is roiling and your rectum won't clench any more. Never again.

Sayeed came in a few days ago to tell us once again, "You will go home soon."

"Why? What's happened?"

"We kidnapped a Kuwaiti, from the embassy. Now they will negotiate with us." He was delighted. Unfortunately, Wajd Domani is not a Kuwaiti. He's the Syrian-born Lebanese press officer at the Kuwaiti embassy, and worth nothing as a bargaining chip. He's also a pest. David is nursing him along, showing a great deal of patience and sensitivity. I try, but not very successfully. He complains constantly and breaks into tears often, lamenting each day how long it's been since he was taken. A whole week! I've snapped at him several times already. Not such a Christian showing, and I'm ashamed of it. But he drives me crazy.

At least he provides a date check: He was taken July 12, 1985. Which makes it about July 19. 125 days.

The electricity is often off, and the room becomes intolerably hot and almost completely dark when the door is closed. Wajd begins panicking the moment the power goes off—he says he's claustrophobic. He has had several long talks with the Hajj, trying to persuade him of his lack of value. He hasn't passed on much out of his talks. Just one small comment that might be useful later. Apparently, the Hajj told him he used to be a bodyguard for Hussein Husseini, while Husseini was with the Movement for the Dispossessed, in 1980 or 1981. Husseini is now the speaker of Parliament—a movement away from radicalism and into main-line politics that the Hajj obviously strongly disapproves of.

We are now allowed to get together once a week for services with Father Martin, Pastor Ben Weir, and Tom Sutherland. David continues to be worried about Tom—says he seems listless, pale, and without spirit. Last Sunday, I got highly irritated with the guards and lost my temper a bit. They kept walking around and singing Shia chants while we were trying to hold the service. I told Sayeed I thought it was outrageous and was preventing us from praying properly. Surprisingly, no anger from him. Perhaps they'll stop.

I made a couple of small chess sets out of the tin foil from the processed cheese we get every morning and evening. Asked Sayeed to take one to our fellow hostages in the next room, which he did, then returned with thanks and the information that none of them can play chess. Neither can David. Oh, well. Nice try.

There's no news of progress toward a release for anyone. The nights are still bad—long hours of praying, soul-searching, regrets. How long? I memorize psalms, read the Bible to David, or to myself. We talk about the few books we have. Not much about our families, or friends. I still go into bursts of physical activity, alternating with days of doing nothing, just lying on the mattress like a lump.

They've begun taking us out, one by one or two by two, onto a walled-in, semiroofed exercise area on the roof of the first floor. There, we can run around the sides a bit, and do some exercises. It's hard, running with your blindfold only half raised. I spotted an extra guard, besides Badr, standing quietly against the wall at one end, with a silenced pistol hanging from his hand. Playing the same tricks again. Do they hope someone will try to escape? Or are they just being careful? No place to go, anyway. We're surely in Hay El-sellum or Bourj Al-Barajneh. Full of checkpoints and guard posts at night, and obviously impossible during the day—what do you suppose would happen to a pale-skinned American in thin, white boxer shorts, running down the street in the middle of a Beirut suburb full of Shiite radicals?

Tonight, something is going on. All the guards are here, and I heard the Hajj's voice. Wajd has been taken out. Is he being released? Sayeed releases my chain, and David's. We're guided out of the room, down some stairs, down a short hall, and into another room. Rough concrete floor. Dirty. Someone in the room, on a mattress. The door closes, and we raise our blindfolds. It's Tom Sutherland. We shake hands, embrace. He is really in bad shape. Worried. Says they've been giving him a hard time over some paper in his briefcase, calling him a spy, threatening him. No sign of Father Martin or Pastor Weir.

Within a few minutes, Sayeed comes back in and tells Tom to pick up his mattress, then takes him out. Almost immediately Sayeed's back, and tells me the same thing. I'm taken down more stairs, into a huge, echoing subbasement. There is a line of cells on the right side of the room, about chest high. Steel doors. I'm shoved into a cell. It's not quite big enough for the mattress on the floor—I have to pull the end up for the guard to close the door. The ceiling is wire mesh, too low for me to stand up. Michel quickly comes back carrying a length of chain. He fumbles around, then chains my feet, a padlock on each foot, passes the chain out through a low, barred opening, and padlocks the chain outside.

"What are you doing? Why?"

He laughs. "You like?"

"No. Why are you doing this?" No answer.

After he's left, I can hear Tom moving around in the next cell. I stand up as far as I can, half crouched, push my mouth up next to the mesh above me, and call out to him softly.

"Tom. Are you okay? What's this about?"

"I don't know. They say I'm a spy. This is some kind of punishment."

But why me? No one has accused me of being a spy recently, not since the first few weeks. I haven't gotten into any trouble in the past couple of days, that I know of. So what in hell is going on?

Tom and I spent one night in the "horse stalls," as he refers to them. The mosquitoes are bad, and some kind of machinery roars all night. The next evening, I'm taken out and back upstairs. David is still in the new cell. He's got no explanation, either. I tell him what it's like. "I don't think Tom can last long down there. It's pretty awful. What can we do?"

We both pray for a while. When Sayeed comes back, I

ask him why he put us down in the stalls, then brought me back and left Tom there. "He's a bad man."

"No, he isn't. He's a professor, not a spy. A good man."

Sayeed explains that they had found a paper in Tom's briefcase—some kind of discussion of Islam. The problem apparently is not so much what was in the paper as that Tom denied having it, said he'd never seen it. That has awakened the hamsters' paranoia. If he's worried enough to deny it, it must be bad, is their kind of logic.

He even showed the paper to David and me when we asked for it. It is simply a copy of an address to some conference that explains basic concepts of Islam. Very academic, totally harmless. We try to tell Sayeed that it means nothing, that it's simply the kind of thing college professors collect. But he's stuck on the idea that Tom's denial means it must be important, and compromising. I go back to arguing the main point.

"You have to get him out of there. He won't be able to stand it long."

"I can't. It's an order. He must stay."

"Do you want him alive? He's not a bad man. Look, if he has to stay, take me back, as well. He can't stay there alone."

The discussion goes on for some time. Finally, Sayeed leaves. Half an hour later, he's back, with Tom. Rejoicing. Embraces among the three of us.

Sayeed explains. "I took a *fatwa* from the Koran." This kind of *fatwa* is a religious ruling made by randomly choosing a verse from the Koran, like sticking a pin in the Bible, and interpreting it as being a yes-or-no answer to his question. This time it was yes. I can hardly believe the explanation. Sayeed is reasonably intelligent, fairly fluent in English, somewhat educated. Yet he believes in this procedure, to the point he will violate his orders. At any rate, Tom is back, shaken and scared, but with us.

Sayeed asks if we would like to have Father Martin and Pastor Ben with us, as well. Five in a room this size? No hesitation. We all answer, "Yes, of course." The next day they are both brought into our cell, and five mattresses are jammed in—four in a row, and mine crossways against one end wall. It's going to be hard to live like this, but we need each other, badly. At least, I need them. Anything to keep my mind going, to keep away those hours of whirling, useless thoughts, to keep me away from myself.

We've worked out some sort of a routine that allows the five of us to exist in this ten-by-twelve-foot room. The companionship has been wonderful—both Father Martin and Ben Weir seem to be gentle, quiet men. They've already formed a deep bond, sharing their faith without paying any attention to the dogmas that separate them. Father Martin conducts mass one day, Pastor Ben leads the service the next.

Tom seems a little uncomfortable, but goes along. From what he's said, he was once a regularly churchgoing Presbyterian, but had just drifted away. He seems to be still in shock, and is worried sick about the pressure he's under from our hosts. He talks about nothing else. We can't persuade him that they're not serious about his being a spy, and in fact, we can't be sure. He's been taken out for interrogation once already, in a small room across the hall. From what he tells us, they were pretty threatening, but didn't abuse him. He takes little part in our discussions, spending most of his time just lying on his mattress. A couple of times he's talked about suicide—putting his head in one of the plastic sacks we get for garbage. I've not been too patient with him—I don't think he's serious abut it, and anyway, it's a damned difficult way to kill yourself. I don't think it could be done even by a very determined man.

David is enthusiastic about the services. He's a regular at the Crystal Cathedral in California, which I gather is some sort of very conservative, evangelistic Protestant group. He seems to be very conservative about just about everything—a solid, Orange County Republican. We couldn't disagree more on just about every issue, and it's beginning to show.

Every morning, after breakfast—almost always cheese on Arabic bread, with one cup of weak, boiled tea—and the trip to the bathroom, we pick up our mattresses and lean them against the wall. Then we pace around in a circle, one behind the other, gradually beginning to run, faster and faster. Father Martin, Ben, and Tom each end up dropping out of the circle and stepping into the center of the room. David and I circle them, picking up speed, leaning further inward, until we're racing madly into exhaustion. Finally, we both give up, sweating and heaving for breath. The exercise is too much for this small room, but it's a purge.

I've tried several times to clean the dirt off the rough cement floor with a small broom the guards gave us. But there's too much of it. I just manage to kick up enough dust to make the air thick and my companions curse until it settles back into the holes and cracks in the floor. I guess I've become some kind of fanatic about trying to keep clean. It's hard. We wash our clothes in the cold tap during our ten-minute stay in the bathroom and try to dry them in front of a fan the guards also gave us. It doesn't work very well because the room is always awfully humid—five bodies put out a lot of moisture. And heat. Sometimes it's so hot, we all just lie limp. I've even taken to lying on the rough cement because it's too hard to sleep on the mattress.

We've gotten some new guards—Fadl and Mahmoud. Of course, like all the names we know, they're just made up. These two men are larger than the others, perhaps twenty-five years old, and friendly. Fadl even puts in a few minutes from time to time with a large piece of cardboard, trying to fan some fresh air in through the doorway. Mahmoud speaks some English, Fadl very little.

All the guards apparently are taking karate, or something similar, perhaps tae kwon do. Some have black belts, others brown.

Several times, Sayeed and I have wrestled—me blindfolded, trying to use the little aikido I learned in Japan against his karate. Not very successfully, obviously. None of this new set of guards—we see little of Badr and Michel

these days—seems terribly concerned about us seeing them.
I dumped Sayeed on the floor once, fell on top of him, and
ended up with a disarranged blindfold, staring into his face
from about four inches away. He didn't even blink, and said
nothing about it. Nonetheless, we've all become pretty careful about keeping the blindfold in place while they're here.
Ben is the twitchiest about it. He's got a set of swimming
goggles with the lenses covered by tape, and every time
there's a noise at the door, he jumps for the corner, faces inward, and snatches his goggles down. He must have had a
bad time earlier. He's been a captive well over a year. He
and Father Martin were kept together in the mountains for
a time, along with Levin and Buckley.

We're all desperate for news. Ben speaks fluent
Arabic—he spent thirty years in Lebanon, much of that
time in Nabatiyeh, the main Shiite town of south Lebanon.
He frequently lies on the floor (at our urging) next to the
door to see what he can pick up from the guards' talk. Not
much—apparently it's mostly what you would expect uneducated young men to say during a stint of boring duty. At
least we can keep track of the date. Today is August 30,
1985. 168 days.

Ben says he believes he heard Wajd down the hall, complaining, so he hasn't been released. And he thinks he over-
heard some French. David said he thought he heard French
being spoken in a room down the hall during his trips to
the bathroom. We know at least four Frenchmen were kidnapped before Tom and David were taken, so maybe it's
them.

Ben is teaching me Arabic. I've made flash cards out of
bits of paper from the few books we have and other things
lying around, and practice for hours. We've got a couple of
Arabic newspapers, or at least parts of one, and he's using
those to try to teach me a little grammar. So far, I've got
several hundred words written down, with appropriate sentences. The pronunciation is hard. One sound, called "ein,"
a kind of swallowing, nasal noise, I don't think I'll ever

get. We practiced it over and over again the other day until the others were ready to kill us both.

We ask often about the news, but get nothing. The guards are apparently under orders to tell us nothing about what's happening outside. It's like they don't know much about any negotiations—they're just guards. It's so frustrating, and I know the others feel it as much as I do. We're just sitting in this hole in the ground rotting, like some kind of neglected pets. No more newspapers, books, or magazines, and our requests for a radio are being ignored.

The electricity's out again, and it's stiflingly hot—too hot for even a small candle to relieve the darkness. We played "Twenty Questions" for a while, like children, but now everyone's quiet, just lying still. I've recited mentally the half dozen psalms I've memorized so far, and prayed. Now what? I don't dare start thinking about Maddy, or the baby I know she's had by now. I'm tired of thinking about my sins. Even my fantasies—about escape; rescue; making a million, a billion dollars—are getting old and worn. I can masturbate quietly in the dark, as I have from time to time. Use it or lose it. But that only takes a few minutes, and there's a whole night ahead. What's a nightlong project? Build a house? Well, design one, anyway. How many rooms? Fireplaces? What do I need in a house? What would I really want? Library. Pool room. Swimming pool? Yes, definitely, swimming pool. Big one.

We're upstairs again, on the ground floor. The guards came in, told us to pick up our mattresses, and brought us one by one back to the same room David and I were in a few weeks ago. But this time, all five of us. It's a small room, perhaps twelve by fifteen. The Hajj has also given us a radio, a little seven-band Sony. We can even get Armed Forces Radio on it, and listen to the half-hour repeat of all the American news reports—the networks, AP, and UPI. Heard Peg's voice the other night—the first time any of our families have been on. I choked up completely, and started crying.

I've started serious study of the Bible with Ben and Father Martin. They've had me laying out the parallel gospels—Matthew, Mark, and Luke—comparing the different ways various episodes and sermons are presented and trying to figure out why they're different. Where is each one aimed, and whom was it written by? I've made a list of the different kinds of references—how often miracles are related, the role women play, other things like that. Fascinating, and a great help in trying to understand.

Still working on the Arabic lessons. I work through the homemade flash cards several times a day, but Ben and I have cut back a little on the pronunciation lessons. It's too irritating for the others.

David and I seem to be bickering a lot. The longer we're together, the harder it is for the two of us to get along. Tom is still very quiet and very depressed.

We've just had a startling announcement from the Hajj. They've decided to let one of us go home, "as a humanitarian gesture"! It's also an effort to persuade the Reagan administration that these people are serious about wanting to negotiate. The most startling part, though, is that he says we're to choose which one. We're all stunned.

Then the Hajj adds that it cannot be Tom. He will be the last to go home, he says. It's impossible to tell if he's serious. He also says it should not be me. We protest. Ben argues in Arabic with him, fruitlessly. He leaves.

How are we going to handle this? Ben, kidnapped in 1984, has been here longest, of course. But if someone is going to be a spokesman, is he the one? He's a very good man, but quiet. We all deserve to go home, and we all want it badly. I can see it on everyone's face, and I know it's on mine. What a terrible, terrible thing to do to us. Perhaps we should refuse to choose. But then, maybe no one will go. No, we will try.

We quickly decide that, whatever choice is made, it must be unanimous, and it should be by secret ballot. We also agree that we will ignore the Hajj's stricture about Tom and me. We walk around in our circle for half an hour. Very little talking. Finally, I speak.

"We all want to go. I think, if it can't be me, it should be David. He's articulate and forceful. If someone is to speak for us, to persuade Reagan to begin talks, he'd do it well."

David's grateful, but says little. Pastor Ben says he does not want to go, that he will stay. Father Martin says the same.

We sit down, tear up some paper, and begin the ballot. First time, one vote for everyone except Ben, two for me. How does Ben feel? His face shows nothing, and he says nothing. Another ballot, same result. We take a break, get up, and begin walking in a circle again. After a few minutes, I ask, "Anybody want to say anything else?"

"Why? You want to campaign?" David snaps. I don't reply.

Another ballot. This time it's two for David, three for me. I'm in a quandary. Should I vote for myself? Or David? How long will this go on? Again. Same. Again. Now it's four for me, one for David.

"Well, that's that," Father Martin says, obviously assuming the single vote for David is mine. "No, Father. It has to be unanimous," I tell him. It takes him a few seconds to realize that both David and I are voting for ourselves. I'm ashamed at the silence.

Last ballot. Five for me. We sit back. I can feel the tears building. Father Martin hugs me, then Ben, Tom. Finally David.

"Thank you," I manage. "I'm very grateful. I also feel guilty. You all deserve to go as much as I do."

I'm also scared. The Hajj said he didn't want it to be me. Will he veto the choice? Dear God, I don't know what I feel. I can't believe it will happen, I feel somehow it's not right. I'm ashamed of wanting it so bad. But they chose, we all chose. I can't allow myself to really believe this is the end.

We call Sayeed, tell him of our choice. He laughs. "We

have already chosen." We ask him why. The Hajj told us to choose. Whom have they picked? "I will tell the Hajj. He will talk to you."

A night of misery, joy, confused prayer. I try as hard as I can not to believe it. But it's no use. I can't help thinking about being free, seeing Maddy, my daughter, Gabrielle. The shame and guilt won't go away. I can't even look at Ben. He's so sincere in his happiness for me. And the others, they must be terribly disappointed.

Finally, the Hajj appears. No discussion, no greeting. He speaks in Arabic to Ben, at length, angrily. Ben gasps. "Oh, no. Oh, no." What is it? I know already.

"He says I'm the one. I'm going tonight. I tried to argue, but he won't listen. I'm sorry."

The disappointment overwhelms me. I expected it. I was prepared for it. It's a relief to have it settled so surely, after all the agonizing. But it hurts. Oh, God, how it hurts.

Ben is quickly given a haircut, clothes. We get a brief chance to embrace him, wish him luck. "I'm sorry," he says to me again. "Don't worry," I reply. "You should have been the one we chose anyway." He's hustled out.

The four of us sit quietly for a while. Then the lights are turned out. I pray, reaching for calm, for acceptance. Slowly, slowly, it comes. Lord, I don't know what you want of me, what you're trying to do. Help me.

SEVEN

PRIORITY;—URGENT—
THE ASSOCIATED PRESS
Copyright 1985 By The Associated Press.
All Rights Reserved.
DATE: September 18, 1985
TIME-STAMP: 11:43EST
DATELINE: Washington

The Rev. Benjamin Weir, one of seven Americans kidnapped in Beirut, has been released after more than 16 months in captivity, the Presbyterian Church said today.

Church officials said Weir would appear Thursday at a Washington news conference. "He's in good health," said Majorie Carpenter of the church's Atlanta office.

WASHINGTON, D.C.
SEPTEMBER 19, 1985.

Peggy Say and her brother Glenn Richard Anderson, Jr., were jammed against each other in the middle pew of the huge Presbyterian church, sweating and nervous. It wasn't just the massive crush of press people around them. No one had had a chance to speak privately with Ben Weir before this press conference. Neither knew whether he had seen their little brother Terry in prison, whether Terry was ill or desperate.

There was an explosion of applause, bursts of blinding light from flashbulbs, and the glare of TV camera lights coming on. Weir walked onto the stage, looking healthy and fit—even normal. The expected questions, until finally The One: "Pastor Weir, did you see the other hostages?"

"Yes. Just a few days ago, and they were well."

Peg began crying. Rich clapped and shouted with the others. Then Weir went on, gravely: "If something isn't done soon, the captors are going to execute the hostages. They have released me to urge the administration to act immediately in this situation, or the consequences will be fatal."

The gravity of the message was nearly buried in the rush of knowing that their brother was alive and well. Later, Peg, Rich, and members of other hostage families met with the Presbyterian pastor. A gentle, kind, and spiritual man, he passed over lightly the worst part of the captivity. Instead, he related personal anecdotes and conversations about the other hostages, passed on messages—all the little details the families were longing to hear.

Peg had come out swinging after the TWA debacle. The Associated Press agreed to pay her travel expenses and phone bills; the hostage families had become a vocal lobby, harassing the government, appearing on talk shows and newscasts almost every day, somewhere. None of them was quite sure what exactly should or could be done, but they were demanding vehemently that *someone* do *something*.

The families demanded a meeting with President Reagan. They got Vice President Bush first, to his dismay.

The meeting was heated and angry. The relatives held Bush personally responsible for the lack of action, and demanded an accounting. They accused, berated, argued, and pointed fingers. The vice president just slid lower in his chair, as if he really felt somehow guilty.

David's son, Eric Jacobsen, later remarked, "I wanted to slap him and say, 'Sit up, for God's sake, man. You're the vice president of the United States!' "

Finally, when Peggy Say accused Bush of being un-Christian, he sat bolt upright, shaking his finger at them all, and shouting in Ben Weir's face: "I don't care what you think! I'm telling you that we are responsible for you sitting in that chair today! It was your government that got you free!"

The response was not quite accurate. The U.S. government was not responsible, but it knew all about the deal that had brought Weir home.

Those 100 TOWs that Kimche and McFarlane had talked about, and President Reagan had approved, magically become 508 TOWs, had in fact been the key. The original Iranian promise to free all the hostages in exchange for the weapons had melted down to their freeing one. McFarlane, at Central Intelligence Director William Casey's urging, had tried to make that one William Buckley, not knowing that Buckley was dead. Naturally, the kidnappers could not produce Buckley, so they had freed Weir.

McFarlane said in a 1993 interview that "Reagan was very disappointed" that only one hostage was released. "But," he continued, the president was "not at all moved to turn it off. To the contrary. He said, 'Well, it is bearing fruit.'"

The Iranians thought so, too. Shortly after Weir's release, Shwimmer and Ghorbanifar were back at the table with Israeli and American officials. Now they wanted Hawks, Sidewinders, Phoenix, and even Harpoon missiles. The Phoenix, the most advanced air-to-air system available, had been sold to the shah before the revolution, but to no one else. Real weapons. And real money.

It was very clear that these things were not intended for any dissident faction in the Iranian army or government. They would be used directly in the war against Iraq.

McFarlane told them they had gone too far. The Israelis and their Iranian intermediaries backed off, but only to work out new terms. No Harpoons, no Phoenix or Sidewinders. But okay on the Hawks. The Americans gave the green light, if the weapons came out of the Israeli inventory.

Of course, being the Middle East, it again was not that easy.

NOVEMBER 18, 1985.

"Colonel North? This is Yitzhak Rabin." The Israeli defense minister. "We have a problem, and Mr. McFarlane says you can solve it."

On an open (nonsecure) phone line, the Israeli official explained, using only a few euphemisms and code words. Israel wanted to send the shipment of seventy-five Hawks to Iran via a discreet route, but didn't have a small plane available that could handle it. "And, obviously, they wanted us more actively engaged in [the swap]. I say that without any proof, but in hindsight, it appears that's what they wanted," Lt. Col. Oliver North asserted in a 1993 interview.

If that's what they wanted, it worked. As the shipment became more complicated, and new glitches popped up, North worked his phones constantly to keep it on track. The tangle spread. The United States was "operationally" involved, far from giving a passive green light.

Everybody involved—and that meant nearly everybody at the top level of the U.S. government—can now remember warning everybody else about what they were doing.

"Has the president really blessed off on this stuff?" North recalls asking McFarlane. "Because we've got a potential mine field here politically."

McFarlane himself remembers warning just about everyone. The Israelis: "To the extent that the U.S. government is authorizing you to do it, and in our law, that engages us as parties and in this case violating a law *unless it's rather carefully done*. It's a distinction without a difference." The president: "Now you understand, Mr. President, that Cap and George are against this?" The cabinet members, including Weinberger and Shultz: "Look, if we were giving arms to terrorists, of course it would be mindless. The point is, is it reasonable to believe what Israel says, that these arms are going to people who want to change the policy? . . . You either believe that or you don't believe that. But it's not a matter of giving Khomeini arms. We must not do that."

Shultz and Weinberger protested even more directly, and wrote memos or had memos written to them detailing their objections. Just for the record, apparently, because none of those warnings or objections was strong enough to derail the project.

North arranged the logistics, through retired Air Force Maj. Gen. Richard Secord, now a free-lance businessman with close ties to the CIA. He referred the problem of replacing the Israeli Hawks to the Pentagon, and to Colin Powell, then a major general and military assistant to Weinberger. He asked the CIA's Duane (Dewey) Clarridge to help obtain clearances for the plane carrying the missiles. Nearly all of the top officials brought in had to be told what it was about. They were too important to be sidetracked with a curt reference to "national security."

A last-minute holdup in Portugal, where the missiles were passing through en route to Iran, required McFarlane to politely pull rank, in a telephone call, on the prime minister of that country. "I said to him, 'Mr. Prime Minister, I am sorry to intrude. My government has encountered a problem in making this shipment of some goods through your airport, and I would appreciate your help. . . . It is terribly important to my country.' And he responded, 'I'm conscious of what it is, and you're telling me that it is important to you. We will do it.' "

The weapons made it to Iran. But once again, this was the Middle East.

"The Israelis [had] put together the oldest and most beat-up Hawks they could find," McFarlane said. "They kind of pawned off the worst stuff on the Iranians [to] get new replacements and kind of improve their own position in the process.

"But as you might expect, the Iranians were livid about it, because not only where they getting bad stuff, earlier models of Hawks, but the Israelis had the effrontery to ship it in boxes with a lot of Hebrew on the outside into Tehran airport."

McFarlane blames the screwup mainly on the arms dealers involved—Shwimmer on the Israeli side, and Ghorbanifar for the Iranians. After all, there were millions of dollars involved. Regardless of who was to blame, no hostages were freed.

13

STIGMATA VI

Evil dealt with daily
becomes familiar, even ordinary.
At first just faceless and
malefic minions, guards
become distinct and separate.
Some are petty, mean, and vicious,
others ordinary, even sympathetic.
Communication can begin,
and some small understanding,
but soon runs into walls of
background, belief, and circumstance.
The logic is too different;
mental language untranslatable.
There's no shared view of God or man.
Oppressor and oppressed,
each sees the other
a victim bound and blind.

BEIRUT. SEPTEMBER 1985.

Since Ben left, relations between David and me have deteriorated. We seem to fight all the time. David keeps referring to the necessary "pecking order," as if we were all a flock of chickens. Tom says almost nothing, and Father Martin is straining to keep things on an even keel. It's as if with Ben gone, the equilibrium in the room has been lost, as if the adjustments we had made to each other no longer work.

This morning, while David was in the bathroom, I asked Tom and Father Martin what was going wrong, what they thought I could do to make it easier. Their answer was a solid blast at me.

"You challenge David all the time. You seem to want to top him, to prove something to him. It's like a pair of bulls trying to dominate the same herd."

I was shocked. Naturally, I'd assumed the others would agree with me that David was causing the trouble.

I thought about it for a bit, and when David came back, I apologized. "If I've done things to offend you, I'm sorry. I'd like to start over." I assumed he would make the same sort of remarks, we'd shake hands and try to get along. What he said was, "Yes, you have. You've been a bastard." That just enraged me again, but I kept my temper.

I've been sitting here thinking about all that. It's not a view of myself I like—argumentative, bullheaded, trampling on other people. Especially in a situation like this. It's hard to accept, but I have to, since both Father Martin and Tom agree. Have I been taking out my frustration and anger on David? Can I do anything about it? Once again, I'm faced directly with the contradiction between what I believe I am and what others see me as. This place is like living in a hall of mirrors. There's no hiding from the others, and there's no ignoring the reflections they give me of myself.

This is the most direct test possible of those things Christ teaches. If I can't control my pride and arrogance, if I can't put into practice the humility and compassion he calls for in a small room with three other men, how can I do it outside when that time comes, please God?

At the same time, David is as arrogant and bullheaded as I am, and less willing to compromise or try to change. Why should I make all the effort? Obviously, though, the other two think that's the way it should be. After all, they unloaded on me, not on David. It's me they expect to change. Is it because I'm more in the wrong? Or because they have more expectation that I can? Anyway, it's necessary. We can't live with this kind of open hostility and constant clashes.

It's as if my head's a pressure cooker, and with all that

anger and frustration and pain steaming away inside, I just
have to clamp down harder, to make even more effort to
control the things I say and do. More effort? How can I try
any harder than I am trying now? But I have to. I have to.

We've been moved again. We were all taken out, blindfolded, some time after midnight and shoved into the back
of a small van with several guards. If we were in Hay El-
sellum or Bourj Al-Barajneh, then I think I followed the
route well enough to know where we are now. Some small
streets, out onto what I believe was the airport road, across
in front of the Sabra and Chatilla Palestinian refugee camps
(some gunshots there, very close, but we don't stop), then
around and up the hill to somewhere near the old Kuwaiti
embassy. That's also where the former Iranian embassy
was.

Out of the van, then led up the stairs in an apartment
building. Strict security, cold orders—"No speak. No noise.
We are ready to do anything." Seven or eight stories. First,
mats and shoes in front of the apartment doors, then nothing, then empty doorways—the building is obviously only
partly finished. Onto the roof, and across to the parapet.
One of the guards helps me sit on the parapet and swing
my feet over. It's only then, as I'm sitting facing outward,
that I realize where I am, and can see under the blindfold
a long, long drop. But the guard places my hand across the
gap to the parapet of a neighboring building. "Be careful."
I step across, and am led into another apartment, then an
empty bedroom. Two new guards, very young men. David,
Tom, and Father Martin are brought in, and the guards
leave.

Raising our blindfolds, we see a large room, perhaps fifteen by eighteen, with four mattresses laid out, tissues in
boxes, water bottles, pee bottles. Steel plates on the windows. No handle on the inside of the door.

Within a day or two, we discover that there are other
prisoners in other rooms of the apartment. Counting steps
and the flushing of the toilet, we figure there are four of

them in the room next door. Even with at least eight hostages, though, the guards seem remarkably casual, as if they are totally unworried about security. They are always armed, and there are always several in the apartment, but often they leave the door of our cell open because of the stifling heat, and even allow us to go back and forth the six or eight feet to the bathroom, one by one, without escort. Of course, we quickly find there is no likelihood of escape. Too many guards, too high up, several locks on the front door of the apartment.

One day, as I leave the bathroom, I hear a hiss from the slightly opened door of the room next to ours. Dropping my toothbrush, I squat down and grope for it, peering under my blindfold. "We are French. Who are you?" the voice says in English. "I am an American. Anderson." Then I quickly stand up and continue the two or three steps to our room.

We have heard on the radio, which we are given from time to time for a few hours, that there are four French hostages, along with several Brits, an Italian, a Korean, and some others. This must be the French. Tom, who speaks fluent French, knocks on the wall to the rhythm of the "Marseillaise," and we hear the rhythm repeated back to us.

Our days quickly settle back into a deadly routine. David and I still argue, but much more cautiously. Instead, he's taken to arguing with Tom, as I do from time to time. But Tom still seems apathetic, tiring quickly of any discussion. Father Martin and I talk about religion, and the Catholic church. He's very liberal, and is giving me a picture of a church very much different from the strict, priest-dominated one I knew as a boy. We talk about celibacy, and women's ordination, about his years working among the oppressed of the world—Australian aborigine alcoholics, California migrant workers, Indian lepers, Cambodian refugees.

He's a kind, gentle man whose personal God is always just that—a kind and gentle God. But he's not always easy to get along with. The strain of this life, this captivity, the petty humiliations we're all subjected to, is as hard for him as for any of us, despite his strong faith and personal dedication.

I have to laugh sometimes. I'm the only other Catholic here, and he treats me sometimes like a particularly annoying altar boy. He snaps at me, and orders me around in a way quite different from the way he talks to David and Tom. I don't mind, though I can't quite say why. I wouldn't accept that kind of treatment from anyone else.

We're now allowed a pen and paper, and I've been able to keep a sort of diary in the form of a long letter to Madeleine in which I write a paragraph or several every day. Sometimes I talk about her, or our child, sometimes about the four of us. We've all grown pretty peculiar, and a psychiatrist would have a ball observing us.

Every day, we walk in a circle, sometimes for hours, one behind the other. Father Martin can't stand to have David behind him, complaining that he creeps up too close and won't stay with the same pace. Tom doesn't want me behind him for some reason. So we always fall in in the same order—David, me, Father Martin, Tom. When someone steps out of the circle to take a drink or pee, then steps back in the wrong place, there's a quick shuffle and rearrangement to get everyone back where he belongs.

David unconsciously whistles show tunes barely audibly. He knows, I think, every movie musical ever made. It's like white noise and drives me crazy. I can't form a single coherent thought. I complain several times, but it's become such a habit, he can't break it.

We've all become terribly possessive about the small space we have to ourselves. When a guard, or even one of the other hostages, steps on my mattress, I feel a quick burst of rage. Tom and Father Martin got in a sharp spat the other day when Tom stood against the wall near Father Martin's mattress to pee in his bottle.

There has been a running fight with the guards over the bathroom. For some reason, they're limiting our daily trips first to ten minutes, then to seven, in which we have to move our bowels, wash, brush our teeth, wash our underwear and plastic dishes, and fill our water bottles. It's especially hard on Tom, who complains he has greasy skin and hates not being able to wash after eating, or several times a day. That's all we get—the one trip to the toilet each morning. If we miss that chance to take a crap, we just have to hold it until the next day. Often by the time the morning trip comes around, we're in physical pain. The humiliation of not being able to go the bathroom when we need to, and being forced to rush through that one visit, is great. There doesn't seem to be any particular reason for it, except the guards don't want to waste more than an hour taking all eight of us to the toilet. Don't know why—they do nothing the rest of the day. Incredibly lazy shits.

Badr and a couple of other guards woke me up at five A.M. the other day to ask me about a Westerner living in my building. It was immediately apparent from their description—"short, wears glasses, lives on the top floor of your building, and works in your office"—that they're talking about Fisk.

"Who is he? What is his name?" Sayeed is translating.

"I don't know who you mean. There are no Westerners in my building. They all left. There are only Lebanese."

"You are lying. We have been watching him. Who is he?"

"I can't guess. It must be someone who just moved in. I don't think there can be many Westerners left in Beirut. I don't know who this man is."

"Who were the Americans who lived in your building when you were there?"

"Oh, I don't remember their names. There were only one or two, and they left a long time ago."

"We know you're lying. You will be in big trouble."

"Look, I don't know who you're talking about. There was an American woman married to a Lebanese, and there was an American correspondent for UPI. Redmon, I think his name was. He left." The name was wrong, recalled on the spur of the moment from another man I knew in Tokyo many years ago.

After some more sharp words and a little shouting, they gave up and left. I'm terribly worried about Robert Fisk. If he's still in Beirut, it's obvious they are following him and mean to kidnap him. I can't think of any way to warn him. Maybe if we can talk them into letting us write letters? Seems unlikely right now, but I'll try.

It's getting very cold outside, and we don't really have enough blankets. Of course, there's no hot water. Still haven't resolved the toilet problem, though we get a little more time. We're constantly being reprimanded and threatened about peeking under our blindfolds at the guards. We always deny it vehemently, and falsely. We've all gotten pretty good looks at the various guards from time to time, though I can't say it really makes much difference. They're all pretty much as one would expect—short, dark-haired, usually with a short, scruffy beard and large, hawklike Arab nose. Nothing that would help very much if we had to describe them to someone.

Even with four in the room, and the talk and activities we try to get going, most of the days and all of the nights are filled with incredible boredom. Hours and hours of spinning, semi-incoherent thoughts. It's difficult to concentrate without an effort. I try to keep a project going in my head—right now, it's a gentlemen's club based loosely on the Foreign Correspondents' Club of Japan, where I was a board member and vice president for several years. I work out a budget, staffing, equipment, services, and so forth, right down to the last ashtray and spoon. I can always make it come out as profitable on paper, or rather in my head. It occupies some time, but not nearly enough.

I make up crossword puzzles on bits and pieces of paper, working both ways, from words to clues and back. But the others all say my clues are too obscure. I think they're pretty simple, but then I know the answers. They won't even try to solve them anymore.

We also have begun to have services twice a day, in the morning and afternoon. Father Martin has taken to passing leadership of the service around. We each in turn choose the verses for the day, and make some comments on why we chose them or what we're thinking about in relation to the day's readings. Then everyone makes whatever other comments he feels, and the service continues. It's interesting, and useful.

It is often hard to take communion and feel anything. Not that I have doubts about my beliefs. It's just that I'm so often angry or frustrated that I can't get my mind calm enough. I'm learning how to put those things aside for a few minutes. But it's not easy. It's been a long time since I felt that closeness, that comfort that I remember so well. It's painful not to have it. I need it.

Sometimes, though, when I'm able to diminish my frustration, or the anger left over from some sharp words with David or some petty humiliation by the guards, I can find a place during this so-simple ceremony where it's close. It's not exactly that near-serenity, that absolute knowledge of a presence that came on me before, when I had so completely surrendered. But it's close. There is a clarity, a suspension of things, a sense of being elsewhere, and a feeling of calm power and peace. It's fleeting, but so strongly attracting that I reach for it every mass, often unsuccessfully, as if the reaching prevents me from getting there. It's so difficult to describe, like a Zen trance, but more.

EUCHARIST

Five men huddled close
against the night and our oppressors,
around a bit of stale bread
hoarded from a scanty meal,
and a candle, lit not only as
a symbol but to read the text by.
The priest's as poorly clad,
as drawn with strain as any,
but his voice is calm, his face serene.
This is the core of his existence,

the reason he was born.
Behind him I can see
his predecessors in their generations,
back to the catacombs,
heads nodding in approval,
hands with his tracing
out the stately ritual,
adding the power of their suffering
and faith to his, and ours.
The ancient words shake off
their dust, and come alive.
The voices of their authors
echo clearly from the damp, bare walls.
The familiar prayers come
straight out of our hearts.
Once again Christ's promise
is fulfilled; his presence fills us.
The miracle is real.

My continual reading of the Bible also helps me, both to keep my mind occupied and to govern myself, though it also is a source of bewilderment and humility. I fall so short of the prescriptions. I've violated so many of the commandments, it's as if they were a list of my sins instead of guidelines to living. But each time I read it, it becomes clearer and there's something new to think about. The voices of Paul, John, the Old Testament prophets sometimes seem to come completely alive, to be those of familiar people, modern people, not remote historical accounts. I've studied and studied Job, trying to grasp the themes and purpose, and suddenly parts of it sound as if I could have written them.

> . . . I am allotted months of emptiness,
> and nights of misery are apportioned to me.
> When I lie down I say, "When shall I rise?"
> But the night is long,
> and I am full of tossing until dawn.

The psalms contain verse after verse that speak directly to me, and about me, in beautiful, clear phrases:

How long, O Lord? Will you forget me forever?
How long will you hide your face from me?
How long must I bear pain in my soul,
and have sorrow in my heart all day long?
How long shall my enemy be exalted over me?
Consider and answer me, O Lord my God!

Still, there is so much I don't understand, or can't accept. I keep reading, and thinking. Father Martin and I talk about some of the more difficult parts, but often it's beyond him, too.

We no longer have any news. We've lost the radio, and the guards won't bring us any newspapers. I went on a hunger strike for about five days recently, just to demand news. When they finally deigned to notice I wasn't eating, and I told them I wanted news, they laughed. The next day, Sayeed promised a newspaper and some news if I would end the strike. I did. He brought the paper—in Arabic. The news was that "everything is very good. The negotiating is continuing." There was also a message from the chiefs—if I wanted to starve myself, it was my problem, not theirs.

The frustration is incredible. There just doesn't seem to be anything that we say or do that makes an impression on these people, especially the younger guards, the ones we call "Junior Jihad." It's not that they are mean, or not most of them, anyway. They're just incredibly lazy and inattentive. I claim Sayeed has a "magic slate mind"—one step out of the room, and it's wiped clean. I asked him for water once, and he actually forgot what I wanted in the four or five steps from our room to the kitchen.

Sayeed is an enormous puzzle. He is genuinely religious, perhaps the most religious one of the bunch. He speaks reasonable English, and seems intelligent, though Father Martin says he's sick. He dubbed Sayeed and Badr "Sicko and Psycho." Sayeed even seems sympathetic to us often, though it doesn't change his behavior much. He told us not long ago, "I can never hate Americans again after being with you so long." How can this man, with his belief in a "compassionate and merciful God," do the things he does every day? How can he justify this kind of cruelty? The Kedde book explained that each Shia is required to take as "exemplar" a religious leader, or mullah, and follow his guidance in every facet of his life. So if someone like Khomeini or even Fadlallah is the exemplar for these people, I suppose it's no wonder they can rationalize kidnapping and murder. But it seems to require a total absence of personal logic or responsibility. And they don't feel responsible. Their favorite reply to such questions is "Nothing can be done" or "It is an order."

They see no contradiction between the Koranic strictures about treating an enemy fairly, or not punishing people for others' sins, and locking us up. The Koran is basically a compassionate book, and its principles are not that different from those of the Bible. How can someone balance a deep belief in the Koran and its principles with obviously evil behavior? It's psychotic.

My diary is getting bulkier and bulkier. I still write a paragraph or two each day, sometimes a page. It's both a comfort and often very painful. I'm learning to control my thoughts of Madeleine, my pain and guilt, and to think only of her grace and beauty and the wonderful sense of knowing each other we had so quickly. Still, I often have to push her into the back of my mind. It's been more than ten months now. I don't find the sexual frustration surprising or too hard to deal with. But I'm still surprised at the intensity of the pain sometimes when I think of her, and what this is putting her through.

We had another rough search of the room. The guards come in, paw through the few things we have—all of which they gave us—and take away anything they feel like. Sayeed took my diary this time. Afterward, when I found it gone, I called him back and asked him why he took it.

"We have to read it."

"It's personal, a letter to my wife. You're not supposed to read it."

"It is an order."

"Are you going to give it back?"

"I must give it to the chefs."

"That's wrong." Then, my anger breaking through, "You're an evil man."

He abruptly went away. But strangely, about twenty minutes later, he came back and handed the diary back to me. "Do you still think I am evil?"

"I don't know. People who do evil things are evil. If you don't, perhaps you're not."

A strange incident. Compassion? Shame? How does a terrorist feel shame for something this petty, when he feels none for the imprisonment itself, or for a hundred other petty humiliations?

As a safeguard, I've recopied all the diary—perhaps forty pages or more, in very tiny writing on a couple of sheets of paper, rolled them up and wrapped them in the plastic from a tissue package. I'll keep it in my shorts from now on.

I've made several rosaries by pulling out the strings that hold together the tattered plastic mat on our floor. I thicken them with a simple kind of crochet, then tie knots to represent the beads, and use toothpicks and tin foil to make crosses. I've given one to each of the others, though Tom and David aren't Catholic. It isn't really necessary for prayer, of course, and I don't often need it. But I was trying to explain to our two Protestants how comforting it is to follow the ritual, to have a formula for prayers sometimes. And it's comforting for me, as well, because it's such a potent symbol of Catholicism. The trappings aren't the substance, obviously, but they are familiar, and there are so few familiar things in our life.

I've just been given another sharp and unpleasant look at myself. I finally got Tom Sutherland talking, and he told me that I was crushing him, that I'd been aggressively argumentative in all our discussions of politics and other things, and that he felt I thought he was stupid. His ego has been crushed by these hamsters' constantly hassling him about being a spy, and he's telling me I make him feel worse. It's obvious that he's been taking the spillover from the disagreements between David and me, and we've both been hammering at him, probably in some sort of transference.

I feel like a total shit. I haven't been paying attention to the effect my "intellectual" exercises have been having on this man, already deeply depressed and suffering. I apologized, and said I would try hard not to insult him, and tried to convince him that I don't in fact think he's stupid, that it's just my style of argument. I've got to be much, much more careful. He seems so fragile. He's not in any shape to take any criticism, or smart remarks and putdowns. These things have no place in here, anyway. But habits are hard to break. I wonder if any of my friends really liked me at all. I seem to come across as an arrogant loudmouth. That's not what I mean to be, and I don't think that really is me. But there's no denying I have not paid enough attention to the others here, have not been considerate enough.

Jesus, though, how much more effort can I make? It's enormously hard just to wake up and get started in the morning, to face another endless day of humiliation and frustration.

I've tried to control my behavior with David, tried not to argue with him too much. Now I'm going to have to watch myself with Tom, and I should probably be more careful with Father Martin, as well. It's just clamping down the lid of the pressure cooker a little more, and I wonder how long I can do it. I'm not a bad man. I'm not. Or at least, I don't mean to be. Do intentions count? Not for much, I guess.

We've been moved again, but only to the end bedroom in the same apartment. It's a smaller room, and when the door is open, as it often is because of the heat and humidity that build up, we have to be careful not to give the appearance of peeking at the guards in the living room, part of which we can see clearly. Of course, we do peek—Tom most blatantly. He's always getting caught and screamed at. It's hilarious the way he leans back and tilts his head, trying to be subtle, but in fact being as obvious as a teenager in the front row of a burlesque show.

I flew into a rage at the guards. Two of them, Fadl and another guy, took me into the living room to show me some pictures. They were of dead children, small children, being held aloft by a screaming, chanting crowd, apparently after a major explosion of some sort.

"America do. Reagan do," Fadl said in his pidgin English.

The pictures appalled me—so explicit, so bloody, such small bodies. But what enraged me was the use of these bodies as a demonstration against the United States, and the gall of Lebanese, mired in their horrible, vicious civil war, especially these particular bloody-handed Lebanese, blaming America for their dead children.

I threw the pictures down on the floor. "No. Not America. Lebanese. Lebanese did this, to each other."*

I refused to look when they picked them up and shoved them at me. I pulled the blindfold down firmly over my nose, and started praying out loud, ignoring their shouting. After a minute or two, they took me back into the room. "I'm sorry," Fadl said.

I was trembling with rage. The others asked me what was wrong. I couldn't describe the pictures, or explain. I just sat against the wall, and put my head on my knees until I could calm down.

I thought of the boy I had seen die at Barbir Hospital in 1982, of the small bodies in the refrigerated truck outside the Tripoli Hospital in 1983. So many children. I never learned to control the awful wrench at the sight of them.

When I last visited Florida, Peg tried to tell me of the abused kids she encountered in her social work. I couldn't even listen to her stories. The thought of child abuse was

---

* In fact the Lebanese who carried out the bombing had been trained by the CIA, as it was later revealed by investigations into the Iran-Contra affair.

so evil, so repelling. Now this. These evil people blaming
their dead children on America, waving their gruesome pictures at me. I will never, never understand.

THE CHILDREN

These are your children,
fierce in hatred, bathed in blood;
the ones you handed guns at ten or twelve
and set against their brothers.
So many died; they can be mourned,
turned into martyrs and exalted.
What will you do with those who live?
The war is over now, you say.
It's time for reconciliation.
They don't know that word,
never having heard you use it.
They're more familiar with
words like "Kill. Destroy."
Put down your guns. Forgive
your brother. Go to work,
you order. Work at what?
They have no skills, except for war.
Many cannot even read.
The minds of others
have been twisted,
scorched by sights and acts
too terrible to tell.
The young are resilient.
Most will probably obey
again, and gladly turn
their energies to peace.
Those that don't you'll punish,
like so many untrained,
disobedient dogs, until
they come to heel.
Some you'll have to kill—

the taste for blood
will never leave them.
But about forgiving,
it's not their brothers
they'll have trouble with.
It's you.

It's two days after my birthday, October 29, 1985. 227 days. The guards told me today that I have a child, and that there would be something about it on television. It's the first I've heard anything, though I knew the baby must have been born in June—four months ago. They brought in a small black-and-white television for the late evening newscast, which had a short montage. Gabrielle standing with a couple of her cousins—I couldn't tell where. Then short pieces of Peg, Dad, and Rich speaking; Judy with someone in a church; and finally, a few seconds showing a baby— just video of a still picture. Couldn't see much—a baby face, big eyes, and quite a bit of hair. There was no sound in English—just an Arabic commentary over the pictures.

By the end of the two minutes or so, I was crying, crouched close in front of the television, peering under my blindfold, trying not to let the guards standing behind me or the others know how much it hurt.

At first, they told me the baby was a boy. I was doubtful, because Maddy always talked as if she knew it would be a girl. The guards went out to check, then came in to say, no, it was a girl. They seemed disappointed. I wasn't.

When they left, I got up and walked rapidly around and around the room. The others were quiet. The thoughts were roiling around in my head—Madeleine, the baby, where are they? What are they doing? The brief shot of Gabrielle— she looked so sad. No indication where she was, either. Suddenly, I stopped and faced into a corner and started sobbing. What have I done to this so-bright and happy child? The sadness on that always cheerful face was like a fist in my chest. Father Martin came over and put his arm around my shoulders. I flinched—I wasn't ready to be consoled or even touched just then.

After a while, I went over and sat next to him. He'd been hurt when I rejected his comfort. "I'm sorry, Father. I just needed a few minutes."

We talked a bit about Gabrielle, and how I felt about that picture. That hurt, that guilt won't go away for a long time, if ever. And there's just nothing I can do about it.

FIRSTBORN

Nothing good can come from bad;
so goes the homely saying.
Soft brown hair, softly shining oval eyes;
open, fresh, inquiring face, just honey-touched;
firstborn part of me, you put the lie
to pedants with a mischievous grin.
Not wholly bad, but badly flawed,
my arrogant, unthinking former self
helped make a being better
than I am, or will become.
I could not credit me in you
were not your features so much mine;
gentled, made lovely and exciting
by your mother's Asian gift;
my flaws reduced, her virtues flowering—
but mine. My father's, sisters',
brothers', too; a family mark,
a tribal brand for all to see.
This shared genetic heritage,
and undiminished love, will help,
I hope, to ease forgiveness,
pain, and miles and years;
to let me touch your heart again,
as you have always touched
and honored mine.

The rest of the day and night was spent in confused thought and memories—Madeleine, the joy of a daughter, the regret and guilt about Gabrielle and her mother.

I had known our child was to be born in June, but have had no news about her. Madeleine was so certain it would be a girl. I had chosen the name Danielle. Traditional, lovely. But the name Sulome came to Maddy in a strange dream when we were together. Equally lovely, and exotic.

In the morning, the guards brought in a newspaper with a picture of the baby and a short story, obviously about the messages that were sent in the television story. With some difficulty, I spelled out the Arabic under the picture: her name is Sulome Theresa. Trust Maddy—stick to the name she chose, but a bow to me. So now I know—another beautiful child. Sulome Theresa.

BUTTON

Button, button, who's
got the button?
Not I, not yet.

Big bright eyes,
small button nose;
my face, and not.
A wondrous thing,
this Button.

Button, button, who's
got the button?
You, and I.
We've got the Button.
Finders, keepers.

EIGHT

14

MADELEINE

Relations between Peg and me had gotten very bad, and I felt I had to get out of the house we had shared in Batavia. I felt she was changing from the pressure and attention of being on television every time anything happened in Lebanon or in the United States concerning the hostages. The worst part for me was knowing she was not telling me everything she was learning from officials she talked to. I couldn't understand it, and felt humiliated. I rented a room in the house of a friend in Batavia, Marsha Barton.

Terry's father and brothers went back to Florida. Judy stayed in Batavia, although relations between her and Peg were also strained. A single mother with three children, Judy also had a full-time job, so I didn't see much of her. It was unbearable living in this situation in Batavia. I became very depressed all the time. Crying was part of my daily life. I felt very sorry for my daughter, whom I was breast-feeding, while crying at the same time. It was very lonely without a family and with my first child, in Terry's hometown without him. Family is very important where I come from. The only family I had was his, and I could not get along with Peg. I was living with a friend, but she was not family. It was time I left.

I arrived in England, where my sister Nahla lived, in October 1985. A mother of two, she helped me a great deal in dealing with my new role as a mother. She took care of

Sulome when I fell sick. She was, as always, very concerned about my mental and physical condition. I had ached for such care and concern ever since Terry's abduction.

Psychologically, I was deteriorating slowly, and when the captors in one statement claimed they had killed William Buckley, whom everyone in Beirut knew was the CIA chief in the Middle East, in retaliation for Israeli air raids on PLO headquarters in Tunis, I began to imagine the worst. Knowing how important Buckley must have been to them, I feared for Terry's fate. His first birthday in captivity had come, and he still wasn't free. His captors had shown no sign that there would be any release. Holding my baby in my arms and crying, I spoke out loud, with no one else in the room, wishing him a happy birthday, doubting my own words, fearing for his condition. Two days after his birthday, a videotaped birthday message from his family and friends in Batavia was broadcast on Beirut TV stations. Stephen Hawley, a high school classmate, showed a picture of Sulome on the tape, telling Terry he had a daughter.

Those few days were the most terrible since he was taken. On November 7, a caller claiming to be a member of the Islamic Jihad said the group would execute all American hostages it held because "indirect negotiations with the United States have reached a dead end." Another caller the same day claimed that all American hostages had been killed and their bodies dumped in a bombed-out factory in Beirut. No bodies were found; it was impossible to figure out what was going on. I thought perhaps the hostages had died in the course of one of the many exchanges of artillery and rocket fire among the various groups in the city.

It was terrifying to imagine Terry dead. How could he die now? We haven't started our life together yet. He hasn't seen his daughter or felt the warmth of her body, as I did every minute of the day. Why is this happening? Why did he have to ignore their first attempt to kidnap him? I was angry with him; I wished I was dead, too, so I could face him with my anger.

One thing I knew: they would not have killed the hostages simply because negotiations didn't work. They would never kill the source of their chance of victory. My Lebanese, whoever they are, have practical, commercial minds. These people were not any different from any merchant who sees success in the value of his merchandise. This kind of analysis was my only refuge, the only way to stave off a mental breakdown.

The next day, letters from the four American hostages were delivered to the AP bureau in Beirut. They denied the claim of their death. Terry's message to me also said that he had seen the videotape made in Batavia, and finally knew he had a daughter, and that her name was Sulome.

BEIRUT. NOVEMBER 1985.

The fighting outside has been getting worse—a lot of shelling, rocket-propelled grenades, automatic weapons fire. The guards are nervous. I have fantasies about this apartment house being blown open, like so many I've seen, the guards being killed, somehow the blast freeing us. Sometimes the fantasy turns into a nightmare of me hanging head down from the wreckage, six stories above the ground, like the man at the U.S. embassy.

We've been shifted for no apparent reason from our large room into the end room, next to the toilet, where the French were. They've been moved into one of the other bedrooms. The room is still scattered with their belongings. Tom found a diary in a coat hanging on the wall. It's written in French, by a Lebanese doctor, a Jew. He was kidnapped by some other group, then apparently "borrowed" by our hosts to treat one of the French hostages—Michel Seurat. It's an emotional, magnificently written thing that makes me almost ashamed to be reading it. But we don't stop, Tom and I, poring over the beautiful French by candlelight, late into the night.

First, the doctor says he knows Seurat is terribly ill. He's not sure from what, and bemoans his lack of instruments and ability to test, but indicates he thinks it's some form of cancer, possibly of the liver or pancreas, and probably fatal. Nothing he can do here, and no chance of getting any outside help.

According to his diary, he is allowed a great deal more freedom than the rest of us, and has occasionally been taken down the stairs to sit in the evening and watch the other residents of the apartment house, touchingly describing children playing. But most affecting are the words he addresses to his son, in East Beirut. Indicating there has been an estrangement, the father tells of his sorrow, and of his longing to be with him, and of the beauty of the fields and flowers.

I wish I knew this man, wish I could talk with him about this country, and how he feels as a Lebanese Jew. I know there has been a Jewish community here for thousands of years, but understood there were only a few families left. His words indicate a man of sensitivity, and intelligence and deep thought. A rare person. And I know, given his circumstances, he is unlikely to live through this. Whom can he call on for help? We have our families, our government, the power of the press and university and medical communities, and even all that seems to accomplish nothing. In whom can a Lebanese Jew in the hands of fanatical Muslims hope? Only God, the same God millions of Jews have called on for so long.

The night is filled with the sound of guns and with the same thoughts all of us who believe in God must confront sooner or later. If God is omnipotent, and loving, where does evil fit in? Where does justice come in? Okay, perhaps I deserve what I'm getting. Certainly I've violated enough commandments, been unloving enough. But what about the children? And free will. If I'm free to choose good or evil, and evil consists, as I believe, in harming others, what about the others I'm harming? It's my evil that brings them suffering, not theirs.

I find it hard to believe in a God who cares endlessly and each moment about every one of us, who monitors our every deed and need, and guides all things. So many things are obviously unguided, and so many others just cruel. The Old Testament God of collective responsibility and proximate, harsh punishment and lavish reward is one that few people accept these days. Okay, the Old Testament reflects as much a harsh, tribal people's view of the Deity as that Deity's true being. The Bible is an account of man's dealings with God as related by man, of man's progressive understanding of His nature. But no matter what God says in His revelation of Himself, we can understand only what we are capable of, and can only relate to others what we understand.

But what do we put in place of that old, simplistic view? The modern, intellectual theist's idea of a God who planted all creation in the seed of the Big Bang, a clockwork universe that, owing to his ungraspable intelligence, is infinitely complex? Nice resolution of evolution and theology, but unsatisfactory. It leaves no room for the God I know, that so many know—the one who touched me, comforted me, the one I felt in my innermost being.

Somehow, I know I'm asking the wrong questions, trying to understand God in my terms. None of this was God's doing. I cannot believe in an accountant God, who weighs my sins and metes out appropriate punishment. These men are not in any way I can understand God's instruments. This is not my punishment for adultery, or indifference, or all the petty dishonesties I've been guilty of in my life.

Nor do I believe it is a deliberate test, that I'm a kind of modern Job, being subjected to some sort of spiritual test. God knows my soul, to its innermost depths, if He cares to. He doesn't need to check, to give me a midterm examination.

This is man's work, the product of a combination of political and economic forces, mixed with the needs and greeds of petty, evil men and the indifference of others. God is there to help me, to give me guidance and solace, and to keep me in the knowledge that no matter how much I may be humiliated, no matter how much I may come to dislike myself as my knowledge of myself grows, His love is unquestioning. He did not place me here, but He will help me get through it, even unto death, with grace and dignity, if I accept His help. But that, strangely enough, is the hardest part—accepting.

None of my speculation is entirely satisfactory. I come up with no sure answers, no definitive understanding. Had I a single grain of humility, I wouldn't expect to. These are things the greatest minds in the ages have grappled with, without reaching any final resolutions. God is essentially unknowable; whatever plans, or purposes, or arrangements He has for us would have to be unknowable as well. But somehow, here, now, I have to work out some way of understanding what is happening to me, physically and spiritually, some way to come to terms with Him, and with myself, to know what we expect of each other.

Once again, the radio has reappeared, without explanation, the gift appreciated as much as its withdrawal is feared. Within days, we hear Ben Weir in New York, in some kind of press conference with a special representative of the archbishop of Canterbury, a man named Terry Waite. Waite offered to act as an intermediary, to travel to Lebanon to talk with our captors. It's the first promising news we've ever heard. Perhaps the Hajj's gambit in freeing Ben is working?

After excitedly discussing it among ourselves, we call the guards. I explain to them what we heard, and suggest they answer the proposal. "He obviously wants to talk to you. The Hajj said you couldn't get anyone to negotiate. Why not answer him?"

Mahmoud and the others listen, then say they'll tell "the chefs."

A couple of days later, a new man appears. He says his name is Ali, and he's very friendly. He talks with a peculiar accent, very American and quite fluent, but with a strange, lisping *s*.*

We will be allowed to write letters to our families, to the archbishop of Canterbury, and to the president and members of Congress. We are to say that if the archbishop wants to help, he should go to Kuwait, not Beirut, and try to get their friends released. We are to urge the president and Congress to do something to end this situation.

It's not entirely satisfactory, but it's something. The four of us compose joint letters. I work up the drafts, and the other three mostly accept them, with a few suggested changes. Then we begin working on our private letters.

I include a will, and a power of attorney for both Maddy and Peg. It will alarm them, I know, but with my divorce likely still pending, and a new child, I can't take a chance. I don't really believe I'll die in here, but there's obviously a real chance of it. The burden of the mess I left my life in has been heavy. As long as I'm alive, I can rely on The AP to take care of Maddy and the child, as well as Mickey and Gabrielle. I dread the idea of leaving them all without any resources if I die.

After a couple of hours, when the guards come to collect the letters, Ali says we must include a denial of a report

---

* Several years later, Ali would let slip in a conversation that he was an Iranian, but had been a longtime resident of Beirut, and had graduated from the American University there. We had deduced from other such slips that he was acting as some sort of liaison between radical factions in the Iranian government and the Hezbollah/Islamic Jihad people, and as an adviser on things American. Sources have since given his real first name as Bassam, but have been unable to supply the last. Those sources say he was the number-two official in the special "security committee" set up within Hezbollah to control the foreign hostages. He was also the official liaison between the Hezbollah senior council and the radical Iranian faction headed by Ali Akbar Mohtashemi, the Iranian interior minister, which encouraged the taking and holding of hostages despite opposition from the less-radical faction headed by Iranian President Rafsanjani.

Bassam also was identified as the man used as go-between for the contacts with Anglican church envoy Terry Waite, before his kidnapping, and in other contacts with the West.

on the radio that we've been killed. He calls it an attempt by the U.S. government to disrupt things—obviously silly. Probably just another hamster making whatever trouble he can—nothing unusual here. We add the disclaimer to the end of our letters.

Ali says they'll be delivered later, and for once proves to be telling the truth. The news is on the radio within hours—the letters were all dropped off at The AP. We're all totally hyped up. Is this the beginning of the end? Will it work? We don't dare hope too much. The letters are not magic bullets. No one is going to say, "Gee, they're suffering. Let's begin negotiating." But it does help increase the pressure on those who might be able to do something to win our freedom.

MADELEINE

SUNDERLAND, ENGLAND. NOVEMBER 11, 1985.

"Madeleine, my love, my heart, I saw our daughter on TV the other night and I cried for joy.... I seem to have left things in a bit of a mess, don't I? ... I never cease thinking about you—I talk to you (in my head) every night and in the early mornings. Those are the difficult times, and thinking of you and our child helps. God has been good to us, and I'm sure this is only an interruption of our lives together, one that if He wills, won't last much longer.... Maddy, love, I'm sorry to have brought you pain, mostly through my arrogance in not being careful enough. It is little return for the happiness you brought me. I hope I can bring you as much happiness in the many years we will have together. Read the Song of Solomon. Chapter 4, verses 1–15, and 7, 1–5. They were written for you."

The letters, the first direct contact from Terry since March 16, renewed my mind and soul and gave me new en-

ergy. Carolyn Turolla, the AP executive assigned to stay in contact with me, was the first to tell me about them, in a call from New York, saying they were sending me a copy as soon as possible.

Then an AP staffer in Beirut, Mona Ziade, called to say she had the letters in her hand, and asked if I wanted her to open them and read them to me. I wanted so badly to hear what he had to say, and told her to go ahead. The first was addressed to The AP, saying that if anything happened, Terry's insurance was to be divided between his daughters. I asked Mona to stop reading. I couldn't bear the idea that he might die. He's not going to die. He is alive now, and that's all I want to know.

There was another, long letter addressed to me and his family. Robert Fisk, who was in the Beirut AP bureau, made copies and flew to Cyprus with them on the next plane. I waited for hours to hear from Robert. Time had no limits anymore. My sister, her husband, and I stayed up all night. I was talking, laughing, crying, and laughing again and crying as though I were mad. I went up to Sulome's room while she was asleep, hugged and kissed her, and told her about the letter from her beloved daddy. I knew she couldn't understand even if she were awake. I felt the need to be with her and feel her. She was part of him. I couldn't be any closer to him.

It was morning before Robert called. He had just sent the copies express mail from London. He said he was encouraged. One of the letters that Terry wrote was for President Reagan, urging him to try to secure their release. Another was addressed to the archbishop of Canterbury, Robert Runcie, appealing for his assistant, Terry Waite, to mediate. At that point, I was sure Terry would soon come home, and all the others, with all these people working for their release.

I don't remember how many times I read Terry's letter—ten, twenty, thirty times. I read it until I could say it by heart, and still that wasn't enough. I could see Terry's face talking to me, telling me again how he felt about me, and *how hurt he was for not being careful enough. The words in the letter were as loving as he had always been, chosen as carefully as when he used to report about the events and people he was covering, considerate and caring about his family and their well-being. In his letter, I saw a man in terrible pain, and yet making sure that his pain was not inflicted on us. I saw a father who could cry with joy only looking at a photograph of his child's face. In the letter, Terry gave me strength that held me together for a long time.*

I immediately got a Bible and started looking for the Song of Solomon. I could not believe there was such love. I had read the Bible, of course, but somehow never paid attention to this book. To be told that these words were meant for me, that Terry felt all this for me, I didn't know what to do with myself. Reading it over and over again, I started imagining that Terry was sending us a message or a code, instead of telling me his feelings. I knew it sounded crazy, but I got so worked up that I called Terry Waite and told him of my theory. I was sure Terry was telling us where he was and who had him. I called Shazi and Robert Fisk in Cyprus, and told them. I managed to persuade them that I was right. Even Terry Waite seemed a bit convinced.

Waite told me he would certainly look into it, and assured me that he would do his best to see that Terry and the others were home by Christmas. He said he was heading to Beirut in a few days, and if he got to see Terry, he would tell him that I was not in Lebanon anymore, and that the baby and I were fine. Waite impressed me as a very sincere and confident man, who knew the risks he was taking and was ready to take them. He also suggested I write Terry a letter, and he would see Terry got it.

All my hopes were high, and I started getting myself ready to receive Terry by Christmas, going shopping for new things and making sure everything I bought would be pleasing to him. The days that followed were extremely tense. Waiting for a phone call or a message that would send me and my daughter to the first plane to meet Terry both gave me a ticket to heaven and brought me to the edge of a nervous breakdown.

> How beautiful you are, my love,
>> how very beautiful!
> Your eyes are doves
>> behind your veil. . . .
> You have ravished my heart, my
>> sister, my bride,
>> you have ravished my heart
>> with a glance of your eyes,
>> with one jewel of your necklace.
> How sweet is your love, my
>> sister, my bride!
> How much better is your love
>> than wine,
>> and the fragrance of your oils
>> than any spice!
> Your lips distill nectar, my bride;
>> honey and milk are under your tongue;
>> the scent of your garments is
>> like the scent of Lebanon.

Song of Solomon

BEIRUT. NOVEMBER 1985.

The comments from our families are coming thick and fast. There's even a picture in the local paper of Tom's wife, Jean, reading his letter in the AP office. The reported comments from Washington are a little slower, and considerably briefer. "No negotiations with terrorists. No pressure on Kuwait."

It's incredibly strange to sit here in our underwear, blindfolds perched on our foreheads, absorbing the abuse and petty humiliations of these young men, then listen to our letters being read and reacted to in Washington and New

York by the world's mighty. Every time the Hajj comes here, I try to convince him we're just not that important, that he's not going to get what he wants for us. This obviously isn't going to convince him. Yet I can't be sorry. We all drink in the attention, huddle over the radio constantly, debate every word among ourselves endlessly. We've been so long isolated, so long cut off, so close to despair. It's impossible not to believe now that something is happening, that perhaps one of us, two of us, all of us, might be going home soon.

In all the news reports, though, there's no mention of Madeleine. I believe I know why. She's Lebanese, a Christian who lives in West Beirut, whose family is also in the Muslim half of the city. And she's incredibly vulnerable—an unmarried woman with a child by an American. There are those here, Christian and Muslim, who would kill her just for that. She does not dare to speak out. I understand completely. Yet I long for her voice, for some word, for some indication, no matter how tiny, of what has happened to her.

There can be no doubt of our love. But how long can a beautiful young woman, alone with a new child, rest her hopes and her life on the few short months we had? I trust her absolutely, rejoice in the knowledge of her intelligence and calm judgment. I know that whatever she does, it will be the right thing for her and our child. But the thought of the choices she might be forced to make brings me great pain.

The days go on, one after the other, mounting up with frightening speed. Each one seems so incredibly long—hours and hours of boredom, frustration. Yet already there have been hundreds of them, most I can barely remember. Still no indication when something might happen, no way to base a real hope of freedom.

Our routine is virtually written in stone. Wake up from a fitful sleep, usually about dawn. Lie quietly, staring at the ceiling, rummaging around in the garbage pile of my memories and thoughts, or following some fantasy. The morning

guard comes in, and we all abruptly snatch at our blindfolds, pulling them down over our eyes. Cup of weak tea
and a cheese-and-Arabic-bread sandwich. Trip to the toilet.
Mattresses leaned against the wall and our morning round
of walking. Usually quiet—nobody wants to talk much this
early. Eventually, we tire of the walking and sit down, first
one and then another. I'm usually the last, and sometimes
continue to pace up and down in the narrow space beside
my mattress long after the others have stopped—just a couple of steps in each direction. It's cold, and I keep my socks
on—I've worn almost the entire bottoms off them, and
have sewn layer after layer of scrap cloth onto the bottoms
until they're more like heavy slippers than socks. It's almost like undergoing hypnosis—the rhythm of the pacing
and turning, pacing and turning, takes my thoughts deeper
and deeper, until I'm barely conscious of the room and the
others. That, of course, is why I do it so often.

Eventually, even I quit. We have a morning service,
then lie back. Sometimes we talk, often we're just alone
with our thoughts. Lunchtime—anywhere from noon to
three P.M.—means another scramble for the blindfolds.
We're so well trained, like eager dogs. Cold rice with
canned vegetables dumped on top, or another sandwich.
The afternoon is no different.

We talk, or argue about almost anything—politics, or
how the rear end of a car works. Tom and I tried to figure
that out for hours one day. Neither of us was quite sure,
though he certainly knew a lot more than I did. Then we
tried to move on to "positraction"—where both rear wheels
are used for drive. Difficult to envision in your head, without pencil and paper.

David and I still kind of skirt around each other. I have
a tendency to go off on a long stream of logic, a mono-
logue, really, following whatever train of thought I've em-
barked on, pacing back and forth and talking. It seems to
irritate him, as if I'm lecturing. I suppose it sounds that
way, but I'm just using my mind to pass the time. I try to
avoid serious discussions with David, and I've stopped

challenging his statements, or "facts," almost entirely. It's not worth it. We just can't get along together when we disagree.

I keep making decks of cards out of the endpapers from the few magazines and books we have. The hard, shiny covers of magazines work best—I've already used the several pamphlets on Islam they gave us. Great covers for cards. When the guards find them in their periodic minor searches, they take them away.

We all huddle around one of the mattresses with a blanket handy to throw over the cards when anyone comes in the door. We play almost entirely Hearts, and play intensely. Father Martin is the most obvious in his mood swings—cheerful when he's doing well, irritable when he's losing, which is often. He and Tom have the least "card sense," David is pretty good, and fortunately or unfortunately I'm better than all three. They're always trying to talk each other into ganging up on me (we play cutthroat, not partners), but can't hold their coalition together.

Father Martin accused me of dumping Dirty Gerty (the queen of spades—thirteen negative points) on him deliberately on every occasion. I quietly keep track for a couple of days and astounded him when I proved it was just the opposite—I was *his* favorite victim, by far, not he mine. I am a pretty vicious player, though. I've always been very competitive; games are totally unenjoyable to me unless I play to win, whether it's points or money. The vehemence of our play is the only safe outlet for our emotions—and I'm not sure it's all that safe.

The cards, though, can take up only an hour or two. The rest of the time, it's back into our heads mostly. It's not a good idea to lie down and nap, because we already have great difficulty sleeping at night. Best to stay awake, but how? Prayers can't take up too much time, though we still have services twice a day. I write a bit in my diary/letter. Mostly we're just supremely bored. Bored until we want to scream. Literally. When is something going to happen? Anything? What in hell is going on?

* * *

Ali showed up this morning, spoke briefly to us, his usual bullshit and lies, then took Tom out of the room. We had no idea what it was about until Tom came back an hour later, badly shaken, holding some papers in his hand.

"It's Buckley's confession," he said. "Ali asked me to copy it out. What are they after? Why does he want me to do this?"

We tried to calm him down a bit, and get him to describe exactly what went on. He showed us the confession—two parts, twenty-five or thirty pages of what we supposed to be Buckley's handwriting. Nothing exciting—he admitted being CIA station chief in Beirut, but described his activities there as very routine. He talked about meeting with his Lebanese counterparts, and mentioned as the only active project an attempt to provide communications equipment to allow the various border posts to stay in contact with Beirut (phone service between the capital and the rest of the country has been sporadic at best for years).

The most interesting part was the list of names he had added, obviously under order. All were former embassy staffers, but the one or two I recognized had left long ago. I couldn't find any names listed of people still at the embassy.

Tom said Ali had first told him he couldn't read the writing—pure nonsense. Tom offered to translate it verbally, but Ali insisted that he write it out, gave him a pen and paper, then left. Tom said he copied one or two sheets, then tore them up, telling the guard who remained with him he had made mistakes. Finally, he said his hand was tired and he couldn't do any more, and was brought back to us.

The four of us analyzed the situation from one end to the other, trying to figure out what the point of this little exercise was, but couldn't come up with anything satisfactory. Were they pursuing their earlier insistence that Tom was a spy, like Buckley? Were they trying to incriminate him, trying to obtain something in his handwriting? For what purpose? To show whom?

Finally, I told Tom, "Look, I can't guess what they're trying to do. But I have to say, whatever it is, it's unlikely to be to your benefit. I don't know what you can do about it, though. If you refuse, they might get rough. Or they might not. I don't know. You have to decide if you're going to go along with this."

He chewed over that for a while. Obviously, he was worried about the consequences if he refused, and about what use might be made of a document like this in writing if he agreed. The first few weeks, when they accused him so vehemently of being a spy, really shook him. He still gets very upset when one of the guards makes even a joking reference to it. He said Ali told him he would be back in the morning.

Then I came up with an idea. "Why don't you agree, then, that every place Buckley writes 'I' or 'me' or refers to himself in any way, put instead 'the writer' or 'the author.' Throw in references on every page to 'the person who wrote this,' or say something about 'I'm not sure what this says, but I think the writer. . . .' "

He was doubtful, but agreed to try it.

Tom was taken out by the guards again the next morning. After several hours, he came back, both nervous and a bit exultant.

"I did it. And I put at the top and bottom of every page 'Transcribed by Thomas Sutherland from the original.' "*

Pacing around the room, one behind the other, more hours just trying to get through. David raised the subject first— escape. The guards have become a bit careless. Sometimes there seems to be only one or two in the apartment, though there's really no way to tell. Could be half a dozen sleeping

---

* Whatever the ploy was, it didn't work. No one—Ali, the Hajj, the guards—ever made reference to the confession, or to Tom's copy, again. The incident eventually just faded away—another of the peculiar events that came at us so frequently, and not the most memorable, since no one got hurt or punished.

in one of the other rooms. We're now in a small bedroom not six feet from the front door, which is heavily locked and bolted.

The other day, when David needed to go to the bathroom during the day, he pounded on the door. A guard came, let him out, and started to escort him down the hall—but suddenly stopped in his tracks, then bolted for the front room, leaving David standing alone in the hallway. David said he didn't understand what was happening (as usual, he was blindfolded, but could see under the blindfold) until the guard came panting back with the silenced automatic pistol all the guards carried dangling from his hand. Then David realized the little shit had forgotten his gun.

"I could have grabbed him right then. There was no one else here, I'm sure," he told us bitterly.

We went on to discuss how to carry off a coordinated escape attempt. Father Martin didn't want to talk about it. There's clearly no way in which he would attack anyone. Tom's never had any military training, and in fact has probably not struck anyone since he was a boy. That leaves David, with his one or two years in the Army, mostly as a dental technician, and me.

I tried to explain that it's not like the movies—people you hit don't usually fall down unconscious, unless you hit them very hard, many times. Much as I'd dearly love to get out of here, there isn't much point in getting killed.

David's self-confidence, despite his six-foot frame, doesn't translate into my confidence in him, unfortunately. Also, I'm terribly reluctant to try to convince Tom to take part. If I want to get myself killed, that's one thing, but talking someone else into getting himself offed is out of line.

I know perfectly well we'd have to kill a guard to get out, and then we'd damned well better succeed. Also, we don't have any idea what's outside. Guard posts? Checkpoints? As near as I can figure, this is a heavily Shiite neighborhood. Are the residents mostly Amal ("moderate") or Hezbollah? No way to know.

All in all, I finally decide for caution. "Forget it, David. I'm not going to get anyone else into trouble, and I'm not going to try it myself, unless a chance comes up that's just too good to miss."

David is clearly disappointed. I suspect he thinks I've chosen the coward's way. He certainly has no doubts about his willingness to kill a guard, or his ability to do so. I hope he doesn't try it. He's likely to be in for a very big surprise and an unpleasant aftermath. These young men may be much smaller than he is, but they're in very good condition, they're young, trained in martial arts, and most are quite strong. Forty- or fifty-year-old men who have been locked up for months aren't likely to be much threat to them.

A couple of the Junior Jihads have taken to hanging around the door to our room, peering through the bars and talking about us. Finally, I told Sayeed when he brought in the food, "Tell your boys we're not animals and this isn't a zoo. We're not here for their amusement. And we don't like being watched."

This occasioned a long discussion among the guards. The first response, through Sayeed, was: "They are men. Do not call them boys. They don't like it."

"Well, they are very young. To us, they are boys. Besides, it's only an expression."

Then one of the guards, maybe twenty or twenty-one, came over and squatted down in front of me. His English was guttural, thick with a Lebanese accent, but understandable. "Before, if I want to see you, I must talk to secretary, and then you don't want to see me. Now, I can see you when I want."

The sense of sudden, unanticipated power these poor and uneducated kids feel is obvious, even for those who are relatively friendly. Of course, it's very common among prison guards. But for them, ordinarily so powerless, without any hope of a better life or even a decent job, it must be heady.

I have learned, over the months, how to talk to the guards—very calmly, keeping anger out of my voice, very slowly and logically. Or at least with what I consider logic.

Their logic doesn't operate by the same equations. But it's hard to talk to someone while you're blindfolded. First, you feel terribly vulnerable, especially when things are tense, when the guards are angry. Then so much of the communication is missing—the eye contact, the reading of body language and expression, the feedback. It all has to come from the sound of their voices. I have even greater sympathy for blind people now. To live in a world where you just never know what's going to come at you out of the dark! Where you're *always* vulnerable.

I find myself leaning forward, straining with my body to make myself understood when my emotions are high, when I'm upset or just trying to make them understand. And so frustrated when I fail.

The control part is hard, too. They don't like to see us showing our anger or frustration, though they understand that we must be angry. They know they are doing wrong to us, know they are hurting us in so many ways. They want to feel justified—not just generally, in the way their chiefs explain, but very personally. So any anger we show is immediately returned, and amplified. It's as if when we get mad, we feed their righteousness. Yet they can go completely off the wall at a moment's notice. I've seen it before, when I was traveling around Lebanon—a militiaman can be talking reasonably, quietly, then he hits a subject like Israel or evil America and works himself up and in seconds is practically foaming at the mouth. They are very dangerous then. With our hosts, of course, I can't take the expedient course—leaving quickly. Sometimes I can't even take the wise course, which is to stay quiet and not show any reaction or anger. Sometimes I just blow my top. That doesn't work very well. I always regret it, and we always lose something—books or pen and paper, or some one or two of the other little privileges we may have managed to get from them.

But sometimes it works. Sometimes it's the only way they'll listen. This time, my complaint seems to have gotten through. The young men give up hanging about the door, watching. They still peek once in a while, but only to keep an eye on us—though what they think we could be doing is beyond me.

Our food is getting worse—nothing but sandwiches, with that thick, chewy Arabic bread that makes your teeth hurt after a while, and some cheese or *labneh* (yogurt) or *halawi* (a Lebanese sweet). Rarely any meat, and very little fruit of any kind.

One thing we do get, though, is our morning coffee. Badr comes in quietly just after dawn every morning with a small pot of thick, black Arabic coffee. Don't know why he does this, and it's certainly weird—coffee in bed, room service from a terrorist.

The roller coaster goes on. We were thrown into deep depression the other day when the hamsters installed, with enormous bustle and hammering and trouble, a heavy jail door in addition to the wooden door of our room. It just seemed to hit all of us at once—if they're going to this much trouble to turn this apartment into a real prison, they must believe we're going to be here for a long time. It does not imply anything good about the negotiations they are allegedly conducting with the U.S. government, or whomever. Still no real information, just a vague, meaningless, "everything is good, and very good" whenever we ask what's happening. Still, we keep on asking.

I got upset with David again. Sometimes when Sayeed or one of the other guards comes in and wants to talk for a while, I try to pump him for information. It's hard work. They're not supposed to tell us anything, and obviously don't know much. But whatever it is, it's more than we know, so I keep trying. But David seems to get bored quickly, and interrupts to ask, "How are your children?" Or to try to persuade whoever it is to bring us something, usually ice cream. That effectively ends any chance of getting any news out of them that time. Finally, I blew a minor eruption after the latest incident. Didn't help things between

David and me at all, I'm afraid. Must be more careful. But it's incredibly hard to sustain that kind of control.

We get the radio for only a couple of hours a day. They come in and take it away every night about eleven or twelve o'clock, and we get it back the next evening. Apparently, the Frenchmen next door get it the rest of the time. Sometimes at night I can see their shadows on the wall opposite our barred door, pacing back and forth, just as we do.

It's close to Christmas, and we've heard on the radio that Terry Waite is back in town. He seems to hold a press conference at least twice a day, and sounds very optimistic. The roller coaster is climbing again. But the downhill part isn't far behind. On Christmas Eve, we hear him telling the newspeople that he's leaving Beirut without having gotten anywhere. Our church services are understandably somber, and there is no conversation afterward. We all just sit or lie quietly on our mattresses.

The depression is enormous, a thick, black blanket smothering me. I can't even begin to think. Despite all our caution, all our effort not to believe anything good would happen immediately, we really did believe it. At least, I find now that I did. To face again the knowledge that it will be weeks, months before there's even a chance of movement, a chance of freedom for one of us, is just too much. I can't do it. Please, God, I have to keep going. Just keep going. It will end. But when?

> Deepest darkness, fumblings,
> uncertainties are frightening.
> More frightening is the
> darkness of the mind,
> when outside lights
> make no impression
> and inner lights go dim.
> Uncertain fumblings here
> disturb surprising things,
> topple icons, awaken

deep monstrosities that
roar and slash, but faced, retreat;
acknowledged, can be bound
and thrust back in their holes,
rekindling light and fixing
holy objects into place again.

MADELEINE

SUNDERLAND. DECEMBER 1985.

*The pain and the disappointment were extreme. Nothing
could have hurt more. It was a big blow knowing that not
even Terry Waite or the Church of England, with the U.S.
government and its ally, Israel, or even Syria, which
claimed to be doing its best to free the hostages, could get
our men home.*

*When Waite had left for Beirut November 13, he had
high expectations that he would be home soon with the hostages. We discussed Terry a couple of times on the phone.
He asked me to pray, and to take care of myself and the
baby. He tried hard not to transfer his optimism to me so
I wouldn't be so disappointed in case of failure. I really believed, like many others, that Waite could do it, that he was
the right man for the mission.*

*I followed his every move in the news, and through Sche-
herazade and The AP. Carolyn Turolla called every day.
Without this wonderful woman, who cared personally and
deeply, I couldn't have borne it. She always let me and Terry's family know what was going on, through the years and
to the very end.*

*The pain I felt when Christmas came and Sulome and I
were alone, without Terry on our first Christmas as a family, was great. I tried to tell myself that life had to go on
for my child. What was more painful was not knowing what*

was happening to her father, how he was getting along, *if* he even knew it was Christmas. I recalled Christmas last year, and the party we gave for the AP staff. How happy we were. Terry seemed infused with happiness every time I looked at him, his eyes telling me how proud he was of me. I was so proud, too, as his fiancée. Everything was so fine.

The loneliness and the fear of the unknown were killing me. How could God give and take like that? Why? I meet a man I know I want to be with forever. I carry his child at the age of thirty-four. I'm one of the happiest women on earth, and bang! He goes away, leaving me with only a memory. A very precious memory, but still just a memory.

The year ended with me in bed, with my daughter in my arms and only my tears protecting us from the loneliness surrounding us.

15

Ali is back with his smarm and bullshit. Brought us several big bags of fruit—bananas and tangerines and apples, more than we can possibly eat before they go bad. He still insists he's not part of this group, just "helping my friends." He has claimed at various times to have attended the University of California at Los Angeles and the American University of Beirut. Possible—his English is pretty good, though he has a strange accent. Sounds a bit like an American, but with that peculiar rolling French *r* found among those who learn French before English. Sounds more Iranian than Lebanese. Whatever the accent, though, ninety percent of what he says is purest bullshit.

He asks us if we need anything—books, of course—and implies that there is movement in the negotiations and something might happen "soon, and very soon." Back on the roller coaster again. It's just impossible for us not to allow ourselves to hope, no matter how many disappointments there have been, no matter how much we distrust this man. He makes my skin crawl, but I still talk to him politely, pretend to accept his friendliness.

During the next couple of visits—he always goes out after a few minutes, saying "I'll be right back," then disappears for a week, or two, or three—the promises of release become more explicit, more direct. A deal is being made, he says.

Finally, we are measured for clothes, and Ali brings in

182

new shirts, trousers, even shoes for the four of us! "A few days," he says. Are we going home? Can we believe this man? Tom bangs out the "Marseillaise" on the wall to the Frenchmen next door, and gets a triumphant-sounding repeat back. We're full of speculation, yet all of us are afraid to believe. He's so explicit, though. He couldn't tell that direct a lie, could he? What would be the point?

Then, suddenly, the roller coaster plunges down. Ali brings in a *Time* and *Newsweek* telling of the bombing of Libya. On April 14, 1986, American warplanes attacked Libya, killing, among others, Moammar Kadafy's adopted child. At first, Ali insists it won't make any difference. He's certainly contemptuous of Kadafy, whom all these people dismiss as a madman who probably murdered their beloved leader, Imam Mussa Sadr, some years ago. But as the days pass and the promises grow vaguer, it's clear whatever was going on has been blasted to bits with Kadafy's headquarters.

Once again, we go into depression, fighting the slide as hard as we had fought the climb. The days gradually drift back into the fog of breakfast, walking, bathroom, lunch, and so on. The conversation by now lags often. We've talked ourselves out, just about.

Then Ali's back. We are going home, he says. The clothes are brought out. I am given a needle and thread; I carefully hem everyone's trousers to the right length. The excitement builds. Ali gives slow, clear instructions. "You will all be taken out to a bus waiting outside. Your blindfolds will be removed, but keep your eyes on the ground. Don't look at anyone. Get on the bus, keep your eyes down. You will be driven a short distance."

We wait several hours, endless. Finally, in the evening, the door opens, and several guards come in. The Hajj is there. Much bustle. David is taken out. A few minutes later, Tom. I reach out for Father Martin, sitting next to me, both of us blindfolded, and embrace him. "Good luck, Father."

"Why are you saying that? Aren't we all going?"

"I don't know. We don't know what's happening. If I don't see you, good luck."

"God bless you."

The guards come in again. I stand up, and am guided out the door, down the hall, and straight into the bedroom at the end.

The guards guide me to a straight-backed plastic chair, and I sit down, enveloped in depression. It was all obviously a cruel hoax. Within a few minutes, Tom says something to the guards, making me aware he also is in the room. But I hear nothing from David. We sit, facing the wall, for an hour, a second hour. The two guards, Sayeed and someone else, grow bored. The two approach and stand on either side, and begin chanting in Arabic. Louder, louder. Then Sayeed leans close to my ear and switches to English. "Death to America. Death to America." The normally friendly young man has gone off on some Shia mind trip, hypnotized by his own voice, by the chant, by hatred. I lean forward, fold my hands and begin to pray, trying to ignore the noise, trying to lift the blackness that envelops my mind. "Dear Lord, grant me peace. You who take away the sins of the world, grant me peace. Lord, help me. Our Father . . ."

After several hours, David is brought in and pushed into another chair. Sayeed and the others have grown quiet. The Hajj appears, gives orders. The three of us are taken back to our room, and the others all leave.

Lifting our blindfolds, we look at each other. Father Martin has obviously gone—home, it seems. But the joy we should feel for him doesn't come.

David tells Tom and me that he was asked to make a videotape for Father Martin to carry. He said he wrote a plea for the U.S. government to do something, and that it was gone over carefully by our captors before they finally taped it. Then he was brought in to us without seeing Father Martin.

We sort through the few things left beside his mattress. He has apparently been allowed to take nothing. The Bible, stuffed with markers. The tiny book of prayers he has carried for so long. We prop his mattress up against the wall, rearrange ours to give us all a little more room. The conversation is brief. Finally, we compose ourselves for sleep.

16

DAMASCUS. JULY 26, 1986.

The Syrian military car pulled up to the crowd of reporters and officials in front of the Syrian Foreign Ministry. Father Martin Jenco stepped out, looking dazed and blinking in the sunshine.

"Where's the sister of Terry Anderson?" he asked the crowd. Those around him moved back slightly, making a path to where Peggy Say stood. The two rushed into each other's arms. Both were crying and laughing as the secret policemen pushed at the surging newspeople and pulled the priest and Peggy toward the building.

"How is Terry?" Peg asked quickly.

"He's okay. He's holding up."

There wasn't time for much more. Jenco was most concerned with the videotape he'd been given by his captors, and the threat they'd made: If it isn't broadcast on television by midnight, the hostages will be executed. The threat was empty, absurd. But no one could ever be sure.

The priest was swept away by Syrian officials to be handed over to the American ambassador, the tape still in his hand.

Peg rushed back to her hotel, where she called The AP to tell them about the tape. After some tussle with officials at the embassy, The AP got the tape and passed it to all the networks, barely making the deadline imposed by the captors for its broadcast.

* * *

When Jenco paused briefly for a news conference at the airport in Damascus, Terry Waite appeared at his side. "It's no coincidence I am here," the Church of England envoy told the reporters. Waite had not actually been involved in any way in the negotiations that led up to the priest's release. He didn't even know about them. He was on a visit to Jordan when Oliver North called him up and told him to go to Damascus immediately. The American figured that Waite's high public profile would provide decent cover for the secret deal. Waite didn't question the orders.

Jenco's release ended Peg's trip to Damascus. She had arrived two weeks earlier as part of her crusade for her brother's freedom. But it was clear that only one hostage was coming out this time.

Peg was a long way from the scared, confused housewife she had started out as sixteen months before. Still scared at times, and even often confused by the whirlwind of media and politicians that enveloped her nearly everywhere she went, by now she was totally focused on the goal that had become an obsession. Find some way to get Terry out.

The obsession had gripped her through the death of her father and older brother, both from cancer, within weeks of each other. It held through exhausting months of television talk shows and radio interviews, through the endless repetition of what was by now becoming almost a standard pitch. "My brother has been held for more than a year. Nobody is doing anything. Somebody do something!"

Peter Kilbourne's death in April had outraged and bewildered Peggy by its casualness. She knew and liked Peter's family. She also knew that North and all the others involved were virtually certain that if the United States attacked Libya, hostages would be killed. They went ahead, and three hostages died—bought from their captors by the Iraqi chargé d'affaires in Beirut and personally executed by him.

At Kilbourne's funeral in California, Peg decided that if Terry died, as he very well might, it would get more than a ten-second clip on the evening news. Nobody deserved to be treated this shamefully. The government would not be allowed to sacrifice Terry. It would, by God, learn to see him as a person.

Peg had also by now lost a good deal of her awe of people in power. She had met with President Reagan, and heard him talk vaguely of "quiet diplomacy." She had met with Yasir Arafat, head of the Palestine Liberation Organization. Margaret Papandreou, the wife of the Greek prime minister, had befriended her, personally intervening to get her a visa for this trip to Syria. Other foreign leaders, ambassadors and officials, had listened respectfully to her pleas. Her meetings with them, especially on this trip, received national press coverage, with articles on the front page of the papers back home every day.

Peg had sat and argued in dozens of meetings with U.S. officials, bluntly expressing her anger and frustration. One of her most frequent targets was a Marine officer she had met in her search through Washington for someone who could tell her something, anything. Lt. Col. Oliver North was an aide to National Security Adviser Bud McFarlane; surprisingly, he was sympathetic and willing to talk to her.

"She was very angry, very upset at the lack of progress, of clear-cut answers," North said later. "You [could] not listen to her long, anguished ordeal and not be moved by it. You'd have to have a heart of steel."

North's heart was not made of steel. He was sympathetic, and he was in fact one of the few men who could have told Peg all about the efforts to free the hostages, if the whole subject hadn't been top, top secret. "I would only say, 'Peg, the State [Department] has told you all they can. We are trying everything possible to get Terry home.' "

"Everything possible" had expanded over the nine months since Ben Weir's release into a tortuously complicated, very shaky edifice involving the extreme stretching, if not outright violation, of a number of U.S. laws; barefaced and repeated lying to the public and one another by top government officials, including the president; and even actions that could arguably be said to violate the U.S. Constitution.

There was little pretense anymore to a broad diplomatic purpose behind the effort. It was now obviously a straight swap, arms for hostages. There was also no attempt to reconcile these dealings with the frequently repeated public policy on terrorism, but vigorously reaffirmed in a major policy study conducted by Vice President Bush: no deals with terrorists. Or to square it with the administration's strong efforts to prevent its allies from selling weapons to Iran.

How could Ronald Reagan sign a secret "Presidential Finding" authorizing the negotiations in the face of these contradictions, backed up by the strongest sort of objections from his senior cabinet members? In the face of repeated failures and the certain knowledge of bad faith and lies on the part of many of the parties involved?

Emotion, according to several of those close to Reagan. Sheer emotion that deepened with each encounter with relatives of the hostages.

"He'd listen to the families, and the dimensions of their pain that he absorbed, more than [anything] I ever saw him absorb from a member of Congress or a cabinet officer or anything else about policy. This was something that *really* moved him," McFarlane recalled.

"It made Ronald Reagan decide to take whatever political risk was necessary," North agreed. "I'd said it to Bud, Regan, [James] Baker—'Don't meet with the families. I don't think that's a good idea.'"

With the president emotionally involved, no amount of protest or objection from anyone was going to kill the initiative begun by Israel so long before. Even the massive screwup of the second shipment of missiles to Iran in November wasn't enough to derail the process, though Weinberger and Shultz and even McFarlane, who was in the process of resigning, thought it had been.

Ollie North had by now negotiated a detailed package of weapons and missiles and a minutely exact timetable with the Iranians, through Ghorbanifar and Shwimmer. The proposal was to receive final approval at a meeting in London December 7 among the Iranians and the Americans.

In a memo to himself on December 4, 1985, North outlined the package:

> ". . . 50 HAWKS w/PIP [product improvement package] and 3300 basic TOWs.
>
> "—Deliveries wd commence on or about 12 December as follows:
>
> "H - hr: 1 707 w/300 TOWs = 1 AMCIT
>
> "H + 10 hrs: 1 707 (same A/C) w/300 TOWs = 1 AMCIT
>
> "H + 16 hrs: 1 747 w/50 HAWKs & 400 TOWs = 2 AMCITs . . ."

The market price was set: One American citizen is worth 300 TOW antitank missiles, or 50 Hawks and 200 TOWs.

Shultz and Weinberger made one last effort to stop the process, and thought they had succeeded. At a meeting with the president, they again forcefully put forward their objections, and this time were joined by McFarlane. Reagan apparently gave in, authorizing McFarlane to go to the London meeting with one message for the Iranians: no more weapons.

McFarlane did so, in a blunt thirty-minute presentation to Ghorbanifar, Shwimmer, and Kimche. North sat in on the meeting. McFarlane reminded them all that what had begun as an attempt to open a dialogue with Iran had become a haggle over human lives. It had to stop. The United States wanted to continue talking to Tehran: It would like better relations. But first the hostages had to come home, and not in exchange for missiles.

The reaction was an outburst of contempt from the go-between Ghorbanifar, who curtly dismissed the Americans' second thoughts and concern with principle.

"You neophyte idiots," the Iranian arms merchant told McFarlane. "You're dealing with very vulnerable people, unsophisticated people who care little about dialogue, or about anything except survival."

Ghorbanifar was a weapons dealer, he said. That was his business. That was what this was all about from the beginning.

"You're a goddamned fool," he concluded. "You're going to get every one of us killed. And I don't want to have anything else to do with you."

An obvious, if unpleasant end, McFarlane thought as he left.

Not quite. The meeting was held in London, but it was still about the Middle East. McFarlane, for all his sophistication and knowledge of world affairs, apparently did not understand the Middle East.

North stayed after his boss left. The two differ on what his instructions were, but the results are not in doubt. The dialogue continued.

McFarlane was replaced within days by Adm. John Poindexter as Reagan's national security adviser. Ghorbanifar came to the United States. The deal was alive again; but the Americans no longer trusted Ghorbanifar. They wanted to deal directly with someone in the Iranian government.

On February 17, a shipment of 500 TOWs was flown from Israel to Bandar Abbas, in southwest Iran.

On February 24, North sat down in a Frankfurt, Germany, hotel room with not just one, but half a dozen Iranian officials. The most important was Mohsen Kangerlou. The former tailor was a senior foreign policy adviser in the Iranian government, and very close to Ali Akbar Mohtashemi, the ultraradical interior minister of Iran.

The meeting consisted mostly of North's speech about Washington's wanting a better dialogue with Iran, and the ritual tirade about the iniquities of the West from Kangerlou. At the end, the Iranian pushed a ten-page list of weapons and parts across the table to North.

On February 27, a second shipment of 500 TOWs was flown from Israel to Bandar Abbas. The unsatisfactory and embarrassing Hawks the Israelis had tried to give to the Iranians in November were still sitting around in their Hebrew-marked boxes. They were picked up and taken back to Israel.

No hostages were released. However, North got something else out of the deal. The Americans had heavily overcharged Iran for the missiles they had sent. But in the complicated bookkeeping involved in the top-secret deal, only the lower, correct amount was credited to the Department of Defense, which supplied the weapons. Even after Ghorbanifar, Shwimmer, and everyone else took their cuts of the $10 million deal, and the Defense Department was paid, millions of dollars were left over, and "off the books"—that is, with no need to account for it, since officially it didn't exist. That money, it occurred to North very quickly, could be used for another project dear to both his and Reagan's hearts: the Nicaraguan Contras.

Congress, enraged by the unofficial war the Reagan administration was waging against the leftist government of Nicaragua, had cut off all official funds for the Contras, the antigovernment guerrillas. North had been deeply involved in the U.S. support effort for the Contras, and would continue to work hard to raise private money for them. It was both a priority of President Reagan, his boss, and a matter of strong personal and ideological conviction for North.

This windfall from the missiles sold to Iran would buy a lot of weapons and supplies for the Contras. It was more than enough to offset the disappointment caused by Iran's reneging on the promised release of the American hostages. The arms-for-hostages process would go on.

In April, Reagan called once again on the now-retired McFarlane. The Iranians were ready to receive a top U.S. official in Tehran—secretly, of course. Would McFarlane go?

"Well, I was pleased. I was surprised, but I told him sure," McFarlane said. "The only thing I asked was, 'Are Shultz and Weinberger involved?' And he said they were on board."

The trip, as explained by North, would involve meeting top Iranian officials, primarily President Rafsanjani himself, for substantive discussions. Hostages would come up only as the prerequisite for any further rapprochement.

And, by the way, North added, the last shipment of weapons would be made concurrent with the trip. Three loads of spare parts for missiles.

The plane that headed for Iran on May 25 probably carried more top secrets than had been assembled in one place in a long time, in the hands of McFarlane, North, Howard Teicher, and George Cave from the United States; Amran Nir from Israel; plus a number of CIA communications experts with equipment that would allow them to talk instantly to anyone in Washington, from the White House on down.

"Looking back on it, it was a terribly dangerous thing to do," McFarlane admitted. All the top officials carried poison pills in case the negotiations broke down and they ended up in the hands of Iranian radicals.

The trip was yet another disaster. The Iranians who met them were low-level functionaries. The plane was taken over by militiamen and unloaded. There was no meeting scheduled with Rafsanjani.

"There was no commitment to meet [high officials]. Ghorbanifar and North had lied," McFarlane said. The official that McFarlane finally talked to clearly believed McFarlane was there to deliver weapons. He had nothing to say about hostages.

"It made it pretty clear that the go-betweens had deceived us both. Ghorbanifar had been overselling his brief to the Iranians . . . and North, out of this can-do spirit and not much brains, said let's go over and try to make it work."

McFarlane blew a gasket. He was not there to negotiate more arms-for-hostages deals. In the end, he ordered the planes loaded with spare parts that were waiting in Israel to unload, gathered up his party, and headed for the Tehran airport, ignoring pleas from North, Ghorbanifar, Nir, and even the Iranians for more time to work out something.

Once again, the whole deal had been blown out of the water. Apparently. Only apparently.

Over the next few weeks, in several direct and indirect contacts, the Iranians were told there could be no further discussions until at least one or two hostages were released. If that was done, according to one scenario set up by North, the Hawk spare parts could be brought into the deal again, and maybe even a couple of radars.

Father Jenco was released on July 26.

On July 30, President Reagan authorized the release of some of the spare parts the Iranians wanted. Three pallets of electronic spares for Hawk missiles arrived in Iran on August 3, 1986.

NINE

PATIENCE

Patience is not a virtue—
it's a necessity, a survival trait,
an ever-filling well from which
I sip, or gulp, exhausted
by the desert of this nonlife.
My faith surges and recedes;
hope sometimes abandons me,
leaving only patience.
I kick and scream and flail
inside my head; patience
offers only soft resistance,
washing gently at my rage.
I know if I dive deeply,
I will find patience, hope, and faith
emerging from a single source,
eternal and unchanging.

17

It has been two days since Father Martin left. The guards all say he has been taken to Damascus, where, they add, my sister Peg met him. That afternoon, they bring in a small black-and-white television. David, Tom, and I sit facing the TV, the guards standing behind us, and cautiously lift our blindfolds to watch the news reports of Father Martin's arrival. Yes, Peg is there, enveloping him in a bear hug. We hear snatches of reports, but Sayeed quickly turns the sound down if it gets too detailed.

Then, a commentator appears. American. NBC? There's a wide yellow banner across the top left side of the screen saying, "SECRET MESSAGE?" The commentator speculates on whether a reference to William Buckley's family in the tape David made, and Father Martin obviously delivered, contains a code. Buckley was single, and had no family, he notes.

I can feel my back grow cold. There is no comment from the guards. When the report is over, they disconnect the television and leave, still saying little.

As soon as they are gone, we grill David. What was that about? He said he sent his condolences to Buckley's wife and children. Where did you learn about this alleged family? "You told me," he says. "No, I knew nothing about Buckley, knew nothing about a family." We're unable to trace the source of the bad information, and speculate whether it will have any effect. If our hosts believe it, I can't help feeling, we're in for trouble.

The next day, the guards storm in, accompanied by Ali and the Hajj. "You are spies. You are evil," Ali shouts. We're submitted to a ten-minute harangue, our protests of innocence ignored. David and Tom are taken out of the room.

"Stand up," Ali says, apparently translating for the Hajj. "Face the wall. Put your arms up." Then they leave.

After a few seconds feeling silly standing with my arms up in an empty room, I sit down, and try to compose my mind. I pick up one of the old paperback books we've had for weeks, and begin to read. I can hear shouting outside the door, but can't guess what's going on. I don't want to think about it.

The door opens a half hour later, and I pull down my blindfold, putting the book aside.

"Why are you sitting down? We told you to stand up!" Ali says fiercely.

"You left. I thought you were finished with me, so I sat down. You want me to stand up? Okay." I face the wall and put my arms up, as before.

There is quick, hard discussion in Arabic, but they say nothing more. Then Tom and David are brought back in, and the harangue begins again, Ali translating for the Hajj. "You are spies. We trusted you, and you betrayed us."

"No, we didn't," I try to interject.

"Shut up. Don't speak." He continues. We will be punished. We may be killed. And so on, and so on. Finally, it runs down. As the two of them turn to leave, I call out quietly. "Hajj."

"What?" It is Ali answering.

"You are wrong."

Ali mutters in Arabic. The Hajj replies. "Shut up." They are gone.

After the door closes, we begin the discussion. Tom and David say they were put against a wall, threatened, questioned. There was a lot of shouting, but no physical punishment. What happens now? No way to know. Just wait and see.

It doesn't take long. The next evening, the guards are back. We are abruptly ordered up, then taken out one by one to the stairway, down the stairs, into a van waiting outside. From the engine sounds, there seems to be two of them, but we can't be sure. A short ride, perhaps fifteen or twenty minutes, then we are unloaded. Near the ocean? Ouzai, by the airport? Hard to tell. The airport has been closed for weeks, so there are no plane sounds to guide us. From glimpses under the edge of the blindfold, the building seems to be deserted, half finished. One by one, we are lowered through a hole in the floor, into a dirty basement, then taken down a short hall and into a six-by-six-foot cell, with a steel door. No light, nothing but dust and filth on the floor, a narrow ledge running around two sides. Bustling of the guards, then we're pushed out and into the cell next door. Two of the same size, knocked together, the remains of the wall between still there. The door slams.

Mattresses for each of us, two in one half, one in the other. Water bottles. That's it. Nothing else. I'm frightened. This place is grim, the worst place we've been. How long are we going to be here? The story of the alleged secret message has poisoned their minds. They must have been planning to move us after Father Martin was released, just as they did after Ben went home. But these conditions? How are we going to make it? What now?

18

MADELEINE

Father Jenco called me a couple of weeks after his release. We talked for an hour. I loved hearing him talk about Terry. Everything the priest said about him made my heart jump. I cried with the joy of the first news from my love. I felt so proud of him, and so sorry for him.

Father Jenco, a very gentle man, told me only the gentle things about Terry and what was happening to him. He told me how much Terry loved me, what he felt about his daughters, and his plans for our future. I knew these things, but it still made me very happy hearing them a year after I last saw Terry.

Father Jenco didn't mention the hard conditions they were all in. He told me that it looked very promising. Everyone else thought so, too.

My sister and her family had been a great support to me in England. I know that without them, that period of Terry's captivity would have been even worse for me. Still, nothing had seemed to ease the pain. I was very vulnerable and needed Terry with me.

Knowing that nothing I could do would bring him home was the most frustrating thing. As a Lebanese and a journalist, I knew there was very little any woman—wife, fiancée, or even mother—could do in these circumstances.

The people who held Terry had no mercy in their hearts. Their loyalty was only to their cause or their greed. Humanity had no meaning to them. Young men who were raised in destruction and ruins, who have seen death done for a loaf of bread at their doorstep, have no mercy for a crying woman. I felt helpless.

At the outset, 1986 had not looked very promising. I wanted to believe that somebody, somewhere was doing something that nobody knew about to end the mess we were in. I always hoped and believed the U.S. government had not forgotten the American men in captivity, even though through experience I knew its leaders knew so little about us and our mentality, or how to even start any negotiations by giving instead of expecting to just take. The U.S. stand was "no negotiations with kidnappers," and the only way to end the problem was to negotiate at some level. My mind would race for hours just so I'd feel I was doing something more than taking care of Sulome.

She was six months old at the start of the year, and already filling my life with joy that I never dreamed of. Her movements were very steady, and her bright green eyes would look at me with love. I didn't know how mothers could feel. Between learning how to be a mother and what to do with my child, I began to feel the responsibility of motherhood.

My sorrow for her grew as she did. I'd grown up without my father. My parents separated when I was a few months old. They never meant it, they always said, but stubbornness and youth made them do it. I always hated the fact that my father never lived with us. Although he would come and visit often, it was not normal to have both parents but live with only one of them. Here, my child was going through the same thing. We didn't plan it this way.

On the first anniversary of Terry's kidnapping, March 16, 1986, there was still no news, no progress. On the contrary, more foreigners were being kidnapped, and more mystery surrounded their captors. I felt I was living in the dark. I began to feel the distance between us. I felt trapped without news in England. Something in me kept nagging at me to move. I had to leave, to get closer to Terry.

I decided to go back to Lebanon, but my family in Beirut

wouldn't hear of it. The situation there was getting worse, even on the Christian side of the capital. But I needed to be close to Terry, to my family. I wanted them to share my child with me.

Scheherazade Faramarzi, who had been transferred by The AP to Nicosia, asked me if I would consider coming to Cyprus. I welcomed the suggestion, and on April 6 flew with Sulome to the island. It turned out to be a very good move. For the first few months we stayed with Scheherazade, who became the best friend anyone could wish for.

Just a few days after we arrived, U.S. Navy jets attacked two military bases in Libya. Although the Shiites of Lebanon have no connection with Libya, they hate Moammar Kadafy, blaming him for the disappearance of their leader, Imam Moussa Sadr, during a visit to that country in 1978. I had little fear for Terry, but I knew that some retaliation by the Libyans was likely, and other people might be harmed by Kadafy's followers in Lebanon.

Within days, there were news reports that Peter Kilbourne and two other Britons kidnapped two weeks earlier had been murdered in Beirut. Kilbourne had been missing two years, and no group had ever claimed responsibility for his kidnapping. It was very painful to learn that someone could be kept that long, then killed for whatever reasons the kidnappers thought suitable.

Sulome and I adjusted to Cyprus quickly. She was ten months old now, almost walking. I wasn't ready to be sociable, but enjoyed the warm weather and the closeness to Lebanon and my family. But mostly, I was close to Terry. I could breathe the same air he was breathing, and if I wanted, I could take a short plane ride and be in the same neighborhood where we always suspected he was, without anyone knowing who I was. I often thought of doing that, but dared not. I could not take my daughter and could not leave her behind. But simply the knowledge of being so close to him made a difference in me.

Sulome and I moved to Larnaca, on the south coast of the island. Summer began, and my family came to visit. Ev-

Aftermath of car bomb, Beirut, 1983. *(AP/WIDE WORLD)*

Incoming Israeli bombs hit an apartment house in West Beirut, 1982. *(AP/WIDE WORLD)*

BEIRUT IN AGONY

A Palestinian antiaircraft Sam-7 fires at an Israeli bomber. *(AP/WIDE WORLD)*

Israeli aerial and naval shelling of West Beirut in the summer of 1982. *(AP/WIDE WORLD)*

Scheherazade Faramarzi, an Iranian reporter, and Anderson at work at the AP bureau in West Beirut, 1982. *(AP/WIDE WORLD)*

Hussein Mussawi *(seated)*, the leader of the Islamic Amal, a radical Shiite faction believed to be associated with both Hezbollah (the Party of God) and its secret terrorist offshoot, Islamic Jihad. Photo taken during an interview with Anderson in Baalbek, 1983. *(AP/WIDE WORLD)*

Madeleine Bassil, Anderson, and Faramarzi celebrate Christmas in the Metn region of the Lebanese mountains, 1984 *(AUTHOR'S COLLECTION)*

Shortly before his abduction Anderson embraces Madeleine at a party in West Beirut, 1984. *(AUTHOR'S COLLECTION)*

Anderson on Marine duty in Des Moines, Iowa, 1970. *(AUTHOR'S COLLECTION)*

Anderson and first wife, Mickey, at their 1968 wedding. *(AUTHOR'S COLLECTION)*

Mickey with daughter, Gabrielle, in Venice, 1977. *(AUTHOR'S COLLECTION)*

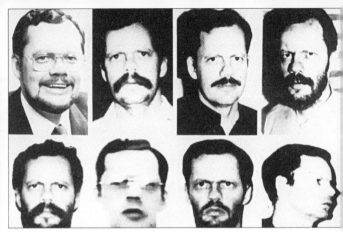

A composite of eight photos chronicling Anderson's near seven years in captivity. Top *(left to right)*: a 1984 pho showing Anderson prior to his capture; photos from 198! 1986, and 1987 respectively. Bottom *(left to right)*: photo released respectively in October 1988; October 1988; Ju 1991; and August 1991. *(AP/WIDE WORLD)*

Head shot of Anderson from May 1985, just two months after his abduction. *(AP/WIDE WORLD)*

Captive, 1986. *(AP/WIDE WORLD)*

Captive, 1987. *(AP/WIDE WORLD)*

Head shot of Anderson released October 24, 1988, three days before his forty-first birthday. *(AP/WIDE WORLD)*

Head shot of Anderson taken from a videotaped message released by his captors four days after his forty-first birthday. Anderson said in his prepared statement, "I am well and being well treated and I received your birthday greetings and as always I thank you very much." *(AP/WIDE WORLD)*

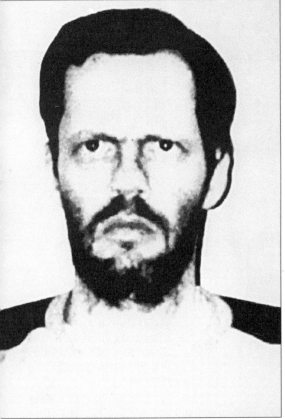

Captive, July 1991. *(AP/WIDE WORLD)*

Anderson's sister Peggy Say, his brother Jack Anderson, and an unidentified child commemorate Anderson's capture in a June 1988 meeting. (PEOPLE *MAGAZINE, TIME WARNER, INC.*)

(Below) The Reverend Lawrence Martin Jenco and Peggy Say. (*AUTHOR'S COLLECTION*)

(Above) Glenn Richard Anderson, Jr., and his wife, Jeannie, who were married two days before his death in 1986. (*AUTHOR'S COLLECTION*)

Left to right: Larry Heinzerling, Peggy Say, David Say (Peggy's husband), and Bill Foley, a former AP photographer, gather at the ruins of the Colosseum in Rome shortly before Peggy met the Pope. *(AUTHOR'S COLLECTION)*

Pope John Paul II shakes hands with Peggy Say during he private audience at the Vatican in February 1990. *(AP/WIDE WORLD)*

Left to right: Don Mell, Peggy Say, and Chuck Lewis, former AP Washington bureau chief. (*AUTHOR'S COLLECTION*)

Peggy Say and Don Mell discuss Anderson's plight with the Reverend Jesse Jackson. (*AP/WIDE WORLD*)

Peggy Say meets with PLO spokesman Yasir Arafat to discuss Western hostages. (*AP/WIDE WORLD*)

Anderson's daughter Sulome visits her father's office for the first time on Christmas Eve, 1990. *(AP/WIDE WORLD)*

Anderson greets the Western press in Damascus shortly after his release in December 1991. *(AP/WIDE WORLD)*

nderson, accompanied by Peggy Say, left, and Madeleine
assil, behind at right, smiles broadly upon his arrival at the
Wiesbaden Air Force hospital in Germany shortly after
nderson's arrival from Damascus. *(AP/WIDE WORLD)*

hree former American hostages—Joseph Cicippio, left;
nderson, center; and Alan Steen—face a crowd of well-
ishers from the balcony of the Wiesbaden Air Force
ospital. *(AP/WIDE WORLD)*

AP President Louis D. Boccardi, left, Anderson, and Sulome arrive at AP headquarters in New York in December 199 *(AP/WIDE WORLD)*

Anderson raises h arm to greet wel wishers who gathere outside A headquarters in Ne York to welcome hi back from captivit With Anderson, fro the right, are A President Louis Boccardi, immediate behind Anderso former hostage th Reverend Lawrenc Jenco, with whi beard; and Madelein front. *(AP/WIDE WORL*

nderson with his daughter, Sulome, Christmas morning,
991. *(COPYRIGHT © 1991 BILL FOLEY)*

ight former hostages celebrate their freedom *(from left to
ght)*: the Reverend Lawrence Jenco, Robert Polhill,
homas Sutherland, Ben Weir, Anderson, Alan Steen, Jesse
urner, and Joseph Cicippio. *(AP/WIDE WORLD)*

Anderson and Giandomenico Picco, center, at the Unite Nations Association award ceremony in Toronto, 199: Picco, who won the award for his efforts to free Wester hostages, was presented the award by Anderson. *(AUTHOR COLLECTION)*

Left to right: Sulome, Anderso Madeleine, John McCarthy, an Jill Morrell in Antigua, 199 *(AUTHOR'S COLLECTIO*

Anderson, Madeleine, and Sulome in Antigua, December 1991. *(AUTHOR'S COLLECTION)*

erything I did felt strange. To be free to do whatever I wanted, to enjoy the sea and sun and sand, felt like cheating. There was a conflict within me. I limited my movements to taking Sulome to the beach and straight home to my refuge. My mother came to visit, and that was my best consolation.

There were many hostage stories in the summer of 1986. Several kidnappings took place, and there were rumors of possible releases. Sulome's birthday was on June 7, and that day, Terry's brother, Glenn Richard, Jr., died in the States. His father had died three months earlier of cancer. During his father's funeral, Rich had had a stroke. While he was recovering from the surgery that required, doctors discovered he also had inoperable, fatal cancer.

I had liked Rich very much. Although I had met him only a few times, he always made me feel we had known each other a long time. It was Rich who had been the first to call me the day Terry was taken. That he died on Sulome's birthday made me feel even closer to this wonderful man.

Peggy came to Cyprus in the middle of July. She had been refused a visa to Syria previously, but with the help of the American-born wife of the Greek prime minister, Margaret Papandreou, she had gotten one this time. We spoke by phone a few times, but did not meet.

On July 26, Father Jenco was released—the first good news since my daughter's birth. Terry Waite appeared with him in Damascus, and it looked as if things were really happening.

It was so good just to see Father Martin emerge from captivity, from where Terry was. Knowing he had shared the same room, the same experience with Terry. It was very sad, and yet a relief, for here he was, free and looking well.

Peggy and I had another argument on the phone, ending with her calling me names and slamming down the receiver. I decided never to have contact with her again.

The optimism generated by Father Jenco's release lasted only a short time. Frank Reed and Joseph Cicippio were kidnapped in Beirut just three days apart, on September 9 and 12. Their captors announced themselves as the Arab Revolutionary Cells—Omar Al-Mukhtar Forces. The strange name only meant Islamic Jihad had increased its membership, and would not stop at anything. It was also a sign that whatever reasons they had to release Father Jenco, they didn't have them anymore.

It was hard to accept that it might be a very long time before we saw Terry again. I was again going into deep depressions. I felt like a yo-yo.

19

STIGMATA VII

A six-foot chain, a six-foot cell
allow two paces: step, step,
and turn; step, step, and turn.
When the body's bound,
the mind leaps free to soar
and twist and turn back
on itself until its very freedom
becomes a kind of prison.
Each emotion's felt in
fierce intensity, swelling,
fading only to return again
on a wild, unpiloted
roller coaster ride
that never ends, ignoring
pain, sickness, even death,
devouring all without a pause.
Time's fragmented, each moment
endless, unconnected to
the swiftly passing years.

BEIRUT. AUGUST 1986.

It's a week, maybe ten days since we were brought here.
August what? 3? 5? The guards will say nothing. We simply sit through the day in the dark cell. Now that David and
I have almost entirely ceased arguing—neither one of us
wants the hassle—it seems that Tom has decided to join the
fray. He's emerging even more from his quiet depression,
but usually to fight with David. He disagrees with nearly
everything David says, and seems to have taken a deep dis-

like to him. I try to mediate, but I'm in no shape myself to play mother hen.

This place is truly horrible, and the guards seem to have taken in the atmosphere of the prison. We're jammed in tight against each other, with no room to move except one by one, in turns. David can't even stand up straight—the cell is only six feet high, and he's a couple inches over that. We've lost everything—books, paper, pen, any access to news.

The cell is filthy with cockroaches, spiders, and various other vermin, and mice and rats can be heard scurrying about at night.

Even Mahmoud seems hostile, and the others are worse. Sayeed has disappeared. He showed up one night, prowled the corridor between the cells and howled like a dog. I recognized his maniacal laugh. He didn't stop to talk. At least two of the new guards seem really vicious. So far, they haven't taken any overt action, but often stand in the doorway after delivering the garbage they call food and curse in Arabic. I can feel the hatred boiling off them like steam.

We can hear others in the cells on either side and across the way, but the guards say nothing about them. Once in a while, we peek through the small fan in the bottom of the steel door of our cell—the electricity is often cut, so it doesn't work—as the others are taken to the toilet. I believe I heard someone ask in a strong English accent for a cigarette. Usually, though, the huge ventilation machine in the corner that brings air into this sealed underground jail drowns everything out. When the power's off, the guards turn on fluorescent lights in the corridor, run by a battery, then set a radio on the floor tuned to that exact frequency that resonates with the lights and produces a cyclical, horrible howl. I guess the idea is that we shouldn't hear anyone else talking.

We've been forbidden to look out the small window in the door, with many threats of dire punishment, but of course we do. We can see the doors of several cells, and we know prisoners are in them, but so far no contact, not even a face or a wave. We haven't been able to figure out if the Frenchmen are here.

We just lie on our mattresses for hours on end. At least there's enough room for one person to pace back and forth—two steps in each direction—but neither David nor Tom seems interested in doing so. I do it for hours at a time, trying to keep my head low enough so the guards won't think I'm looking at them as I pass the window. Mostly they stay at the end of the corridor, in a small room, with another steel gate separating them from us.

Tom and I have taken to working on French irregular verbs. With no paper or pen, it's just a matter of memorization and recitation. I know David gets bored listening to it, but it's virtually the only mental stimulation we have. Otherwise, I'm lost in black thoughts. I try to believe something is happening out there, that some sort of progress is being made toward our release, but I keep lapsing into profound pessimism.

Tom asks regularly about my faith. He is still groping, not really believing but unwilling to give up that faint hope that if our government can't get us out, something or someone called God might do so. There isn't much I can do to help him. I don't believe in that kind of miracle anymore. My faith has to do with a knowledge, a deep assurance that there is a God, and a Christ, and that He requires something of me. What, I'm not sure of. I know I still have not become the kind of person I am capable of being, and should be. I know that Madeleine helps me toward that goal, just by being herself. I can't reconcile that with the strictures in the Bible about having one wife, about divorce not being permissible. Nor can I reconcile the idea that I'm loved, accepted by God for what I am, though I have committed many, many acts that are without doubt sins.

I've moved beyond the kinds of questions Tom asks. Does God answer prayers? If so, why am I still here, after having prayed so long and so hard for freedom, or sometimes death? How can God's plan include the kind of evil these men are committing? Why are there so many contradictions or seeming anomalies in the Bible? How can a belief in its holiness and truth be consistent with what we know of evolution and history?

I can make a case to "resolve" any of these—I'm nothing if not a skillful debater. But my concerns now are all internal. I've consigned Madeleine and my daughters and my family to God's hands. I can do nothing for them, except pray and trust in Him to care for them as I do. Most of my thoughts are spent rooting around in my mind and my past, trying to understand myself, who I am, why I do the things I do, how to recognize and root out the evil within myself, how to deal with the hatred and anger in my soul. For long periods, I just try to repress all of it, try to float through the days and nights in some kind of minimal awareness.

David is gone from the cell. First, he was asked to write a letter. He was taken out for some time, into the guards' room, and when he came back said they had dictated exactly what he was to write—a demand for negotiations. He said he made some spelling errors to make sure those who read it would know it wasn't voluntary. A day or two later, the guards were back, and this time very angry. Apparently news stories had noted the errors, making exactly the conclusion he wanted, but broadcasting it all over the world. We could hear the angry discussion down the hall. David sounded very shaken. He was not brought back to us, but was put in another cell on the other side. We can hear him say a few words now and then to the guards, but can't see that particular cell. I'm worried about him, but find the relative peace a relief. He and Tom had been arguing almost constantly for the past three weeks.

The two of us rarely argue, though our "discussions" get a little heated sometimes. Mostly we practice French, speculate about our possible release, or play a simple version of the Japanese game Go that I made out of olive pits and taught to him.

It's been raining pretty hard—unusual for late summer in

Beirut, and the walls are streaming with water. We have asked the guards to do something about it several times, with no joy. We're afraid to ask to be moved. It seems like there aren't any more double cells in this small basement, so it might mean we would be separated, and neither one of us wants that. Finally, one day Mahmoud came in, took our mattresses and water bottles, then returned to move us into a large cell adjoining the guards' place. I nearly lost my grip. I couldn't bear to be under their direct gaze all the time, and while the new cell is dry, it's also filthy. I shouted at Mahmoud: "Why don't you kill us? You're a Muslim, we're Christians. You're supposed to kill us."

After an hour or so of this, Mahmoud took us back to our old cell, growling, "Don't complain anymore." I'd rather have the water all over than have them watching us, peering at us every time they get bored. But I was shocked at the way I lost control. I've been clamping down so hard on all that anger, all that frustration, just pushing it down and down. To have it burst out that way is both embarrassing and startling. It makes me realize that it's all still there, nearly five hundred days of it, an enormous weight, a total waste. How much more will I have to swallow before the end?

We know the name of at least one of the other prisoners— Sontag. He's an old man, apparently hard of hearing, and is being given a bad time. Every time he speaks, to ask for the bathroom for instance, he speaks loudly. Then the guards tell him to shut up, speak quietly. He always replies even louder: "My name is Sontag. My name is Sontag." It seems as if he's taunting them, or trying to convince them he's crazy. He has been thumped fairly severely a couple of times for crapping in the little plastic wastebasket we all have in the cell. I've had the temptation myself when the guards are slow to take us to the bathroom.

I've still got my diary, and have managed to keep one pen hidden in the mattress, but I don't write anything anymore. There's nothing to write. My mind sometimes seems as empty as this cell, and it scares me. Absolutely nothing is happening, nothing, and there's no hint that anything will. It's August now, the height of the Mediterranean summer. If the fighting has ended, or even died down a little, the beaches will be full. Where is Maddy? I know she wouldn't want to leave Lebanon, but I hope she has. Maybe she agreed to go for our daughter's sake. But where? The States, my family? Her sister in England? What is she doing? How long can her love last? We had so little time together, so little for her to hold on to. I know she loves me, and she's fiercely loyal. But she's also young and beautiful, with a good mind and a wonderful personality. And a life to live. I know she's waiting for me, but how long?

I have long depressions that sometimes reduce me to tears at night. I try to hide them from Tom, but I know he feels them, and has his own. We spend long periods not talking, just lying on the mattresses through the day and night. Then we rouse ourselves to some activity—pacing for me, sit-ups or squats for Tom, or a game of Go, or a French lesson.

I was sitting with my back to the wall a week or so ago, thinking about various incidents in my life. I recalled our trip to Florida, when Maddy and I went to see my father in the hospital just a couple months before I was kidnapped. For some reason, an incident at Kennedy Airport in New York came to mind: A deaf man approached us and gave me a card with the signing alphabet sketched on it. He was raising money. I gave him some, looked at the card, remembered I already knew the alphabet from high school, and put it in my pocket.

Sitting in the dark, I tried to recall the signs, learned from two deaf friends when I was fifteen or sixteen and never used since. Surprisingly, I could remember perhaps two-thirds of them. I tried out some alternatives for the ones I couldn't recall clearly, then showed them to Tom. He wasn't really interested, but I suggested he learn them, too, in case we were forbidden to speak, for instance. He didn't want to, but I persuaded him, and drilled him for a while.

Over the next few days, we practiced a bit, becoming fairly fluent in the simple spelling out of words. No particular reason—just an exercise, a way to pass the time, of which we have an abundance. Even, as my dad used to say, a superfluity.

There are mice all over this place, and even more roaches and spiders. I hate spiders. We tear up the tissues we get from time to time and stuff them, wet, into the holes and cracks in the walls to try to keep the bugs out. But it doesn't do much good. When the power's out, the mice come in through the little fan in the bottom of the door. One got caught when the electricity came on halfway through the fan, and got knocked for a loop. I caught it with the trash can and kept it for a while, then let it go. Another came in while I was dozing and jumped up on the mattress in front of my nose. I woke up in the near-darkness to see this little beastie sitting up two inches from my eye. Scared me to death. Him, too, when I jumped.

Dozing is nearly all I do, still. Tom seems to sleep reasonably well. At least he snores a lot. I just drift in and out, day or night. I probably sleep ten or twelve hours a day in total, but I still feel tired all the time. I pray less frequently now. Somehow, I can't seem to focus my mind. It's been a long time since I felt that touch, that closeness I long for.

Hallelujah! We've established contact with two of the other prisoners—John McCarthy and Brian Keenan! Tom spotted them looking out the little window of their cell across the way some days ago, and waved. They waved back. Then Brian held a piece of paper out the window—dangerous— that said "I am Irish, my friend is English."

Standing on tiptoe to see out the window of our cell, which is just a little too high for my five-seven, I tried to say "We are American" and spell out our names, tracing the letters in the air as large as I could. Didn't seem to work too well. I dug my pen out of the mattress and wrote a long note on a piece of my diary paper. I tried to be witty about our lodgings, castigated the guards a bit, told them who we are, and signed it "Up the Union."

Then I held the note up and told them with gestures it would be in the bathroom we all use, at the end of the corridor.

The next morning I stuck it in the pipe under the sink, with a thread from my blanket tied to it and hanging out the end. This all made Tom pretty nervous, and to be truthful, I didn't want to think about what the guards would do if they found it, but they didn't. Brian and John got it, then put a reply in the pipe the next morning. In it, Brian made it very clear, even blunt: yes, he's Irish, and a Protestant from Belfast, and his mate is an Englishman. But in fact, he said, he's a fervent nationalist, and a supporter of the armed struggle, and not in any way in favor of the union of England and Ireland!

Not an auspicious beginning. The old Anderson step-two: one foot forward, the other in my mouth. Anyway, in the next exchange, I suggested they learn the signing alphabet, and we spent two days, with the help of a couple of notes, showing them through the bars. Now we can talk! And we are doing so, at length. I've quizzed John, who's a producer for WTN, about Maddy, but he knows nothing, and about my friends at The AP. He couldn't help me much, said he was only in Beirut a month, and didn't know them well. But apparently I was replaced by Ed Blanche, who stays mostly in the office and the Commodore Hotel across the street.

Brian was an English teacher at the American University—strangely enough, hired by Tom's wife! He was able to tell Tom quite a bit about Jean, which has cheered Tom up considerably.

It's fantastic to be able to talk to someone else, someone who at least was outside more recently than we were. John was taken April 17, and Brian a few days earlier, April 11—just four months for both of them. They were dismayed to learn we were all being held by Islamic Jihad. No one has told them why they were taken or by whom. To learn they have been tossed in with two people who have been held more than a year, with no immediate prospect of getting out, wasn't the most cheerful news they could have had. But they both seem amazingly upbeat, full of jokes and cheerful chat.

Another new hostage, an American by his voice, has also joined us. He's in the cell to the left of ours, and none of us can see him. But we hear his voice all the time. He seems to be a Muslim, and prays often during the five-times-a-day prayer periods. But the prayers are very strange, full of announcements of his good works and charity, and pleas that are more like demands of God that he be released.

That makes seven of us here, among what seem to be eleven cells. There are probably half a dozen or so guards, and both Tom and I suspect there may be more upstairs, in the half-completed building above us.

The guards have spent the last several days installing a new tile floor on top of the sand that was there. Ingeniously, they dug a hole, leveled the sand floor, and dumped the excess in the hole to fill it up. Then they laid heavy tile on a cement base. They also put new tile in the cells, sealing up many of the holes that the bugs lived in. At least the place is a little cleaner now, if not more hospitable.

I nearly had a hassle during the cleanup. They took me out of the cell and told me to do some exercises in the hallway. Then I noticed them beginning to move things out of the cell. I immediately stopped, announced I was tired, walked back into the cell without waiting to be escorted, and sat down on the mattress. They got quite upset and insisted I continue the "sport." I insisted I couldn't. What I was after was the pen in the mattress—I was afraid they'd find it. Finally, with much wiggling, I worked it out of its hole and stuck it in my waistband without their noticing, then agreed to go back into the hall for more "sport." Close.

One thing hasn't improved—our food. Real garbage—

hunks of mutton bones, cold rice, dry cheese sandwiches on Arabic bread, and the like. McCarthy says they give the meat to their dogs, and the bones to us.

The guards' attitude hasn't improved, either. They're still surly and uncommunicative. Some continue to be hostile and threatening. But so far, no violence, though it feels like it's close all the time. The friendly relations we had with a couple, like Mahmoud, have evaporated.

David has made a videotape. The guards turned off the fans, even though there was electricity, and in the dead, underground silence, we could hear him reading a script in the guards' room—a demand for negotiations, some threats, an emotional appeal to the U.S. government. Tom and I speculate on whether that means negotiations are under way, or if it's another effort by our hosts to get them going. Probably the latter, I think, though of course there's no way to know. It's September now, and we've been more than two months with no news at all. Nothing.

I'm alone now. "Trust Me" Ali, as we refer to him, showed up the other day and told me I had to make a videotape. He dictated a bunch of stuff to me in a very arrogant way, all of it propaganda: rationalizations of their actions, attacks on Reagan, vague but ominous threats, couched in harsh language. I thought long and hard about whether or not I would do it. I wasn't really afraid of what they would do if I refused—there isn't much more they can do to me without killing me. There were lots of things in my mind about aiding and comforting the enemy, the old stuff from the Marine Corps about how to behave as a prisoner, and so forth. Certainly, I don't agree with most of the crap he wanted me to say. But in the end, I decided nobody would believe any of it, nobody would really think these were my opinions, and it was likely to be the only way I could reassure Maddy that I'm alive and well. So I did it.

Ali promised me flatly that I would continue to stay with Tom. They took me out of our cell and into the guards' area, where they set up a video camera and I read the script. Then they brought me back to a different cell, six feet by six feet by six feet, facing a wall so I can't see or communicate with anyone. I've been here a couple of weeks now. It's obvious that I won't get the books Ali promised, or anything else. I'm so filled with rage and frustration and loneliness, I can barely think.

I've got to keep my mind disciplined. I've got to hold on. But it's hard. Already I slip frequently into deep depressions, lie for hours on the mattress, just wallowing in misery. This isolation is almost more than I can bear, and I don't know how long it will continue, or even why I was separated from Tom. The guards will not speak to me, except for brief orders. I can occasionally hear Tom's or John's voice, but there's no way to contact them except with notes in the bathroom. We've exchanged a couple, but they are getting very nervous about it, and obviously don't want to continue unless there's something important to say. Of course, there isn't anything to say.

I've been asking for the Bible since I was put in here, and finally they brought it to me. But it's very hard to read it. There's no light in the cell, just a fluorescent lamp in the corridor that flickers on and off. I have to stand next to the door and hold the book up by the window to see anything, and even then can barely make out the words.

The guards sometimes lock up the doors at the end of the corridor and disappear for hours. They've also taken away the bottles we had to pee in, saying it was unhealthy to keep them in the cells. Now we have to ask several times a day to go to the bathroom, and often they won't take us. I suffered a bout of gastroenteritis while they were gone the other day, and started beating on the metal door and shouting. Finally, Mahmoud showed up, yanked open the door, and demanded, "Why you shout?" I just darted out of the cell, brushing him aside and almost ran for the bathroom, peering under the blindfold to keep from stumbling. I barely made it. I don't think I could ever have imagined being this miserable.

* * *

My diary is gone. I tore it up and stuffed it into the cracks that run along one side of the cell, where there's some kind of sewer pipe. I was frightened they would find it. I'd been carrying it rolled up in plastic in my shorts for the past several months. This morning, as I came out of the bathroom, Fadl and another guard stopped me in the corridor and ordered me to take off my clothes. "Why?" I asked.

"We have new clothes for you."

"Okay. Give them to me, and I'll change in the bathroom."

"No. You must do it here, now."

We argued for a bit. Finally, using the only tactic I could think of, I said, "I can't do that. It's *haram*." It's religiously forbidden. The Shiites are extremely body-conscious, even among men, and nakedness is condemned. It didn't work, but Fadl eventually gave me a towel to hold around my waist. Slipping my hand inside my shorts, I tucked the diary up between my legs as far as it would go, and did a kind of "dance of the veils" to keep it there, hold the towel up, and wriggle out of my shorts and underpants. Then I slipped the new ones on awkwardly, dropped the towel, and pulled them up quickly, catching the diary before it fell. It was, in fact, funnier than hell. But when I got back to the cell, I decided quickly that it just wasn't worth it. If they find it, I know I'll get thumped severely. I'm not sure I could handle that now without defending myself and getting in worse trouble, and more trouble than I've got right now I don't need. So I got rid of it. It hurt, but it's undoubtedly the right thing to do. "Cling to nothing," Father Martin used to say. That's how he's lived his life, and that's how I'm going to have to be here.

I'm not here most days.
I stumble wearily through Indochinese jungle,
soaked with sweat and fear, trembling with
adrenalined excitement, peering through thick brush
for unimpressive men with impressive, hating eyes.
I sit slouched in a Bangkok bar, toying idly with

the midnight curls that top Thai beauty,
listening to soft, coaxing, broken English,
she and I both eager to trade her small perfections
for my dollars, fulfilling needs and greeds for both.

I leap exultantly from a Cessna's step,
defying body fear, flinging arms wide,
stilling with my will the frantic urge;
feeling wind rush, watching earth hurl madly at me
till finally I let my fingers fly
and wait one heart-stop for the wrench
and swing and sudden quiet,
my still-incredulous body swinging in the straps.

Sometimes I sit cross-legged
in Enkakuji's ancient calm,
watching, listening,
feeling the carp swarm silently,
jostling, bumping, round mouths flexing
as I tap the feeding call with a pebble
on the flat stone step.

I lie on Levantine sand, pale next to
the near-chocolate of my other self;
no Asian almond eyes, but huge Semitic ones,
dark with love, not kohl; proud Saracen nose
shouting of towers, and Damascus,
red lips, white teeth whispering of
pomegranates, and ivory.

I'm not chained; there's no steel door,
no bitterness, no anger; those are
much less real than these.
There's pain in past and present both,
but there is also joy, and love.

I'm not here most days.

* * *

I decided a few days ago that I would get over my spider phobia. I get along fine with most animals. Snakes don't bother me at all, or mice or even rats. Most bugs don't scare me, but for some reason, I've never been able to stand spiders, and there are a lot of them here. So I stopped killing them, and just sat for days watching them build their webs in every corner and cranny of the cell, until there were more than a dozen of various colors and sizes all around me. I even stood up to look at them from close range, just a couple of inches, studying them, watching them kill flies and mosquitoes. This morning, I crushed them all with my fist, one after another, in a few seconds. I'll have to live with my phobia.

I find myself trembling sometimes for no reason, and occasionally crying silently, just sitting on the mattress. It doesn't seem to happen because of anything in particular I'm thinking about. Often my mind is just a blank, then I become aware that I'm shaking. I can barely speak to the guards. The food revolts me. When they brought lunch today, I refused it. The guard insisted. "You must eat."

"I don't want it. I'm not hungry."

"You must. Take." It was another bowl of revolting, fat chunks of mutton over cold rice. I picked it up and threw it at the wastebasket, or where I thought the wastebasket was. Of course, I had pulled my blindfold down when the guard came to the cell door. The dish hit the wall, and the food splattered on the floor. The guard cursed in Arabic and left. A few minutes later, Sayeed came in. He's not around much anymore; I don't know why. He sat down and said, "Why did you do that?"

"I don't want to eat. I'm not hungry. And it's bad food."

"You must not throw it away." The Shiites, like many groups in the Middle East, consider food sacred. To waste it is a sin.

"They want to beat you," he added. "I have told them they cannot. But you must not throw the food." He left before I could ask him why he won't let them thump on me. He never seemed to consider it very important before.

I'm afraid I'm beginning to lose my mind, to lose control completely. This solitary confinement is killing me. There is nothing to hold on to, no way to anchor my mind. I try praying, every day, sometimes for hours. But there's nothing there, just a blankness. I'm talking to myself, not God. All that iron control, all that anger and frustration I've been bottling up, holding down for so many months, just wells up and drowns me. Then it leaves me empty, aching and tired, and so terribly lonely. I never realized how dependent I was on other people, how much I needed to be around others, to feed off them mentally. Do I have anything of my own inside me? Is there any core there? Is everything I thought I was just based on a reflection of others?

I've searched through my mind for so long, hours and hours of thinking about everything I've done, everyone I know. I've pulled out and looked at all the impulses and urges I could find, especially those I'm ashamed of. There's a bit of everything in there, all the sins on the list in all their shades and permutations. And a few ideals, still. Some morality, tattered and worn, but there. There *are* things I won't do, things I can't accept, things I would die for. Or kill for.

Incredibly, after all these humiliations, after the thorough recognition and acceptance of the bad things I've done and the selfishness and arrogance and even evil I've found in myself, there is also a great, stubborn rock of pride. The greatest sin, or my salvation? Or both?

I wish I could die. I ask God often to finish this, to end it any way that pleases Him. I can't do it myself. I can't spit in Maddy's face, say to her, "You don't matter enough for me to live." But I'm just so tired.

Things sure get weird around here. The guards brought in a birthday cake on my birthday, October 27! A huge, two-layer thing. They took me up to their room, sat me down, and told me they were going to tape me eating the cake.

This after weeks of absolutely horrible food. I sat and watched under the edge of my blindfold as they stuck thirty-nine candles on top of the cake, then tried to light them. Of course, being hamsters, they lit them from the outside in, burning themselves half a dozen times trying to light the last candles on the inner ring. I started giggling, then broke out laughing when half the candles melted from the heat and slumped over before they got done. They pulled them out and tried again, only to have the same thing happen. Finally, they brought out the camera, but the light wouldn't work. Keystone Kops! Anyway, I got a piece of cake and some fruit, asked them to divide up the rest among the other prisoners, and went back to my little cell.

My second birthday in captivity. 592 days. I hope Maddy sees the tape.

I've seen Sulome! Two days after my birthday, the guards brought in a small black-and-white television, put it in my cell, and showed me a tape of my daughter. She was so beautiful that it was painful to watch. Maddy spoke over the tape, a birthday message full of such love, and such sadness. Then Sulome came on, playing around outside a house, then holding my picture and looking at it, saying "I love you, I love you, and I love you." A magnificent birthday present. I could barely see it the first time because of my tears. I asked them to play it again, and they did. Then I was allowed to write a short note they said would be sent to my family. I don't know if any of these letters—they've allowed us to write three or four over the past year and a half—have gotten through.

Each time I see something like this, or hear from the guards that Peg has been in the newspaper, or my colleagues have held a public meeting to ask for my release, and especially when I get some word about Maddy and Sulome, it's a blend of great joy and great pain. It shatters the little world I live in, in which I try to build a routine, try to channel my thoughts, try to keep my emotions on an even keel, and sends me careening between euphoria and love and enormous depression and regret. I would not give up these messages from the outside for anything, and yet sometimes they hurt too much. But at least the pain makes me know I'm alive.

My prayers are terribly mixed up now. God must be confused. Sometimes I'm so grateful for what I've had—an exciting life, so many wonderful people—family, friends, colleagues, even finally a great, passionate love that was and is returned with equal intensity. Then I feel, okay, if it ends now, I've had my share and more. I've returned little for all that, and I have many, many things to regret. Mostly the hurt I've given others who did not deserve it. I can't ask Him for more, having used so poorly what He's given me.

I'm beyond the promises and pleas now—"Just get me out of here, I'll be good, I'll do this, or that." They don't mean anything. It's acceptance I'm working on now. This is just the way it is. I can't change it, just as I can't change the things I've done in the past. When the frustration and rage boil up again, I have to just go through it, ride it out. Pushing it away doesn't do any good. I can't bottle it up anymore. That doesn't work. God knows I have reason to be angry and frustrated if anyone does. I can't predict when the pain of being away from Maddy and my daughters and my family will well up, overwhelm me. Or my feelings of guilt and shame.

There is almost a relief in knowing that I can't do anything about these things, in finally accepting that nothing will be changed by any of this—guilt or shame or rage or frustration. It's a surrender, of responsibility, of the need to push myself more and more, to try to be something I'm not and never can be. I find it easier to say to God, "Whatever you want will inevitably be. I have no choice but to accept, do the best I can with these circumstances, with what I am." That's where some peace lies. It's not easy, and doesn't always work. Often I just want to scream, to make it end. But I can't.

My mind feels tired with the effort of making itself work, of finding things to think about that aren't painful.

Often now, it just goes into neutral, and I sit or lie for hours thinking of nothing. Then I rouse myself, pace back and forth, two steps each way, for hours, until my body is tired enough to allow me to doze off. It's easier to think of things when I'm pacing. The farm project Tom and I worked out for weeks—a dairy farm, staffed by juvenile delinquents, or "youths at risk," or whatever the politically correct label is these days. Schedules, equipment, budgets, and on and on. Building a house board by board, first the design, then the construction. Plans for stories, books. All neutral things. Anything to stave off those times of depression for as long as possible. Sometimes it works for two or three days before the roller coaster takes off again.

The guards are mostly leaving me alone these days. Not much harassment. Just the daily trip to the bathroom, food deliveries three times a day, and that's it. Be grateful for small favors, I guess.

Frank Reed, the guy we've heard praying all the time, is even worse than I thought. He seems to have gone completely off the wall. Sayeed came in the other day and asked out of the blue if I wanted to meet another hostage. Of course, I said yes. He told me Frank's name, and said he was sick and they wanted me to talk to him. Sayeed and a couple of other guards took me out of my cell and across the way to Frank's. I sat down and peeked under my blindfold. I could see Frank backed into a corner and all hunched up. Sayeed stood just behind me in the doorway. "Hi. I'm Terry Anderson," I said first. He didn't reply. I just kept talking, and reached over to shake his hand. He didn't offer it, and I had to grope around to find it. "I'm a hostage also," I said. "They have said we can talk." He still wouldn't speak.

"I think it would be better if you left," I told Sayeed. "I don't think he wants to talk with you here." He went out and closed the door, but I'm sure he stayed just outside, beside the door. I lifted my blindfold. "You can raise your blindfold," I said to Frank. "They're gone."

He still did not move. "It's okay. They're gone. You can look at me," I said.

Finally, blindfold still well down over his eyes, he muttered, "I don't want to talk."

"Do you want me to leave?"

"Yes."

I knocked on the door, and Sayeed came to take me back to my cell. "He's very sick," I told him. "I don't know what you've done to him, but he's not well. He wouldn't talk to me."

That was it. I can't imagine a hostage in these circumstances refusing to talk to another American. He's almost catatonic. Must have had a very bad time. God help him.

I'm back in contact with the others. I've been moved to another cell down the line—no reason given. They just came in, said, "Stand up," and moved my mattress and bottles, then came back and took me two cells down. There are five cells on this side of the basement, then another five facing them on the other side, though I can't see the two on the end because of the angle and a partial wall in the center of the room. I can see John and Brian across the way, and they can see Tom, who is just next door to me in another cell. While we can't see each other, he can also see John and Brian across the way. We've been talking again with the hand language, with the two of them taking turns relaying messages between Tom and me.

John says Tom is in pretty bad shape, very depressed and talking about suicide again. They're worried about him. He and Brian seem okay, still sounding fairly cheerful.

I told them about my brief contact with Frank. They also think he's gone nuts. No word on Jacobsen. Nobody can see his cell, which is around the wall that blocks off half the cells. Sontag's still there. John says they can see him occasionally and wave to him, but haven't been able to teach him the sign language. He just doesn't understand what they're trying to do. Otherwise, I don't seem to have missed much in my isolation.

It's an incredible relief to be able to talk to someone

again. The last few days alone were hard. I was trembling a lot for no reason. If everyone's got a weakness, I guess I've discovered mine. It's a shock to find how much solitary affects me. Dear Lord, keep me sane.

David has gone home, I think. That's what one of the guards said to me, though of course there's no way to know if he's lying. But there was a lot of bustling around the other night. I asked to go to the bathroom, but at first they wouldn't take me. I insisted, and they gave in. As I was being escorted through the guards' room to the bathroom, I peeked under the blindfold and saw David sitting on the floor against the wall, fully dressed. We've now counted the number of people going to the bathroom by listening to the cell doors being unlocked and relocked—we don't dare peek out the windows while the guards are in the cell area. David seems to be gone. Sontag is also missing, though none of us noticed him being taken out.

Good luck for both of them, but why David? They had seemed to be going in order of kidnapping—Ben Weir, then Father Martin. I should have been next. Dear God, if they skipped me this time, does that mean they'll keep me to the last? That would mean months more before Tom, then maybe John and Brian. I asked the guards, but got no information, except "Things are good, and very good. The negotiate is good." It's November, I think—just about a week since my birthday. Nearly two years now. Three or four releases in two years. Not a rapid schedule. But maybe things have broken, maybe they have come to an agreement. Maybe we'll all get out of here soon. Please, God.

20

Jacobsen was pushed out of the car on the Corniche Manara, in front of the Riviera Hotel, just one hundred yards down the Mediterranean seafront from Anderson's old apartment. The area was a Druse neighborhood, and militiamen from the main Druse force, the Progressive Socialist Party, quickly took him in hand. The PSP had always had close ties to the American embassy in Beirut, providing most of the ambassador's bodyguard. With a couple of phone calls, a motorcade was organized to whisk Jacobsen across the Green Line to the embassy, in the eastern hills overlooking the city.

Jacobsen's release was the perfect example of the flat, unadorned purchase of an American hostage by the American government. It was exactly what everyone involved, including North, McFarlane, Poindexter, Shultz, Weinberger, Bush, and even Reagan—everyone except Central Intelligence Director William Casey and the Israelis—had indicated was unthinkable. The price: a mere five hundred TOW antitank missiles, FOB Tehran.

The details of the deal were worked out in two meetings in Frankfurt, Germany, between North and a nephew of Iranian President Rafsanjani, Ali Bahramani. The Americans had grown tired of Ghorbanifar's lies and, more serious, his failure to deliver. The Iranians were also sick of him. One referred to the arms dealer, in the presence of North, as a "crook."

225

With the help of a few go-betweens and considerable delicacy, North had succeeded in bypassing Ghorbanifar and setting up what he referred to as the more direct "second channel"—to Bahramani.

The weeks-long process had nearly broken down when Islamic Jihad snatched two more Americans off the streets of Beirut—Frank Reed, the head of a private international high school, and Joe Cicippio, comptroller of the American University. There was no way the Americans were going to accept an unending process—pay for one hostage, see another kidnapped. They said so, loudly, to their new contact.

But Bahramani vehemently denied that the Lebanese radicals had broken the understanding reached through the earlier deals. They didn't have Reed or Cicippio, and didn't know who had taken them, he insisted. North, through naïveté or reluctance to see his carefully built initiative go up in smoke, accepted the assurances.

They were, as you might expect, total lies. Reed and Cicippio were already in the hands of the same people holding Anderson and the others.

In their eagerness to develop this new contact, North and several other U.S. officials had already agreed not only to the official market price—five hundred TOWs for each hostage. They had thrown in considerable U.S. intelligence information about alleged Soviet designs on Iran and the Gulf, as well as intimating other military equipment might be forthcoming, if the Iranians could pay for it.

That, it seems, was important. Though the congressional ban on funding the Nicaraguan Contras was expiring, and North no longer needed the secrecy of transferring excess Iranian payments to that project, the idea of more free, unbudgeted, uncontrolled money for that particular cause was a powerful incentive to keep things moving.

With a couple of minor hitches and delays, the whole thing went smoothly. The TOWs were loaded on pallets in the States and shipped to Israel on October 27, after Iran made a four-million-dollar payment into a secret account.

On the next day, they were moved on by the Israelis to Iran.

Six days later, Jacobsen was unceremoniously dumped from a car in front of the Riviera.

Among the party greeting the dazed, confused ex-hostage was Lt. Col. Oliver North. The first two debriefings had gone disastrously for the government. Weir had refused to cooperate at all, showing considerable hostility to the officials of various intelligence agencies who were pressing him for immediate information. Jenco had been somewhat more cooperative, but still extremely wary of giving any information that would lead to a rescue attempt. Both men feared greatly any such action. The hostages had discussed the possibility many times, and nearly all agreed that given their jailers' alertness and willingness to die, any attempt at rescue would quite likely result in many deaths, including the deaths of some of the hostages.

The fear was a valid one. The American government had a fully prepared, trained, and eager rescue team from the Special Operations Command—popularly known as Delta Force—loaded on helicopters and standing by in the eastern Mediterranean when Weir came out, hoping that he would give them some clue that would lead them to the location of the remaining hostages. The same team was waiting again when Jenco came out, and had gone on full alert a third time for Jacobsen.* All they needed was the right information. They hadn't gotten it from either Weir or Jenco.

"Part of the advice from the guys at the State Department task force had been that they're not getting handled right from the start," North said later. "Here's our chance. We'd blown the first two. Let's get cooperation this time."

---

* In February 1993, after a speech I gave in New Orleans, a heavily muscled man perhaps thirty years old approached me backstage. He was in obvious emotional distress, and after his first few words, was openly crying.

"I was with Delta Force. For six years, we trained for your rescue. It was all we focused on. We never got a chance to do it. I can't tell you what it means to see you here."

He listened to my stammered thanks, then walked quietly away.

Cooperation they got. "David was totally exhausted. Emotionally drained. He talked nonstop all the way back. Right from the start, he wanted to talk, wanted to help. Wanted his captors brought to justice," North recalled. It was a great relief.

"Here's a guy who's going to give us everything. [But] ... he didn't have enough." David simply didn't know where in Lebanon or Beirut they had been held prisoner. "And ... within days, they were preparing pamphlets in Tehran."

The pamphlets being distributed in Tehran's bazaar detailed the arms-for-hostages negotiations, including McFarlane's trip to Tehran. They were a major shock to the Iranians—their revolutionary government had been dealing with both the Little Satan (Israel) and the Great Satan (America). The revelations were an even bigger shock in the West—to the American people, who had heard Ronald Reagan trumpet "No deals with terrorists" so many times; and to America's allies, who had been subject to frequent and loud lectures about the evil of selling arms to Iran.

By the day after Jacobsen's release, the pamphlets had been published in Beirut by a pro-Syrian magazine, *Al-Shiraa*. Western agencies, including The AP, picked up the story.*

* The pamphlets, and the subsequent news stories, were the result of the power struggle going on in Iran between Ayatollah Montazeri and the speaker of Parliament, Hashemi Rafsanjani. In late 1986, Rafsanjani had the son-in-law of his rival, Montazeri, arrested. The man, Mahdi Hashimi, was accused of having been an agent of the shah's secret police, Savak. The charges included murder, smuggling, and conspiracy against the Islami State. All carried the death sentence. Hashimi was quickly executed.

Within days, Montazeri had the pamphlets distributed in the bazaar in Tehran, revealing that Rafsanjani had been buying weapons from the United States, and his followers had met with McFarlane and North, among others.

Rafsanjani survived the attack, later becoming president. He took his own revenge by leaking to France and Germany, among other countries, the names of all the agents working in the terror network Montazeri had labored for years to build throughout Western Europe. The networks were quickly rolled up and destroyed, although the French allowed the head terrorist in

That shaky, terribly complicated structure North and the others had erected came crashing down. There would be no more American hostages released for nearly four years.

their country, Wahid Ghrodji, to return to Iran for fear of an attack on their diplomats at the French embassy in Tehran.

21

MADELEINE

**LARNACA, CYPRUS.
NOVEMBER 1986.**

*Even after Jacobsen's release, we held on to the hope that
Terry would also be coming out. The rumors had said for
two weeks that two Americans would be released.*

*The tension had begun to build again on October 3,
when a videotape of Terry and David was released by Islamic Jihad. Terry looked fine. I didn't know how to feel. It
was strange to see him on tape, so close and so far. He
looked strong, with his will unbroken. His gaze was
straight, and he was wearing glasses. That made me happy,
because I knew he couldn't see beyond his nose without
them.*

*After the videotape, the rumors multiplied. From the
earlier releases, it seemed the ones held longest would be
next out, meaning Terry and Jacobsen. Journalists flew in
to Cyprus to cover the event, including our friend Bill
Foley, working for* Newsweek.

*The AP called to advise me to get ready. For three days
I packed, unpacked, and packed again, trying to make sure
I missed nothing. I was very nervous and scared. After
eighteen months of captivity, how would Terry be? How
would we feel, being together again? It was a torment to
wait for days with no real assurance he was coming out. I
struggled to believe, and to pretend not to believe so I
wouldn't be disappointed. Trying to protect myself from my
own feelings, to stay in control. Does he know he is to be*

freed? I hoped not, so he would avoid the pain of disappointment.

I waited in the house in Larnaca, tickets for Germany in hand. We would take the first plane after we heard he was out. I didn't want to go to Syria, where he would go first. The Syrians' role in all this was hardly an innocent one. I always believed that Syria and Iran had started the hostage taking. The Syrian military was in control of most of eastern and northern Lebanon, and by now, most of Beirut. Nothing could be done there without their knowledge, if not participation. But the growing power of the Shia, which led to clashes between them and the Syrians, had lessened Syrian influence in the Shiite-populated southern suburbs. That meant that the Syrians could not gain the release of the hostages. But they still had enough power to easily block it if they chose.

Then David came out. Everyone was excited, hoping Terry would be next, soon. The atmosphere was overwhelming; I felt I could fly without wings. My mother kept crying from happiness, and even Sulome knew something was happening. She clung to me, and I had to take her everywhere I went.

I stayed in the office till late. My mind was racing with hope and disappointment. I bit my lips till they bled. I worried that Terry was also waiting. I wondered if he knew, and what it was doing to him.

The next day I went back to Larnaca, still waiting for something to happen. There, I heard about the report in Al-Shiraa about the arms-for-hostages dealings.

Shortly after I arrived in Larnaca I had met with a well-connected person who knew a lot about the hostages, including, it sometimes seemed, their whereabouts. I didn't know his connection with the kidnappers, but the information he passed on to me from time to time proved accurate and was encouraging. He had information about Terry's health and the conditions in which he was being kept.

This source proved to be a kind friend who felt my need to know about Terry and who thought it was important.

I had learned through him about the arms-for-hostages deal while it was going on and that Reverend Weir's release was the result of those dealings.

When I first heard of the deal I didn't know what to think or do. If it was true, Terry should be coming home soon. I certainly could never find out for sure, until a few months later when it was disclosed by Al-Shiraa.

When the name Imad Mugniyeh was first mentioned in a newspaper report as being involved in the kidnapping of Westerners many months after I had heard the name from my friend and source, I was shocked about how much I knew and how little I could do. Mugniyeh wanted his brother-in-law freed from jail in Kuwait, where he had been convicted for his connection in the bombing of U.S. and French installations in Kuwait. My source knew all this and more. It was very difficult to keep my promise never to reveal to anybody what I knew. Yet it was a promise I had to keep. I could not tell a soul of it, but was very grateful to have had the chance to know anything about Terry that would rest my mind and give me something to tell my daughter when the right time came.

If there had been a chance for Terry's release, the report in Al-Shiraa killed it. Even if the captors knew of such a deal, though I doubted it as a Lebanese, they would never want it known that they were not really in control of the hostages, that Iran was the boss. Their demand for the release of their friends in Kuwaiti jails would be jeopardized by this. They wouldn't have a way to save face anymore.

I fell into another deep depression. I felt as though I had been battling with a very strong power for days, and I was exhausted. I felt like a failure for not being able to prepare myself emotionally. I knew I could not afford to give in to depression again. My responsibility to my daughter was weighing heavily on me. I wanted to run away from my thoughts of Terry. Once again, I blamed him for everything. For not giving us a chance to live as a family. For being stupid. I would cry alone and angrily call him names. But nothing eased the deep pain of my loneliness.

TEN

GROWING THINGS

I dream of growing things,
not in meticulously ordered gardens,
but in abandoned wild profusion.
I think of cutting fallen trees
for firewood with an axe;
cleaning a small, leaf-choked
stream, and watching water
running clear and free again.

I think of all the small, wild creatures
I hunted as a boy and shake my head.
Too many wars, mine and others,
have left me unable to see
any gun without recalling
men's, women's, children's faces,
and the sweetly horrifying
smell of bodies in the sun.

I long for life so fiercely,
and I wake to chains.

22

Things have gotten very bad. Frank managed to get out of his cell and wander up and down the hall for a while, talking to everyone. I was asleep, but later John told me what happened.

John said Frank noticed that the guard had forgotten to lock his cell door, reached through the bars on the window, and unlatched the door. But he couldn't get through the steel doors at the end of the hall, and eventually went back in and shut his cell door. The guards must have been watching. Nothing happened immediately, but after a couple of hours, a chief showed up and they dragged Frank out of his cell and into the guards' room, where they beat him badly. That's when I woke up. I heard the shouting. "You want to escape?" someone asked him loudly. Then I heard a heavy blow, as if he'd been hit in the chest with a stick, followed by the sound of a body falling to the floor. The beating seemed to go on for hours, but probably lasted thirty or forty minutes.

Eventually, they took him back to a small, half-size cell on the end of the row and left him. A few minutes later, he started shouting. "I want my clothes. I'm going home. Bring me my clothes!"

Two of the guards rushed in and beat him some more. He was yelling, "Sayeed. Help me! Help me!" He must be under the delusion that Sayeed is his friend. Finally, it stopped.

It is impossible to describe how it feels to hear someone being beaten like that. To hear the ugly, dull thumps and slaps and the shouting, and be able to do nothing. I felt physically ill, and so utterly helpless.

Now Tom's gotten it. He got caught looking out his cell window. They took him into the guards' room and beat him for what seemed like half an hour. Then they brought him back, put him in his cell, and closed the steel flap that covers the small window in the door. One of the guards, Michel, apparently was away from the prison during the first beating. He returned a short time later, decided he wanted his share of the fun, and opened up Tom's cell door to begin beating him again, until another guard stopped him. Tom is completely in the dark now, and we have no contact.

The guards have gotten really ugly. After those months in the previous prison, where our relations gradually become mostly correct, if not friendly, they seem to enjoy this atmosphere of anger and hatred. The physical surroundings, dark, wet, and dirty, seem to contribute. The guards are ready to use the smallest excuse to start the beatings again. One or two have taken to standing in the door for several minutes after they bring the food, then cursing in Arabic before they leave. So far, though, they haven't touched me, I guess because of Sayeed's order while I was in the other cell. I don't know if I'm grateful or not. I don't want to be beaten, but to be exempt while others are is not a good thing.

Brian's joined the list of victims. They decided to give us all haircuts, as they have from time to time—very short, almost a skinhead. I don't care—I'm not going anywhere—but Brian objected to getting his beard cut. He's had it since he was sixteen. They beat him up, then shaved it off. This is getting out of hand. If it goes on, someone is going to get seriously hurt. At least Tom's out of *purdah*. They opened the flap covering his window again after more than a week, and we can talk. He's really shaken, but seems to be recovering.

Tom got it again. We were all shifted around for a few days, and I ended up in a cell next to him. One of the guards, whom we call "the Ghost" because he likes to sneak around under the cell windows to spy on us, claimed Tom and I were talking. It was pure bullshit, and we denied it vehemently, but I couldn't explain that we don't talk, we use hand signals to relay messages via John and Brian across the way. Fadl slapped Tom around a bit and questioned him, then came into my cell and questioned me. But again, he didn't touch me. I told them the Ghost was lying. They moved me back into another cell on the other side, but luckily I can still see Tom's cell and he can relay messages to John and Brian. The Ghost came in and asked me in French why I said he was lying. His French is very good, mine still poor. But I said, *"Je ne veux pas parler avec vous. Je ne comprend pas pourquoi vous direz ça. Nous n'avons pas parlé. Je ne veux pas parler avec vous."* I don't want to talk to you. I don't understand why you say that. We did not talk. I don't want to talk to you.

I refused to speak anymore, and he left. I don't know if the chiefs believe him or me, but I think it's fairly certain they'll take his word, unless they know he's a liar.

A grim Christmas Day. They asked if I wanted to send a Christmas message to my family, and gave me a pen and one piece of paper. I just couldn't think of anything to say. Finally, I wrote a two-line note: "I miss you all very much. I'm still well, but very tired." They took the pen away again with the note.

Then, I tried to write a note to pass to John and Brian and Tom, using the pen I've been so carefully hiding all this time, and it ran out of ink.

Finally, as I was talking with the hand signals to Tom, I took off my glasses briefly. They slipped out of my hand and fell, and the lenses got smashed. Now I can't read

Tom's hand signals. I'm sure the glasses will get fixed eventually, but it's likely to be a while. Not much to celebrate this year, except I'm still alive and healthy.

23

MADELEINE

SUNDERLAND, ENGLAND.
JANUARY 1987.

*I couldn't take the loneliness in Cyprus after my mother
had to return to Lebanon. I couldn't go with her because
Sulome had an American passport, so in mid-December, we
came to England to spend Christmas with my sister and her
family.*

*Just before Terry Waite left again for Lebanon in Janu-
ary, I talked to him on the phone. He said he would continue his efforts, but he knew his mission was more difficult
now because of the disclosure of the arms-for-hostages
deal. The reports that he had been meeting with Oliver
North were sure to make the kidnappers believe he was
working for North, or the CIA. These people are so suspicious that even an innocent contact with a government official will make them believe you are a spy. Everyone was
surprised that Waite had decided to try again to meet with
the kidnappers in Lebanon. About this time, they issued
another picture of Terry, with the usual threats against
Americans for various reasons.*

*I was sitting in the kitchen listening to the radio on Jan-
uary 20, when the announcer said that Terry Waite had not
returned from a scheduled meeting with the kidnappers the
day before. I called AP London, but the bureau chief there,
Myron Belkind, said no one knew if Waite was still negotiating or had been kidnapped. He also told me Waite had
been advised not to go back to Lebanon.*

When Waite still didn't show up two days later, it was clear he had been kidnapped. I was told by one source that Islamic Jihad had warned him not to come back unless he had something to offer. Waite didn't. He could not produce the seventeen men in Kuwait, and had been refused a visa to Iran. Some rumors had even linked him to American intelligence because of his meetings with North.

The only person I thought could still bring Terry home was a captive himself now. They must have been really angry to make such a move. I was more worried about Terry because when all efforts failed, his captors might try to prove that they were still in control. I didn't believe they would kill him, but they could make his life hell.

For days, I was on the phone with my friends Scheherazade Faramarzi and Robert Fisk, the London Times *correspondent in Beirut and Terry's close friend. It was a devastating time. Nobody knew anything. One thing was clear—it was the end of this effort to bring Terry home. Another disappointment and another depression.*

You think you get harder in time, that you won't let anything touch you or affect you. I was still very fragile, and Waite's kidnapping was like a slap to my face by fate. I kept wondering if God had planned all this from the beginning, from when I met Terry the very first time at that party. I was always going back to how I had met him. How ready we were for all this. Terry was in the best of shape physically and emotionally. He had started looking back to his Catholic religion, searching for meaning after having left the church as a teenager. I had always felt the presence of God, but had never been as happy as I was with Terry, when I was pregnant with my first child, and feeling extraordinarily well. Why did it all have to be destroyed? WHY?

I would sink so deep in depression that it almost annihilated my spirit. After each hope and each disappointment, life had so little to offer.

WASHINGTON–LONDON–NEW YORK.
JANUARY–FEBRUARY 1987.

Waite's last trip to Beirut was roundly criticized by everyone with any knowledge of what was going on. The stink over Iran-Contra/arms-for-hostages was so strong in the American capital, it could almost be seen trailing after the various top-level officials as they marched in and out of congressional hearings and the offices of various investigators. As usual when scandal hits, each official told a different story, accusing the others of lying. In this one, even President Reagan had to come up with several versions when his own cabinet members pointed out to him that he was lying to the public.

Waite had clearly been used as a front man by North, set up to take credit for the releases and detract attention from the secret dealings between Washington and Tehran. The fact was pointed out in both English and American newspapers. The mere linking of his name with North's was dangerous. The Church of England envoy had been told flatly by his Islamic Jihad contacts during his last trip to get out of town and not to come back without something to offer. He had been able to get nothing from anyone. The Americans no longer waited to talk to anyone about possible deals. The Iranians and Kuwaitis both refused him visas.

Waite knew it was dangerous, and gave clear instructions to his family and others on what to do if he was kidnapped: Make no deals on his behalf. He mentioned his fear of being taken to at least two reporters who had become friends. But he was determined. His reputation had been stained. And he had not accomplished what he had set out to do more than a year before—get all the hostages out. He would try again.

In hindsight, Waite would admit to being reckless. Not for making another attempt, but because he had dismissed the guards he had been provided with by the Druse. He had to argue with them to get them to allow him to go to the meeting with the kidnappers' representative alone. But they eventually gave in to his stubbornness.

As day stretched into day with no word from Waite, rumors flew madly. He was in serious negotiations in the Bekaa Valley. He had been taken. He was close to success.*

---

* One man already knew for certain Waite had been kidnapped. Ray Barnett, a Canadian who was head of a humanitarian organization called Friends in the West, was in West Beirut at the same time as Waite, and even followed him in meetings with Sheikh Mohammed Hussein Fadlallah, the "spiritual adviser" of Hezbollah. But Barnett's meetings were much more discreet, as was his style.

Barnett had been involved for some time in efforts to do something for the hostages. His organization had provided food and other aid for more than twenty-four thousand Shiite families in southern Lebanon during the 1982 Israeli invasion. Using contacts developed then, he had traveled in and out of Beirut at his own expense during the most dangerous times in the past months to try to gain some information. He had gotten very close to the kidnappers and had certainly gained valuable information, but was unable to get officials in the U.S. government to pay attention.

In this latest visit, he was simply paying a courtesy call on Fadlallah to inform him of a prayer campaign he was attempting to start in the United States, and ask the Shiite leader if he would receive a petition from families and friends of the hostages requesting Fadlallah to aid in gaining their release. He had been met at the airport by Hezbollah representatives, who took his passport to be stamped, then drove him off in a black limousine. During the visit, his most reliable and informed contacts told him Waite would be kidnapped because Hezbollah believed him to be a spy. "Mr. Ray, Terry Waite will not be going home," one said. They knew, since they were involved in the arms-for-hostages deal, that Waite's statement claiming he was involved in Father Jenco's release five months before was not true. They knew he had nothing to offer, and had warned the Anglican church envoy not to come back.

Barnett flew out of Beirut on the same Middle East Airlines plane Waite had been due to take. The only seat empty was the one next to him, in the first-class section. It had been reserved by Waite.

Barnett attempted to tell Lambeth Palace, seat of the archbishop of Canterbury, of the information he had been given. He was dismissed with the brief explanation "Mr. Waite is in secret negotiations with the kidnappers."

Barnett, with the approval of the board of directors of Friends in the West, would continue his efforts for the next five years, making repeated trips into West Beirut, to Damascus and Geneva, and elsewhere. He never succeeded in gaining the release of hostages, but developed contacts with the radical Shiite fundamentalists that provided valuable and welcome information on the hostages' welfare to their families.

In Washington, sources Peg Say believed to be reliable told her that a deal had been cut, and Waite would bring Terry Anderson home. She went into hiding at a hotel to avoid being asked to comment by the media.

On January 17, a West German businessman was kidnapped in Beirut. Three days later, another West German was taken.

On January 24, four American professors at Beirut University College disappeared in a well-organized, coordinated abduction operation.†

A third German and a Saudi were snatched off the streets in Beirut. The U.S. Department of State banned all travel to Lebanon, and ordered the 1,500 American citizens in the country to leave immediately.

BEIRUT. JANUARY 25, 1987.

Sayeed has brought me new clothes! Shirt, pants, shoes, socks. He dumped them on the mattress, told me to get dressed, and left. As soon as the door closed, I knelt and began praying. "Dear Lord. Thank you. Let it be true this time, please, God. Don't let it be another hoax, another of their terrible jokes. This is the third time they've brought

---

† The kidnapping of the Beirut University College professors was another carefully planned operation by Imad Mugniyeh and an associate, Abdel Hadi. They bribed police and other guards at the university, then sent four men in police uniforms in a Nissan Patrol jeep, the vehicle preferred by many security units, to the campus late on Saturday afternoon. They explained to university officials that they had been sent to protect the Americans. Once they were taken to the professors, they pulled guns, bundled them into their vehicle, and drove away.

Professor Alan Steen fared especially badly at the hands of his kidnappers. He had for some reason been labeled a spy by Ali's Center. He was beaten severely, including repeated kicks to the head that left him with permanent brain injuries and periodic convulsions. Eventually, a Hezbollah doctor was called in to prescribe medicine to keep him alive.

me clothes, the third time I've really believed I'm close to going home. Please, God."

They've taken us to a new place—an ordinary apartment somewhere just south of the Corniche Mazraa, on the edge of the southern suburbs of Beirut. First I was taken out of my cell, blindfolded as always when the guards were around, and my arms were loosely taped to my sides. With one guard pushing and one pulling from the top, I was hoisted up a ladder to the ground floor, then pushed into a small van. It was freezing cold—it's January, and it was after midnight. Then Tom was pushed into the van with me, and then a third man. He was seated between Tom and me, the three of us jammed tight together. The new man's shoulder and arm, pressing against me, felt thin, almost birdlike. He was much smaller than me—maybe Brian's size, but much thinner. We were all trembling from the cold, and the man next to me nudged me several times and tried to whisper something to me. But a guard standing just outside the open van door caught him. He hit him several times, then yanked him out of the vehicle and hustled him back into the building. We never encountered him again, and never learned who he was.

Finally, Frank Reed was brought out and put into the van with Tom and me. A couple of guards got into the back with us, giving us the usual warnings ("Don't speak. No noise. We are ready."), and we drove for about ten or fifteen minutes.

When we arrived at this building, we were hustled into an elevator and up to about the fifth or sixth floor. We're lying on mattresses in a back bedroom. New apartment, carpet on the living room floor. There don't seem to be any steel sheets covering the windows, and the door is just an ordinary bedroom door, no special lock. From the sounds, it seems there is a couple living here with one or two small, often crying children.

The guards stay in the room with us, and we're not allowed to sit up or speak above a whisper. Is this a staging point, while they complete the arrangements for releasing us? What's going on? They can't keep us like this for very long. A few days? A few hours? The guards say nothing.

We've been here two weeks now. Still blindfolded constantly, still required to lie on the mattress all the time—no standing, no exercise. And, of course, no information.

The three of us are lying side by side along one wall. I'm next to the door, then Tom a few inches away, then Frank on his other side. The guards are always in the room, even sleeping here at night, on mattresses against the opposite wall but only a foot or two away from our feet. It's a horrible strain being with them all the time. They're bored, and watch us. It's like being onstage twenty-four hours a day, in front of a dangerous audience you can't see.

When the guards were momentarily out of the room and left the door open, we lifted our blindfolds slightly and saw another bedroom across the hall, with the door also open. Lying on another pair of mattresses against the wall were John and Brian. We ventured a cautious wave, but didn't dare speak or look at them directly.

Tom and I can talk in whispers. Frank is close enough to do the same, but doesn't say anything. He's constantly being harassed by the guards because he doesn't seem to understand the rules, or what he has to do. For instance, we're allowed to lift our blindfolds slightly to sit up and eat (better food, by the way—almost the same as the guards are eating, or so they say). But he seems to be afraid to lift his blindfold enough to see, and spills his food all the time. That makes the guards upset.

I've persuaded Tom to begin giving me college courses from his specialties—agriculture, animal breeding, statistics. We just go through the course outline, lecture by lecture, hours at a whack. It passes the time, and is actually interesting. He's got an incredibly well stocked mind. Frank takes no part.

* * *

The guards have brought a radio into the room for themselves. It's always tuned to Arabic stations, and we're not supposed to be given any information. But we can hear our names all the times on the news—and Terry Waite's. Mahmoud occasionally translates a bit here and there. He says Waite is here to try to negotiate our release—Tom's and mine. No mention of Frank, but since he's with us, it seems he's to go also. But it's taking a very long time.

The emotional roller coaster takes another plunge. After all that expectation, it seems everything's off. First, there was a burst of Arabic on the radio about Terry Waite. I asked Mahmoud what it was about, and he said, "We kidnapped him." That's impossible to believe—who would kidnap a negotiator? But Mahmoud insists it's true. Something has gone terribly wrong. Two new guards showed up with large steel sheets and riveted them to the windows. Then they put a steel plate on the door. The guards don't stay in the room now, and we're allowed to lift our blindfolds and move around, but it's no joy. They're obviously fixing the place up for a long stay. Dear God, what happened? What is going on? What are you trying to do to us? I can't take this incredible depression, this horrible black feeling. Help me.

24

MADELEINE

LARNACA, CYPRUS. MARCH 1987.

*The second anniversary of Terry's kidnapping went by with
no news. In the States, Terry's family was holding prayer
services and meeting with officials. The AP kept me informed of all the efforts on his behalf. Sometimes I thought
they were exaggerating, and that they were not doing Terry
any good. The captors and the country backing them, Iran,
were hearing of the criticism the captives' families were
making of their own government, their own president. They
didn't need a public relations man. They just had to keep
the captives longer to keep the criticism going.*

*The longer Terry was held, the more determined I be-
came not to give the kidnappers any satisfaction by showing them how desperate we were. I continued to refuse to
speak to the press. But on every one of Terry's and Sulome's
birthdays, I would make a videotape and send it to Beirut
television stations, hoping he would see it, would see how
Sulome was growing up.*

*I heard so little about the wives of the other hostages,
and always wondered how they were managing. In a way,
I envied those who had stayed in Lebanon and not uprooted
themselves as I had. They still had their homes that they
had shared with their husbands, and their families and
friends around them. They weren't flying from one place to
another, with a child and nothing to belong to.*

*I felt very lonely, living in furnished apartments where
nothing was familiar, where there were no memories. I*

hated being a stranger in what was supposed to be my home. From the day Terry got kidnapped, I had lost my security and stability. I had never before been unsure of my ability to take whatever life offered.

Here I have the most precious gift God had ever given me, a daughter, and the wonderful man who fathered her, and yet I can't enjoy them. I was raising Sulome as a duty, not a pleasure. I was waking up in the morning because I had not died at night. I could not bear the fact that nothing I could do would affect the situation. I felt trapped. Everything around me was beautiful, and within hand's reach, but I was not allowed to touch. I could not touch.

Sometimes I would close my eyes and escape to old memories, long before Terry, because that's where I would find security. Going back in time to when life was gentle and peaceful.

God was billions of miles away. I could not bring myself to accept His presence. He deserted us when those men took Terry, and I was not going to let Him in my heart again, as I had grown up doing, when God was my security. As a child and an adult, every time I was in distress or had a problem, I called on God for help. Even if my problem wasn't solved, I knew my prayers were heard and answered. But today, God had no place in my life. It was frightening that I hated thinking about Him. I feared Him today more than ever because of what had happened. And I blamed Him for everything. That made me feel more lonely than anything else.

At the end of March 1987, I returned from England to Cyprus and found an apartment. Sulome turned two years old on June 7, a day I shall never forget. During the taping of the video for Terry, Sulome got irritated with the way I was pushing her to say something that I thought would please Terry. I kept insisting, while all she wanted to do was play with the birthday cake. The more I asked her, the more difficult she got, and the more angry and sad I became. Nothing I did was right.

After the taping, I was left alone with her. She continued to act up, and I didn't know what to do. I sat there looking around me for what seemed to be forever. Alone in a sixth-floor flat I hated. No drapes or shades. Dark outside. I felt desperate. I couldn't handle this anymore. The balcony was there. I could end it if I wanted to.

The thought of jumping lasted only a few moments. I knew I needed somebody to come between me and my daughter, between me and myself. This was not just another of the many depressions I had gone through. I had reached a breaking point. I could feel the danger of a complete breakdown.

I went to the phone and called Cassandra Ludington, wife of the new AP bureau chief. I could hear her surprise when she recognized my voice. Since she had arrived, she had tried endlessly, in a quiet and caring way, to get me out of my solitude. Even when I never called her or accepted invitations to her house, she kept in touch, not pushing but persistent.

"How are you?" she said.

"Fine, thank you." My usual answer. But you are not fine, I told myself. That's why you are calling her.

"No, I'm not fine, Cass." I started crying. She told me to stay where I was, she was coming to get me. I don't know how, but she was there in minutes. We went back to her house, where her two sons, who were visiting from the States, took Sulome out to the garden. I sat with Cass in her living room, crying for more than three hours.

From then on, I began to go out of the apartment more often, and after the first few times Cass asked, I agreed to go to church with her. In the beginning, it felt as if I were intruding on somebody's privacy. I didn't feel godly at all, while everybody was part of it. When others were praying or singing hymns, I was crying. It didn't feel right, and yet I knew I needed to reach some sort of peace with God.

The more I cried in church, the more I felt at peace. I don't know what it is, what happens to us when we are in the house of God, in His presence, but I felt tranquillity whenever I left church. I was still fighting to accept that

*our situation was not created by Him, that there was an-
other power somewhere out there that did the things that
made us suffer, that we blamed God for. All I knew was that
I didn't seem to be alone anymore.*

25

Release anytime in the near future is definitely off. We've been moved deep into southern Lebanon, seemingly into the middle of what used to be called the Iron Triangle. The name referred to a group of fervently Hezbollah villages just inland from Sidon and bordering the ten-mile-wide strip of Lebanon still occupied by Israel. This had always been the center of Shiite resistance to the Israeli occupation, the source of many of the attacks on and ambushes of Israeli troops.

We certainly didn't come from Beirut first-class. Frank, Tom, and I were moved out early one morning, just before dawn. This time, we went only a short distance in the trunks of cars, separately, then were loaded into trucks. But first, we were all wrapped from head to foot with plastic shipping tape. Completely and tightly, with only a small space for the nose to allow us to breathe. I was literally packed into a tiny compartment under the floor of a van, with two guards shoving on me to get the lid of the little coffinlike enclosure sealed.

Then we drove for several hours—obviously south, because that's the only way you can go that long on a relatively flat, good road in Lebanon. I even noted when we passed through Sidon, going around the little traffic circle in the center of the city.

The trip was hell. It was raining, and I got thoroughly soaked and cold from the puddles we splashed through.

Plus, the fumes from the van's engine made me feel desperately ill. Every time we hit a pothole or a bump, and there were a lot of them, my nose banged into the metal floor above me.

When we finally arrived and were taken into what seemed to be a mosque or Husseiniyah (Shiite meeting hall), my nose was bleeding and I was shivering constantly.

Tom and Frank arrived at the same time, apparently in the same convoy. Don't know what happened to John and Brian. We stayed in that place just overnight, then were put into car trunks again and driven a short distance uphill (therefore inland from the coast) to another, similar large building. The guards have fixed up a secret basement room here, with a door in the floor of a closet. Our cell is about twenty feet long and perhaps eight or nine feet wide. It was unfinished when we arrived, and they've been sealing up the walls with cement. We each have a cot, and we're each chained to a U-bolt in the wall.

We're constrained to near-total silence and allowed little movement. The guards seem paranoid about anyone's noticing us. On some nights of the week, meetings are held upstairs, sometimes apparently women. When that happens, a guard is put in with us with an AK-47, the metal grille that closes off the entrance in the ceiling is locked, and a wooden cover is placed over it. We are forbidden to move or even cough, with dire threats, for several hours.

Even when there doesn't seem to be anyone in the building above us, we have to be very quiet. We are taken to the bathroom about dawn, very briefly, and hurried through our ablutions—less than five minutes—and sometimes again at night, late.

This place is metaphorically, as well as literally, a hole. It's dirty and full of mosquitoes. The light, a bare bulb hanging from the ceiling, is never turned off. The guards are suspicious and unfriendly—one is "the Ghost," whom we've already had so much trouble with. He likes to sneak up to the opening of our cell above us and spy. Frank's cot is lying almost under the opening, and it's hard for him not to look at it under his blindfold, when he lies down. Whenever the Ghost appears, he accuses Frank of trying to see him. It's making Frank even more paranoid than he is. I offered to change places with him, but the guard wouldn't go along, for no apparent reason.

Once again, the depression is enormously deep. Only our physical misery distracts us from our black, endless thoughts. It's now March in southern Lebanon, and growing too hot for the heavy blankets we've been given, especially with three people's body heat raising the temperature even more. So it's a dilemma, either being stifled while hiding from the mosquitoes or being cooler and bitten in a thousand places.

It's so quiet most of the time, and the mosquitoes are so numerous, that just their combined whine keeps me from sleeping.

The chains are a very heavy emotional and psychological burden, as well as a physical one. Just to feel them even when I'm not moving drags me near to despair. And now they're very tight. The guards had been leaving them loosely around our wrists until the Ghost spied me managing to pull mine (with considerable effort and some pain) off my wrist. From then on, they were fastened tightly enough to sometimes cut off the circulation. Not that we could go anywhere even if we could get them off, with the metal grille and wooden door between us and the guards, and the guards between us and the outside, and a Shiite village surrounding us.

I've been feeding a tiny mouse that appears in the dead of night occasionally. I call her Mehitabel. She will sit for a while under Frank's bed, absolutely still, before dashing at an incredible speed to the foot of mine, then almost teleporting herself to the ledge beside the cot and finally close enough to snatch the little piece of bread I place next to my head on the pillow, usually while I'm dozing. When the hamsters sealed up the cracks in the wall with more concrete blocks and cement, she disappeared. Tom and Frank tried to convince me she was sealed up in the wall, but I refuse to believe it. She must have gotten away.

The Ghost's a true psychotic. He brought down a small FM radio the other day, placed it between Tom and me, and tuned it to classical music. Then he warned us several times not to touch it, and went away. When he came back an hour or so later, different music was playing, and he insisted vehemently that we had changed the station. Just flat would not believe we hadn't.

He has talked with us in a friendly manner a few times. Says he's from southern Lebanon, the son of a Lebanese teacher of French. His French is certainly excellent. He even brought us a few books in French—classical folk tales and some old poetry. But it's scary to talk to him even when he's trying to be pleasant. He's an absolute fanatic, who claims to have killed Israelis. I don't believe him at all—he's too young and too much of a coward to have ever taken part in a real battle, as he claims. Besides, there haven't been that many real battles against the Israelis, just ambushes and sniper attacks. He makes my skin crawl, and it's impossible to tell when he'll go off into one of his paranoid attacks and turn instantly mean.

Neither Frank nor Tom is in terribly good psychological shape, though certainly Frank is the much worse of the two. He just lies there for hours, without moving or raising his blindfold even when the guards are not around. Seems to still be semicatatonic. Tom is just enormously depressed and pessimistic. With very good reason. I try to make things sound better, and keep saying that something must be happening. But it doesn't convince him, or even me.

I wake abruptly sometimes from the light dozing that passes for sleep these days, sweating and frightened. The dream is often the same: I'm free, and wandering through Beirut, or at the office, talking to Robert or Nick or some other friend, but I know I have to return to this prison. "I don't want to go back," I cry. "Well, just don't go back," is the bland reply. But they don't understand. There is some terrible compulsion, some obligation or promise I just can't ignore, and I have to. I just have to. "I don't want to wake with a chain on my leg again." And then I wake up, and at the first movement, I can feel the chain pulling at my ankle, and my heart plummets inside me.

I dream of Madeleine, too, and can feel her so clearly, the curve of her hip, the way she fits to me, the smell of her hair. It's so clear, so real, and I wake up to a terrible emptiness in my arms. I still can't think of her for more than a few moments at a time with the pain welling up, threatening to engulf me.

I can often feel the panic sneaking up, the weight of the months and years that have gone by while we lie on these mattresses, the incredible waste. I push it away, and busy my mind with mental games, or frantic efforts at conversation. Tom keeps careful track of the time—"This is my five-hundredth, six-hundredth, seven-hundredth day. It's twenty-three days till my birthday, till Christmas, till Easter." I ask him, snarl at him—"Don't tell me, Tom. I don't want to know." I can't stand to think about all those weeks, months, piling one on top of the other.

I pray. "God, give me strength, courage. Above all, calm acceptance. I'm grateful for my life, for all the things I've had. Even those so-short months with Madeleine were a gift. I've done so much, traveled so much. If I die tomorrow, okay, my life has been full. But this purgatory, endless, gray. Don't ask more of me than I can give. But I have to. If this is Your will, I have to."

Sometimes the acceptance comes, and I know I can just go on. Then the black misery comes again, and I try to push it away. Even when it does break through the deliberate busy-ness of my mind, and overwhelms me, I know by now that it will pass, retreat. It's hard to be so completely miserable all the time. But it never disappears completely. It's always there, in the background of my mind, waiting.

Another move, but only a short one. We were taken up and put into an ordinary passenger van late one night and then driven further into the mountains. It was raining hard, and the van got stuck in the mud, clear up to the floorboards. We sat for an hour or so, while they radioed for another van. The guards were very nervous—it would be difficult to explain three blindfolded men in your van if someone came along. Eventually, the other van arrived, and we were transferred to it and taken on to this place, some kind of small villa maybe five miles or so from the place we were just in. We can hear animals—goats and cows and chickens, so it's probably near some small village.

It's slightly better than the last place. First, we three were jammed into an unused toilet area, with our mattresses. Then, when the guards had time to "fix up" a bedroom, we were moved to it. We're each chained to ring bolts in the floor, with two padlocks, and to each other. They've put up very heavy steel doors to cover a pair of French doors in the bedroom, with no fewer than five padlocks and a chain on them. There's no door to the room, just a blanket hung up to screen us from the guards in the next room—very nerve-wracking, since we can't tell when they'll sneak in and peek around the blanket. No exercise again, and just one trip to the toilet a day. Damn few showers, as well.

But John and Brian have rejoined us. We can hear them occasionally. They seem to be in the disused toilet we were in at first.

A few things are better. We can talk quietly, and the Ghost even gave me some cardboard and a pen. I made a Monopoly game and a Scrabble board, with little bits of paper for the letters. We play every day, stretching out our legs to get close enough to each other. The games seem to be helping Frank emerge from his shell. He seems to be interested in them, and I've even been able to persuade him to talk about his work. He ran a couple of small private elementary schools in Beirut, with a Lebanese partner. He's into a system called Mastery Learning, which is interesting. Tom, though, doesn't believe in it, and we have long discussions that sometimes turn into arguments between the two of them.

But Frank remains obviously very frail, narrowly balanced on the edge of sanity. He won't read anything, even when we have books, and spends long hours just lying still, with his blindfold over his eyes.

We're allowed to watch a small black-and-white television sometimes, but only the entertainment programs. The guards turn it off ten minutes before the news comes on, and back on ten minutes afterward. That means, of course, even the entertainment programs and dramas we are allowed to see are truncated, and we rarely learn how any of the stories end. Nonetheless, I watch it whenever we have it. Frank's not interested, and Tom is farsighted and can't see it well.

The TV has confirmed our location, anyway. The main channel we see is Middle East Broadcasting, a Christian Broadcasting Network station that we all knew was located in the Israeli-occupied border zone. The 700 Club with Pat Robertson, and the like. We even see Israeli channels once in a while. None of the channels could be seen in Lebanon outside the far south, near the Israeli border.

They even gave us back two of our watches, taken from us so long ago. Tom's is electric, and the battery has run down, so it's useless. But mine, an old self-winding gold watch Madeleine gave me, is still going. At least we know what time it is, and that pleases Tom, who seems to need to know. I don't much care—we've got no appointments.

Tom wakes up every morning cursing darkly and constantly in a low monotone. It drives me batty. Finally, I told him, "Look, I wake up every day in a depression. It's all I can do just to get through the day. I do not need you manufacturing a bigger fucking black cloud for me every morning."

It slowed him down a bit, anyway.

He got terribly ill for about a week recently. He suffered from recurrent high fever and could not eat at all. I badgered the guards for several days before they finally went and got some medicine for him. Then he wouldn't take it. He said it made him sicker. I spent every day and night pushing and persuading him to take the medicine when he was supposed to, and to eat something every meal, even if it was only a few bites. Got the Ghost to bring some fresh eggs. Those he could keep down. Most everything else he threw up. All this frightened me badly, especially the last couple of days of the fever, but he's come out of it now.

Taking care of Tom, and trying to work on Frank, get him interested in things and talking, is at least keeping me occupied. Prevents me from spending too much time in my now familiar black depression. I spend most of my prayer time on them, though there's plenty of time left over for mea culpas and pleading for acceptance and some kind of inner peace on my own behalf. There's absolutely no news, nothing.

The Ghost has had a truly ridiculous fit. Came in first thing in the morning and noticed a small crack of light leaking in around the steel doors next to me. Too small to see out of, but certainly blazingly obvious with the lights in the room out. He then accused me of bending these giant steel plates in an attempt to escape. Did no good to point out that I was still chained with two chains and two padlocks, or that even if I got out, I was dressed only in a pair of thin, white boxer shorts, and there are undoubtedly dozens of armed militiamen and villagers outside. He was practically frothing with anger. I argued, but finally just shrugged my shoulders and said, "Thanks. But I'm not Superman." He gave up eventually, without any physical violence.

But we then had another verbal tussle. As he left, he took away the few books we have, and the television, the games, and the pen. I asked him why, but he didn't answer. Finally, he said, "Because I have something wrong with my head."

"I guess so," I snapped back. Then I remembered I had said in our argument that anyone who thought I could escape from my chains and bend the door had to have a problem with his head. Blew it again, and again Tom and Frank have to pay with me. We got the stuff back after a while. But I'll have to watch my tongue, as always.

* * *

I think the Ghost is on the edge of going completely mad. He blew up at Brian in the hall. We could hear the shouting. Don't know what Brian did, but sounds like he tried to shove back when the Ghost shoved him on his way to the toilet. The next thing we knew, there was the terrible sound of a heavy beating from down the hall. When it finally stopped, the Ghost came stomping heavily into our room, knocking a thick wooden stick on the floor. "Does anyone want to fight?" he demanded toughly. We said nothing. He stomped around and cursed for a while, then left.

Don't know how bad Brian is. The violence just seems to hang in the air. Somebody is going to get badly hurt if the Ghost stays around here. He's a total psycho.

I'm finally out of that mess in southern Lebanon and back in Beirut, though now I am alone. No explanation. They just came in and told me to stand up. Again, they taped me up completely, until I couldn't move. Then it was into the secret compartment again, this time under the floor of a bigger truck and north for several hours. It was not a pleasant trip.

I did have a couple of seconds to hand my watch to Tom. I'd like to have kept it, since it was Maddy's present. But he needs it worse than I do.

I'm chained to the wall again in one of the apartments we lived in a year or so ago. No news, no TV. I have some books, and read them over and over, mostly by candlelight, since the electricity problem in Beirut seems to be worse than ever. We have power only a few hours a day. I even have the red Bible again.

They leave me alone. Just bring me meals three times a day—still the usual rice and canned vegetable garbage mostly, and take me to the bathroom once each morning. It's a relief.

My mind seems fairly stable. I try not to get optimistic about any imminent release, and truly don't feel it likely. Of course, there's no evidence either way. Just a feeling.

I occupy myself with the Bible, and prayers. They're

more optimistic now, more accepting. I sometimes feel that closeness to God I've missed so much. But the loneliness is still there, the frustration at the endless weeks. It's somewhere around October 1987, as best I can figure. Thirty-one months. Nearly three years. I remember telling Tom so long ago, "It's all downhill from here. It has to be."

"Why?" he asked.

"Because we've been here eighteen months. There's no way they'll keep us for three years. They'll either kill us or let us go before that."

> The word rushes, trembling,
> full of hope and fear,
> shaken by great happenings.
> I sit chained and still,
> full of rage and pain,
> shaken by the smallest things:
> An oft-remembered, much-loved voice;
> a passing, pointless memory
> of sun and laughter,
> strong, black hair,
> soft, smooth skin, and
> soft, smooth words.
> I sit chained and trembling,
> full of pain, and pain's full kin—
> faith and hope awakening.

26

The doors that had opened so readily over the past two years for Peg Say were now all firmly shut. No one in the Reagan administration wanted to even hear the word *hostage*. Even when she did succeed through cajolery or stubbornness or outright threats in getting into someone's office, the faces were all new. The men she had come to know and even persuaded to trust her were all gone.

In one such meeting, to which she had been told to enter via a back door of the State Department building, a new "liaison" man named Michael Mahoney told her bluntly: the hostages were being "devalued." The kidnappers were to be persuaded that their victims had no value to the United States. And, by the way, the family members of hostages, who had so easily won the ear of Reagan, would never again have access to high government officials.

Peg was dismayed and angry. Sure, the families had demanded that something be done. They had not demanded it be illegal, foolish, and ineffective. Three hostages had come home through North's efforts. Six other Americans were now hostage. The net result was not exactly a win. But it was not the families' fault. Nor that of the hostages.

She had even publicly defended the president in an article in *USA Today*—earning a return phone call from Reagan on Air Force One in which he had expressed his gratitude.

But as the administration was trying to push the whole

issue off its collective desk, the kidnappers were pushing it back to center-front. Several death threats were made in January, and tension rose to the point that a U.S. Navy task force was sent into the eastern Mediterranean to hover off Beirut. A message was sent via the Palestine Liberation Organization to Hussein Mussawi, head of Islamic Amal in the Bekaa Valley, and closely tied to the kidnappers. If a hostage was killed, America would very definitely strike. The threats died off.

The issue was briefly pushed off the front pages by renewed violence in Beirut. The Shia Amal militia and the Druse PSP went to war against each other. The damage in the brief but vicious fighting was tremendous. It ended only when seven thousand Syrian soldiers poured into West Beirut, taking over more than fifty militia offices and shooting anyone who resisted.

Interest in and sympathy for the hostages was growing in the small towns and cities across America. Cards and letters from schoolchildren and adults were piling up in the offices of No Greater Love, an organization set up by an energetic lady named Carmella LaSpada to help the families of victims of war and terrorism. Friends and relatives of the hostages were on this or that talk show or news show every day.

On March 16, 1987, the second anniversary of Anderson's kidnapping, the American Baptist Church held a prayer ceremony in Valley Forge, Pennsylvania. Other ceremonies were held in churches in other cities, including Anderson's two hometowns—Batavia, New York, and Lorain, Ohio.

Local committees were formed in all the hostages' hometowns. Ray Barnett, head of Friends in the West, had thousands of "prayer bracelets" made, each carrying the name of a hostage and the inscription "Hebrews 13:3—'Remember those in prison as if imprisoned with them.'" Soon they were on thousands of wrists across the country.

Several of Anderson's colleagues and friends organized his peers into the Journalists' Committee to Free Terry Anderson. Its list carried the names of nearly every famous newsperson in America. The Friends of Tom Sutherland committee was formed in Denver. Others set up shop in other towns.

On May 28, Barnett organized the World Day of Prayer for the hostages, with evangelist Robert Schuller as spokesman.

The Reagan administration must have known its effort to "devalue" the hostages was doomed when even the dignified and powerful Democratic senator from New York, Daniel Patrick Moynihan, joined the crusade. He vowed that Anderson's name would appear in the *Congressional Record* every day until he was free. He made sure it did.

No one wanted a repeat of the Iran-Contra/arms-for-hostages debacle. Everyone wanted the government to do something.

In Beirut, Lebanese television carried a videotape of Anderson's two-year-old daughter, Sulome, blowing out the candles on a birthday cake. "Our hearts are broken. Where is Daddy?" she asked, waving a picture of her father. The Lebanese announcer came back on the screen wiping tears from his eyes.

MADELEINE

NICOSIA, CYPRUS. JUNE 1987–MARCH 1988.

Another day, another shock. Charles Glass, an old friend and former ABC bureau chief in Beirut, was kidnapped on June 17. I couldn't believe that he was still going to Lebanon. Charles, whose family is originally from Zahle, in Lebanon's Bekaa Valley, was a careful man who used to avoid going out on the streets of Beirut during the fighting.

His wasn't the only kidnapping during that period. Four American professors, three Germans, two Saudis, and several Frenchmen were also taken. Their captors used different names, but most were clearly linked to Hezbollah. Some of those taken were freed later in the year. Some were not. Threats to kill them were frequent, but their executions were always "postponed."

Every time the kidnappers needed to prove their identity, they would release a picture of Terry. Sometimes he looked angry, sometimes he was smiling slightly. In all of them, he was without glasses. We never knew whether they had been taken that day, or a year ago. The pictures gave me security, knowing Terry was still alive; still important to them; maybe, just maybe the next to come home.

Sulome was beginning to understand that there were really three in our family, not two. She would take his picture, hold it to her chest, and blow kisses at it. "Daddy Telly, where is Daddy Telly?" she would ask, looking at me with shining eyes. Her questions were like knives in my heart.

I arranged a family reunion in Cyprus, the first one in more than sixteen years. My sister came from England, my brother from Norway, my mother and other sisters from Lebanon. There were nine children now. I can't explain the happiness that surrounded us that summer. Sulome got to meet and play with her cousins from Lebanon, and had a chance to feel like a Lebanese. She even learned to speak some Arabic, something I had tried to teach her without success. It was a special time, and revived my spirit.

Charles Glass was freed August 18, and we celebrated. We even went out dancing, something I love but had not done since Terry was taken. But I also cried for Terry, and felt guilty for the happiness I was feeling with my family while he was still in his cell.

When summer ended, my family went home, except for my mother. The AP arranged for some of the furniture from our apartment in Beirut to be sent to me.

October 27, 1987. Terry's fortieth birthday. We had no news about him, except another picture that had been released in August—the same one released a year ago. I hated his kidnappers more every time they released a picture or a statement of demands. They were robbing him of his life, two and half years of his life, and they showed no remorse.

Two Frenchmen were released November 27, apparently because the French government had met the kidnappers' demands. In Paris, Iranian diplomats were allowed to go home, and their French counterparts were returned from Tehran.

On December 24, just as we were moving to a new house, Reuters News Agency called to say they had received a videotape of Terry. They couldn't get me a copy immediately, so I got my first glimpse of him on Greek Cypriot television that evening, only a few seconds. The report was in Greek, and my Greek is poor, so I couldn't really understand it. The AP called that night and read me the text. Terry sounded sad, but well and very much in control. It was like him, always in control. He amazed me with his deep voice and confident manner. I could only love and respect him more. I could feel his plea for freedom. The videotape was sort of a Christmas present for us. To know that he was alive and well was more than I had expected.

That Christmas Day, with boxes strewn around the living room and the rest of the house empty, I began giving Sulome presents I told her were from her father. She had been asking about him, and whether he loved her. She needed evidence of that love. The presents were proof. She was happy and proud of him. She would tell friends what he had sent her, saying he couldn't come himself because of the people who were keeping him. Many times, I heard her say that her father loved her, and wanted to be with her and Mom, and it was the fault of "those people" that he couldn't.

I found more peace in the new house, somehow found myself again with the furniture we had bought together around me, and the memories it brought. To touch his clothes and feel his presence was enormously strange and beyond my understanding. I used to feel him just by looking at his books and remembering how fast he read and how envious I was of that. Fixing up the house and putting things in order, I felt I belonged, my feet were on the ground again. Most of all, giving Sulome a home, and being able to share with her Terry's invisible presence and tell old stories about him, I felt some security. The stories were important to Sulome, especially the one about how he used to put his head on my belly and feel her move, calling her an "active little bugger." She would laugh and ask me to tell it again and again.

The new year, 1988, began with more kidnappings, but somehow I wasn't touched as much by them anymore. I was sorry for the men, but it didn't affect me as badly as before. I was stronger, and could think better, analyze what was happening, and go on with my life. I was certain by now that they were never going to hurt Terry. He obviously might be the last to be free, but I felt he was least likely to get hurt. Keeping that in mind, I could feel strong.

Sulome started nursery school in January, and life became a bit easier. I was more mobile, and met other mothers, made more friends. Cass Ludington was always there, the best of friends. Best of all, I had returned to church, thanks to her. It was still hard to feel there was justice on earth with Terry and others captive, but I was ready to accept that things were as they were, and hope to understand.

The kidnapping of Lt. Col. William Higgins, a member of the UN peacekeeping forces in southern Lebanon, made me wonder if the United States knew what it was doing. It was said he was a spy, or was working to free the hostages. How little the Americans knew about these men! It was clear that they had learned nothing from the arms-for-hostages deal and its effects on the hostages, and us. The rumors said Higgins was meeting with several Shiite factions or groups who might be ready to help free the hostages. If the colonel really was planning some kind of military action, then we were all in deep trouble. It was the first time in a long time that I worried about Terry's fate.

Terry's fourth year in captivity began March 16, 1988. It was a day again of depression and loss. Nothing had changed, and everyone around me reminded me of it. An-

*other year of the same thing, humiliation and deprivation.
Another year of being unable to do anything for him. It is
not easy to be helpless when you know the one you love is
suffering.*

BEIRUT. NOVEMBER 1987–MAY 1988.

I'm less frightened of being alone this time. The conditions
are better: the room's clean; the food is acceptable, if not
too good; I have the Bible and a few books; and the guards
are less threatening. I didn't have the chain last time, but
I'm almost used to it. Not quite—sometimes the very feel
of it on my leg makes me crazy, and I yank on it and tug
at the bolt in the wall, even though I know it would take
a tractor to pull it out.

I even have an automatic pacing pattern that uses just the
full five-foot length of the chain without quite jerking at the
end, and with a particular turn at each end that keeps my
foot from getting tangled in it. I wonder if that peculiar
two-step will stay with me long after I'm out, like an old
sea captain who keeps to the confines of his deck even
when he's ashore.

I've also developed a strange sitting slouch from leaning
against the wall so long. In every cell, I sit the same, knees
up to hold the book, spine curved to keep my weight off
whatever sore spot I've developed on my butt. There's almost always one, usually that bony place at the end of my
spine.

My mind is more directable these days. I can set myself
a task or a subject and keep to it for days, though when I
doze off and wake again, I frequently forget just where I
was, and then details slip away. But I can usually keep the
emotional frenzy away. When it does come, I just let it
wash over me, cry my tears or curse, and then wait for it
to go away.

Sayeed gave me a cheap, plastic set of worry beads the
last time I saw him. They have a lot more beads than a ro-

sary, so I took it apart and retied it in the proper way, five decades and five singles, one-three-one. Then I wrapped a piece of copper wire I picked up off the floor around matchsticks to make a cross. I've managed to keep it through all the moves since by wrapping it around my wrist.

I use it frequently, with my own formula. Instead of the Sorrowful Mysteries of the Blessed Mother, as Father Martin used to use, I pause at each decade to think about and pray for certain people, or on certain subjects—whatever I'm thinking about at the time. It's a kind of discipline, I guess, and I like the ritual nature of it.

I rarely ask God for freedom anymore. He knows how much I want to go home—I've already told Him so many times. Instead, I pray for patience, acceptance, and strength for myself. I give thanks for what I've had. I haven't become a saint, or anywhere near it. I still rage, and sometimes I want to scream in frustration. But less frequently. I'm still deeply unhappy and lonely. But I know I'll live through this. I will be free someday, and I will use what I've learned about myself properly.

PRIDE

Pride goeth before a fall, they say.
I fall often, but my pride remains.
My dignity is tattered,
my reputation a bit bespattered.
My hair goeth, and my teeth.
My belly saggeth; my arches, too.
But Pride stands regally,
a stubborn Ozymandias
astride his crumbling kingdom,
my, and man's, despair.

I've a surprising new companion. I was moved from the bedroom I was in to another just down the hall in the same apartment, where one of the Frenchmen, Marcel Fontaine, has been kept for some time. We're now chained to the same wall, our mattresses lying head-to-head on one side of the room. He's a small man, several inches shorter than I am, thin, and very quiet. Of course, we told each other our stories immediately. Fontaine was kidnapped just a week after I was—March 22, 1985. So we've both been held for thirty-three months. There were four Frenchmen held together for some time, and they were the ones who were in the next room in the apartment Tom dubbed "the Marseillaise." But Michel Seurat died of some kind of cancer while we were all there. I remembered the letter we read from the doctor who was treating him so long ago, saying Seurat was dying and the doctor couldn't help him.

It seems Fontaine was separated from his two companions, Jean-Paul Kauffmann and Marcel Carton, some weeks ago and has been here alone since. He doesn't think they've been freed, but has little information.

It's almost pleasant to have someone else here after three or four weeks in solitary, especially a man as undemanding as Marcel (the guards call him Fu-fu for some reason). We play dominoes with a set he has, and hold services every day out of an English Book of Common Prayer that turned up in the latest batch of books.

He talks little. His English is limited, and he has a very thick accent. He's from the island of Réunion, and was a consul at the French embassy in Beirut. He seems very conservative, almost right-wing, and likes books about conspiracies: *The Hundred Families That Rule France* is one of his favorites.

We have a number of French books, and he's helping me with my vocabulary (though he says my accent is atrocious and he can hardly understand when I speak French).

The hamsters bring in the little television once in a while, but only for entertainment programs. We're still forbidden all news. No explanation.

We do get half an hour or so off the chain after the toilet trip each day for exercise. I jog back and forth across the room, do sit-ups, and so forth. I feel pretty weak. All the large muscles in my arms and legs and chest have shrunk or turned to flab. Got to stay in shape. But it's often difficult. I exercise hard for a week or two, then get lethargic and do almost nothing for days at a time. I just can't seem to keep it up steadily for long.

These days, we seem suspended, just floating through the weeks, trying not to think much about the hard things, trying not to notice the time going by. Nearly three years.

I almost cracked. For no particular reason, except frustration. I was trying to persuade the guards to get the chiefs to let me send a message home for Christmas. Nothing. No response. "We will tell the chef." "We have told the chef." "We have no orders." Just nothing.

Suddenly, as I was walking around during the exercise period, thinking about home, about Madeleine and Sulome and everyone, my mind started spinning out of control, thoughts just spinning and spinning. I couldn't stop it. I walked over to the wall and began beating my forehead against it, hard, and harder, trying to make it all stop. After a couple dozen thumps, Fontaine knocked on the closed door for the guards. Mahmoud came in, ran across the room, grabbed me by the shoulders, and pushed me down on the mattress. "What are you doing?" It wasn't until then I noticed my head was bleeding.

He chained me up again, got a cloth and wiped off the blood, then asked me, "Why are you doing this?"

I didn't know why. "Don't ignore me," I said. "When I talk to you, give me an answer."

"You must not do this." That was all. The next day, one of the chiefs or subchiefs came in and examined my head, but did not speak to me.

I thought I was doing so well. I thought I had myself under control, and could deal with all this with some dignity. Now I don't know how long I'll be able to make it. Unless something changes, unless we get some news, I'm afraid I'll lose control again. I'm just scared, not of them, but of myself.

Fontaine had a bad time New Year's Eve, just because of the guards' stupidity and laziness. Apparently, every year the French families put a message on Radio France International at midnight, and the four French hostages have always been allowed to listen. This time, he told Mahmoud about the upcoming message several days in advance and asked him to get permission to give us a radio for it. Mahmoud said the chiefs will allow the guards to tape the message, but we can't have a radio.

New Year's Eve, we reminded them several times, and they promised to do the taping. "Be sure, be sure. I promise, on my eyes." At midnight, we called a guard, who said, "Mahmoud is sleeping."

"Well, wake him. He has to tape the message."

"I can't."

That was frustrating. What was worse, though, was that on New Year's Day, Mahmoud brought in a tape machine, saying he had done the taping. But when he pushed the play button, we all discovered that the batteries had been too weak. Only a few words were understandable. Total loss, until next year, God forbid.

It is so enraging to be at the mercy of these young men, and to find them not vicious, just stupid, lazy, and indifferent. They cannot imagine what those messages mean to us. There's no reason for them not to give them to us. I know there have been dozens for me over the years, and I've received only four or five. It's just so uselessly stupid.

Weeks of nothing but boredom. They've brought a few more books, but we have had no news. It's spring now, not that it means anything to us. It's a bit warmer in the room, but the steel on the windows is too tightly sealed for us to see anything but a small line of daylight around the sides. I've seen the sun once now in three years. Back in 1985, after I'd been held only three or four months, the guards took David and me into a room with an open window and let us look at the sky for about five minutes. That's it.

There was no message on the anniversary of my kidnapping. At least, the guards said there wasn't anything in the papers. I don't believe them, but there's absolutely nothing I can do about it. To bluntly tell them I think they're lying and were just too lazy to get permission to give it to me would be stupid.

We were watching some dumb comedy on the television the other night when it was interrupted by a live news flash. A CNN reporter suddenly appeared on the screen, standing on the tarmac at the Cyprus airport, reporting on a Kuwaiti plane that had been hijacked by Shiite fundamentalists and diverted to Iran, then on to Cyprus. They're demanding release of the seventeen Shiites held in Kuwait—the same guys our hosts want in exchange for us. Must be Islamic Jihad. First news of anything in the world we've had in months and months, and it turns out to directly concern us. The guards in the other rooms apparently didn't see the news bulletin on their TV, because they didn't come in to turn it off.

We're absolutely forbidden to watch any news, and we both got very nervous about the report. But neither one of us could turn it off. I turned the sound down low and crouched in front of the screen so if the guards came in I could switch it off, and we watched until near the end, hoping to hear something about us. No mention, just the usual hijacking drama, and finally our nervousness overcame our fascination. With Fu-fu's agreement, I turned it off. We never did find out what happened. One minor benefit, though—we got the date. April 8, 1988. 1,119 days.

Fontaine's gone. They told us one day that one of the two of us was going home. He was convinced it would be me. I once again tried, not very successfully, not to believe it. That night, several of them came in, including the Hajj. As always, I recognized his voice immediately. They told me to stand up, released my chain, and took me out of the room, but only to the other bedroom. I stayed there for a couple of hours, then they took me back, and Fontaine was gone.

The Hajj came over to talk to me. He took my hand, as he usually does, and held it gently while we talked. "*Keefak*, Terry?" How are you?"

"*Salaam aleikum*, Hajj. What is happening? Has Fontaine been set free?" Mahmoud translated. The Hajj said that all the French had gone home. "Everything is very good. There are good negotiations."

I asked him when I would go home, and he said, "Maybe one month." Then he left.

So once again, the roller coaster starts up. There have been so many "good negotiations." So many near-releases. Please, God. Enough.

27

MADELEINE

On April 8, 1988, a Kuwaiti airliner was hijacked by Islamic Jihad. The plane was taken from one airport to another around the Middle East, and two Kuwaiti passengers were killed, before it finally landed at Larnaca. The hijackers were demanding the release of the seventeen Shia jailed in Kuwait, and threatening to kill their American hostages, including Terry, if any attempt was made to attack the plane. They displayed a photo of Terry to prove they were the ones who held the Americans. Eventually, the passengers were released and the hijackers allowed to go free.

I was again, of course, worried and depressed. But this time, the depression lasted less time because I had my friends, and the church, and the refound belief that we are given only what we can stand, not one bit more. I felt God was helping me, my daughter, and my family.

That assurance was confirmed on May 4, when three French hostages were released. I went to Paris to meet Marcel Fontaine, who had been imprisoned with Terry. Hearing him talk about Terry, how it was during the six months they were together, up until Fontaine's release, gave me hope and courage.

Fontaine looked pale and seemed withdrawn, but he reassured me Terry was in good shape and in good spirits. Like all the freed hostages before him, Fontaine also told me of Terry's love for me, how all these years he has never

274

ceased thinking of me. The joy that these words can give a woman is extraordinary. To know that you and the one you love are on the same level of feeling for each other without the look of the eyes and the touch of the flesh. My love for him grew deeper every day.

Fontaine also told me how Terry, feeling depressed when the captors failed to give them something they needed, banged his head on the wall until it bled. When Fontaine could not stop him, he called the guards. I know this news should have made me very unhappy, and it did, but it also told me that Terry had not changed, that he was still fighting for whatever rights he felt he must have, even as a captive. For him to do that meant that no matter what these people did to him, he would always win over them.

According to Fontaine, Terry, with his stubbornness, always managed to get the guards to give them what they needed, and their conditions had improved during the six months they were together. Again, as always, I was very proud of Terry. But also very angry and sad that he was now left alone in his cell to deal with those animals.

I had maintained my refusal to talk to the news media since the day Terry was kidnapped. I knew appeals to the kidnappers in the media would do no good, and I would not give them the satisfaction of seeing me plead. I thought a lot of news coverage just made them feel important. But the day after I returned to Cyprus from Paris, I asked ABC to tape a message I wanted to send to President Reagan. With Sulome on my lap, I wanted the president to see the family that Terry had left behind. The daughter who was growing up without her father. The loneliness that surrounded us. I knew this tape would make very little difference, but I wanted the president to know that the arms-for-hostages deal with Iran had prolonged Terry's captivity, and that he should do something about it now, before anything more happened to Terry.

We were very lucky Terry was still in moderately good shape, according to Fontaine. I was afraid we would run out of luck. I was afraid that with the situation deteriorat-

*ing in Beirut and its surroundings, as the fighting increased
among the various Muslim factions, somebody might make
a mistake or the captives might get caught in the bombings.*

There was never a time through all the years of Terry's
captivity that we could hold high hopes for more than one
or two months at a time. Something always happened. One
of the worst of those times was the day the U.S. Navy
cruiser Vincennes shot down an Iranian commercial jet.
July 3, 1988.

Terry's captors apparently didn't know how to react to
the incident, in which 290 Iranian civilians died. In similar
situations in the past, innocent people would be killed in retaliation. But as time went by and there was no reaction, it
became apparent that relations between the Lebanese who
held the hostages and Iran had gone bad. There were a lot
of rumors and opinions, but the one source I could trust
confirmed the situation. There were many secret clashes going on between the two allies, and that was one of the reasons the hostages were being kept for such a long time.

For years, our fate—Terry's, the other hostages', their
families'—had depended on other people's actions and re-
actions. Friends and enemies. The fear of a friend's mistake
was as great as the fear of the captors. That kind of fear,
of what we might do out here that could endanger Terry's
life, drove me to thinking illogically at times. Deep inside,
I always rejected the idea that any deal the United States
might think of or could accept would bring Iran out of its
revolution and into democracy—something known only to a
few in the Middle East. Now I was wishing for a deal, any
kind of a deal, that might bring Terry home.

On August 18, there was another picture of Terry released by the kidnappers, and a warning that none of the
Western hostages would be freed unless Israel withdrew
from southern Lebanon. When the last of the German hostages was freed on September 12, 1988, I knew someone in
Germany had made a deal with the devil.

For Sulome, until now, at the age of three, the absence
of her father was natural and not yet a major element in

her life. But now I saw her begin to feel the meaning of it around her friends and their fathers. She would watch them play, her mouth open and ready for a giggle to match the one her friend was making. Or she would see them go off to do something exciting together, knowing she had no part in it. Her eyes would drop sadly, and she would look around for me, seeking protection from her own discovery, from the hurt she didn't understand. Every time I saw that look in her eyes, I wished I could enter her heart to soothe it with my love. I had no way to stop her from hurting. This was a new category of pain that I began to experience. My task became building a shield to protect my daughter from her father's kidnappers, not allowing them to hurt her by keeping him captive.

I realized now was the time to explain about her father and the reasons for his absence. I didn't know if it would make sense to her. But I prayed I could bring her closer to him by telling her about him whenever we got a photo or a videotape. I never told her he was in danger.

Every time the captors threatened to hurt the hostages, as they did again on October 21, 1988, they dug a deeper hole of hatred for them in my heart. That reflected my feelings about all Lebanese. A picture of Terry accompanied every statement they made, and the Jihad had made it clear it had no intention of releasing him soon.

On his birthday that year, October 27, the Jihad's statement included a picture of him with a birthday cake, bending to blow out the candles. I couldn't tell if it was a smile on his face, or a look of sarcasm. He appeared thin and feeble, different from all his other photos. Humiliated and withdrawn. I cried until there were no more tears in my eyes. How difficult it must be for him to stand there next to a cake, with some hooded man taking his picture to show it to the world, show how well he was being treated.

I drove Sulome up into the mountains of Cyprus, far away from everything and everybody, and told her about her daddy's birthday. By a tree next to a small river, she and I found a strange kind of peace that only nature could provide. Sulome asked to write her name on the tree. With a knife I carved her name and the date. October 27, 1988. We would do the same thing each of the next three years on that day.

A few days later, on October 31, a videotape came. He looked stronger than in the photo, but resigned. He appealed to the next president, Bush or Dukakis, to end his captivity, saying he found it difficult to keep his spirit and courage high any longer.

BAALBEK, LEBANON. MAY–DECEMBER 1988.

It didn't take them long to move me again after Fontaine left, and it was a memorable move. They woke me before dawn on May 6, according to my figuring, just two days after he was set free. No nonsense about my going home this time. They taped my hands lightly, then placed small, round Band-Aids over my eyes. The Hajj picked up my prescription sunglasses—virtually the only one of my possessions they've hung on to—and put them on my face. Then they dressed me in a *chadoor*—with the black hood covering my head completely. There was a piece of gauze set into the front of the hood, over the eyes, where a woman would ordinarily look out. After the usual interminable wait, I was taken down in the elevator and put in the backseat of a car, a Mercedes that seemed identical to the one they used for my kidnapping thirty-eight months ago.

The Hajj drove the car himself, with me and a guard sitting in the back. They never noticed, through the veil, that the Band-Aids came off my eyes almost immediately. With the prescription glasses, I could see everything around me. We drove through the narrow streets of southern Beirut for about twenty minutes, dodging rubble in the roadway, edging past burned-out cars, bumping through shell holes. The devastation was incredible. I hadn't heard much fighting in the past few days, but obviously this area had been hit hard, and repeatedly, over the months.

Finally, we backed into a driveway and up to a large truck. Dear God, I thought. It's the coffin again. They pulled me out, pulled off the *chadoor*, and wrapped me up in the shipping tape, head to foot. Then they slid me into the secret compartment, and this time one of the guards got in with me.

The ride was a long one, five or six hours, and extremely hot. Up out of Beirut into the mountains, on narrow, damaged roads, finally over the top and into what was obviously the Bekaa Valley. For the last two hours, I was ill from the heat and exhaust fumes, and frightened of throwing up. I had to concentrate totally to keep my stomach under control—with all the tape over my mouth, I would have choked to death on my own vomit.

The truck stopped eventually, and I was taken out, unwrapped, and left lying on the ground, outside what seemed to be an isolated villa. I was too weak to move for several minutes. One of the guards poured a bottle of water on my head, then gave me more to drink. Then they took me inside the villa, through a door cut in the back of a bedroom closet, and down into a secret cellar. A chain was placed on my wrist, and they left.

There was a moment of silence after the door closed. I assumed I was alone, but as always was cautious lifting my blindfold in case a guard was still there. I peered around and saw Tom Sutherland and Frank Reed sitting against the wall, staring back at me. Tom spoke first. "I thought you'd gone home, but the Frenchmen said they were sure you hadn't."

Reed had been kept in isolation for the last year or so, since we saw him last. But Tom had been put in with Jean-Paul Kauffmann and Marcel Carton for about six months—the same length of time I'd been with the other Frenchman, Fontaine. We couldn't figure out why they'd shifted everybody around that way.

It was both good to have company again, especially Tom, and terribly depressing to know that there was no likelihood of release. They wouldn't have carted us all out here to the Bekaa if they planned to let us go soon.

The basement cell we are in is long and narrow, perhaps twenty or twenty-five feet by twelve. There is a walled-off toilet in one corner, but of course we can't reach it because of the chains. We have a light in the ceiling that is on all the time we have electricity, and a fluorescent bulb on one wall that they use when the power's out. In one corner is a long pipe leading up to the surface, with a small fan that brings in air. No chink of daylight, except at the end of the pipe.

The guards have nothing to say—no news permitted. But they have promised an occasional video, and of course we keep asking for books. No luck so far. Mahmoud's here, and a couple of the others we know. Otherwise, it's much the same as any of the other cells we've been in. Very hot, a lot of cockroaches, some spiders. No rats so far.

Tom and Frank are at daggers drawn. They bicker constantly. Tom seems to have developed a deep dislike for Frank, and Frank is, as usual, seemingly oblivious to everything. He sits for hours at a time, slouched against the wall, his blindfold down over his eyes. Occasionally, he rouses to join a discussion for a few minutes, usually to disagree over some "fact" or other. Of course, we have no way to check anything, so it's just one man's "fact" against another's. Pointless to argue.

Sometimes it gets downright ridiculous. While the power was off the other day, Tom and Frank somehow began arguing about whether the little fan in the corner was drawing air into the cell when it was on or pushing air out. Would seem simple to solve—just look at the fan blades. But then they argued about whether the fan turned clockwise or counterclockwise. Went on for half an hour, and ended with Tom berating Frank: "You're so stupid." Not calculated to improve the atmosphere.

Tom and I argue, as well. But usually it's an academic argument, a debate. Since we've been separated, he's gotten a good deal more self-confident, even aggressive at times. Apparently, he got on very well with Kauffmann and Carton. Seems to admire Kauffmann very much, and talks about him often. It's good to see him get back some confidence. His self-esteem was badly shattered over the first few months by the guards' violence and suspicion, and he never really recovered. I didn't help, with my steamroller style of discussion. He began to think he was stupid, and even after I realized what was happening, I couldn't really convince him that I like and admire him, that his knowledge of so many things and obvious kindness and liking for people makes me a bit jealous. He is a good and gentle man who just was not prepared for this kind of hell. Who could be? Kauffmann seems to have done a great deal for Tom's self-esteem. Must also be a very kind and caring man. Tom often says we would like each other and get along well. I guess that's a compliment, and I'd like to meet Kauffmann some day.

I've lost a good deal of my aggressiveness, I think, after so much time alone, and the very quiet months with Fontaine. But I'm still hungry to use my mind. Tom and I talk for hours about anything that comes to mind—how to wire a house for electricity, how a three-way switch works, the endless and even tinier details of the dairy farm for teenagers we worked on for many weeks in the Beirut prison. Genetics, the proper constituents of cattle feed. Anything.

Suddenly, our long-repeated pleas for a radio have again borne fruit. The guards brought in a small Sony, and now we can listen to all the newscasts we want. No reason given once again, either for their taking it away or for its return. There isn't much about the hostages these days. Seems everything is still stalled by the Iran-Contra aftermath. But we're able to follow the presidential campaign in the States. Of course, Tom is a good Republican and supports Bush. I remain a liberal Democrat, and for Dukakis. Though I have to confess I don't know much about him. He seems very dry and cold.

We speculate off and on whether the election will mean anything for us. Bush's getting elected means no change likely, though he may be freer as president to do something a bit more controversial. Like get us the hell out of here. Dukakis, being a Democrat and unschooled in foreign policy, is probably too pro-Israeli to accomplish much. It's clear, though, that our case has been ruled out of bounds for the election. Neither the Republicans nor the Democrats will stray from the mantra: "No negotiations with terrorists." Correct policy, but discouraging.

I still have my Bible, but don't read it much. Just dip in from time to time to look for a favorite passage, or grasp for reassurance—mostly from Paul. My prayers are almost mantras, as well. I have no expectations of God. Just some vague hopes of coming closer to His expectations of me. Someday.

John and Brian are with us! Just a week after we arrived here, the guards came in and dumped two more mattresses against the wall, then banged a couple of metal staples into the cement. When we asked who would be joining us, they just laughed. The next day, they brought them in. We had to pretend to introduce ourselves, still blindfolded while the guards were in the room. Couldn't, of course, acknowledge that we'd already been talking for months in the Beirut prison, with the sign language.

They seemed delighted to be with us; of course, we were, as well. They are in good spirits on the whole, but have had no indication whether there has been any progress on their release.

The first couple of days with them were great—lots of talk, exchanging stories of the past year. Both John and Brian have kept their marvelous senses of humor. John is an incredible mimic, a fanatic fan of the Goon Squad and the *Saturday Night Live* crew, who has enough comic talent to have joined them on television. Strangely enough, he took American studies at his university, but has never visited the States.

Brian is still the tough Belfast boy. He's an English major with a thorough knowledge of literature. Good, deep mind, slow and careful in his expression. Very funny at times.

The two of them have developed an incredibly close relationship, despite their vast differences. Makes the rest of us a bit jealous.

They've been put off quite a bit by the aggressive quality in our discussions. They don't understand the game in it, and of course don't understand that for Tom, it's still a bit of therapy, a way for him to express his just-refound self-confidence. As for me, it's still often just a habit, and I try to cut down.

The two of them are fresh meat for Tom and me. All those months of probing each other's minds, of discussing so many things. John is diffident in the talks, rarely holding the floor for long. Brian needs to be coaxed a bit, but once started has a great deal to say, about books, Northern Ireland, and other things. I'm afraid my eagerness also puts him off. He looked at me late one night, after one discussion of books, and said: "You just suck my mind dry."

Even Frank joins in now and then, emerging from his shell, usually when we're quiet for a while, and talking about Boston. He's got a lot of very funny stories to tell about the characters he knows there, waterfront types, bums, rich people. It's too bad he's so fragile. Don't know how he can sit there for hour after hour, sometimes for days, never lifting his blindfold.

I've still got a picture of Sulome tucked inside the Bible. Sometimes I take it out and just look at it for ten or fifteen minutes. She's beautiful, with huge eyes. Looks more like me than Maddy, but much improved. She's almost three now. I wonder where they are. Beirut? Probably not. The States? England? What is Madeleine doing? Haven't had a message from them in so long now. The guards have brought in a couple of newspaper clips telling of various rallies and events. John said he saw, accidentally, part of a television program on him—a rock concert hosted by the

Friends of John McCarthy. I know there are a couple of similar committees for me—Journalists' Committee to Free Terry Anderson, and so on. Tom gets depressed because there's little mention of him. Frank has never had a message, or any acknowledgment on the radio except his name included in the list of American hostages now and then. No group has even claimed him publicly. How does he deal with that? He never says anything about it. Doesn't even talk much about his Lebanese wife anymore, just occasionally his son, Tarek. What's going on inside that head? Where does he go during those long withdrawals? How badly has he been damaged?

We heard on the radio today that a U.S. Navy ship shot down an Iranian passenger plane over the Gulf. At first, all we could think was "Shit! Now they'll take the radio away." But strangely, the guards don't seem to care very much. They just take it as proof of America's evil, and of course assume it was deliberate. Tried to persuade Mahmoud that such things, horrible as they are, happen by mistake sometimes. But ran into that old problem again: Despite their hatred for America, they are convinced it is all-powerful, that anything it does is deliberate and planned. He did say that he didn't think it would affect us at all. They still maintain their only goal is to gain the release of their seventeen compatriots in Kuwaiti jails.

It's July 3, 1988. We've been here two months now. Very little mention of hostages on the radio, and no messages from our families. The radio is on constantly, with at least one of us listening virtually round the clock. We mainly monitor the BBC, with some programs from the Voice of America and two hourlong newscasts a day in French, from Radio Monte Carlo or Radio France International. The rest of the time we talk, or play poker—the guards finally gave up confiscating the cards I was making and brought us a cheap pack.

Late at night, after some of us start to doze off, there is generally a quiet talk going on between whichever two of us can't sleep. One of the problems in being locked up in a small room has always been no one ever gets to talk about the others in the room, unload his frustrations or peeves with one or the other of his cellmates. In the past, our bitching only came in a rush when the individual we were irritated with made his daily ten-minute trip to the bathroom. Tom would dump all his anger at Frank or, earlier, David on me at once, the other would do the same when Tom went, and I'm sure I got heavily discussed while I was out of the room.

Now, with a slightly larger room and more people available, at least some of that can be worked out in these late-night talks. Frequently, it's John and I whispering to each other at three or four o'clock in the morning as we share one of our four daily cigarettes. I began smoking again, after three and a half years, while I was with Fontaine. He smoked those horrible Gitanes, and I couldn't stand it. Now the guards give John, Brian, Frank, and me each four a day, and we usually share them. Tom doesn't smoke, but doesn't complain. Says he doesn't mind. Undoubtedly selfish of us to inflict this on him, but it's one of our very, very few indulgences, and we can't give it up now.

John is an enormously civil man, I'm discovering. He rarely complains, and I've never seen him angry. I know he's as lonely and discouraged as any of us, but he just keeps his cool, and his sense of humor. Doesn't talk much about his feelings, unlike the rest of us.

I enjoy probing Brian's mind. It takes patience, because he forms his sentences slowly and carefully, and sometimes takes a while to get to the point. I have to carefully curb my impulse to interrupt or run off with a thought, and the conversation. He hates that. But when he does arrive somewhere, in an analysis of a book or a play or something about Ireland, it's generally a subtle and penetrating idea.

We've talked several times about his politics. A Protestant and a nationalist—odd to outsiders, but many of the early leaders of the nationalist movement in Northern Ireland, including the IRA, were Protestants. What I can't understand, and have told him I can't, is how a man with such strong feelings for people, so intelligent and humanistic, can support an "armed struggle" conducted by thugs? We both know that much of the war in Northern Ireland has become a pointless orgy of violence led by men on both sides who do it simply because they love violence. The politics, the supposed aim, is nothing but an excuse to them. There were a number of reports recently about the IRA men who kidnapped several civilians in their cars, loaded the cars with explosives, and forced their victims to become suicide bombers in attacks on British army posts. They threatened to kill the families of those men. Horrible and vicious.

Brian knows he can't defend these things, yet can't bring himself to renounce the cause and the "armed struggle." He seems terribly torn. I don't think he's ever engaged in violence himself. He was a social worker in Belfast. I don't think he's capable of violence, other than a drunken punch-up in a bar for amusement.

He is finding it very, very difficult, I think, to make the daily compromises we all have to make in our relationships with the guards. He hates them, hates what they've done to him, as we all do. But he sees it as absolutely necessary to his own integrity to let them know he hates them, to somehow let them see his defiance. He can react to this situation only in terms he learned growing up in the different violence of Northern Ireland. There, the confrontation with the British and the Protestants is total. Open defiance and openly expressed hatred are the rule. Here, he sees us talking with these young men about politics or religion, as we sometimes do, and even making jokes with them. He understands intellectually that there's no point in constant antagonism when everything we have depends on their whims. He understands the polite fiction we all engage in most of the time, that they are just ordinary men doing a job, not fanatics or terrorists, and we might as well get along. But he can't bring himself to take part in it. He tries from time to time, makes a feeble joke, or debates something with Mahmoud. It doesn't last long, though, and it's labored.

For a couple of days, he even went "on the blanket," as his fellow nationalists do in British prisons. That means refusing to wear any clothes supplied by the enemy, and sitting naked in a blanket in your cell. It's very cold now, and the guards just didn't understand what he was doing. Finally, one asked him why he wouldn't wear the pajamas they had given us. He tried to explain, but they didn't get the point, and finally he gave up and put on the clothes. If they couldn't understand his gesture as defiance, it was useless.

I think John, with his urbanity and wit and ability to get along, has been Brian's buffer. In return, Brian's steely integrity and toughness has helped John in those times we all have, when we question ourselves. Have we been tamed? Are we meek, well-mannered little hostages? Shouldn't we make it hard for them, not easy? We're so well trained now. We yank our blindfolds down when they come in, we stick out our legs for the chains. Sometimes, when they forget to lock us up, we even remind them. All of us have at least once found ourselves shut in for the night with an open padlock on the chain, knowing that if they come back in the morning and see it, we'll be in for a bad hassle, even accused of trying to escape. We've all done the same thing, feeling sick and helpless and weak: locked the chain around our own leg. And hated ourselves for it.

We accept so many assaults on our dignity: shoves and pokes, yanks on the chain, a piece of fruit tossed at us as if we could see and catch it while blindfolded. Accusations of misbehavior, peeking, talking too loudly. The guards are ignorant, uneducated, and unsophisticated. Their manners are bad, and each small rudeness is another wound. Each time they ignore a request or, as they frequently do, promise something and then fail completely to do it or bring it, we have to just swallow our frustration and anger. It does no good to get mad, usually. Just brings anger back, and their anger affects us a great deal more than ours affects them.

I still get angry from time to time. Each new guard has

to be taught: I will not eat bread thrown on the floor, like a dog. I will not accept manhandling for no purpose. I will be treated and spoken to with a decent minimum of respect. I am a hostage, not a criminal, not an enemy. And, first of all, I am a man, not an animal.

Most of the guards who have been with us for some time accept these things, for all of us. But they forget, or get irritated; or a new man comes in, and we have to start over again with him. The really vicious guards are gone now, though one or two surly ones remain. There are frequent small clashes, arguments between us and them. We have no power, of course, except moral pressure. They can do what they like, as long as they don't injure us or drive us crazy. The bosses wouldn't like their nest eggs damaged. But the bosses aren't around much, and when they do come and we complain about something, it's our word against the guards'. Their own people.

On the other hand, after all this time, I think they know it wouldn't take much to drive us to despair, to not caring about consequences or punishments. And in fact, the guards do have some sympathy for us. They know us now, know we are not bad men and have done nothing to them. They don't usually want to make things more difficult. They just don't understand how much their every move, every fit of irrationality or unthinking stupidity or absentmindedness, affects us.

> Satan is a name we use
> for darkness in the world,
> a goat on which we load
> our most horrific sins,
> to carry off our guilt.
> But all the evil I have seen
> was done by human beings.
> It isn't a dark angel
> who rigs a car into a bomb,
> or steals money meant for others' food.
> And it wasn't any alien spirit

that chained me to this wall.
One of those who kidnapped me
said once: "No man believes he's evil."
A penetrating and subtle thought
in these circumstances, and from him.
And that's the mystery:
He's not stupid, and doesn't seem insane.
He knows I've done no harm to him or his.
He's looked into my face
each day for years, and
heard me crying in the night.
Still he daily checks my chain,
makes sure my blindfold is secure,
then kneels outside my cell
and prays to Allah, merciful, compassionate.
I know too well the darker urges in myself,
the violence and selfishness.
I've seen little in him I can't recognize.
I also know my mind would shatter,
my soul would die if I did the things he does.
I'm tempted to believe there really is
a devil in him, some malefic,
independent force that makes him
less or other than a man.
That's too easy and too dangerous an answer;
it's how so many evils come to be.
I must reject, abhor, and fight against
these acts, and acknowledge that
they're not inhuman—just the opposite.
We can't separate the things
we do from what we are;
hate the sin and love the sinner is not
a concept I'll ever really understand.
I'll never love him—I'm not Christ.
But I'll try to achieve forgiveness,
because I know that in the end,
as always, Christ was right.

* * *

The guards have brought us videotapes several times: always a terrible kung fu, violence-drenched thriller. Finally, we couldn't even find them funny and told them not to bring any more. They couldn't understand it—they love these movies, and they know we're mostly bored. But we all agreed without even discussing it. We'd rather be bored than watch that crap.

We heard on the radio today that Islamic Jihad has set free the last German, Rudolf Cordes. None of us has ever run across him in any of the prisons we've been in, though Tom and I speculate he might have been the "ghost hostage" we heard going to and from the bathroom in one of the Beirut apartments we were held in. We hadn't even heard before that he was being held by our hosts.

The announcement said he was freed because of "guarantees for the settlement of the Hamadi brothers problems," referring to two Lebanese Shiites in jail in Germany. None of the chiefs of this group has ever indicated the Hamadis had anything to do with them, either. They always talk about the seventeen Shiites in Kuwaiti prisons.

At any rate, it seems like at least vaguely encouraging news. Somebody's going home, even if it's not one of us. Mahmoud says the "negotiate" is good, but then, they always say that, even when we all know nothing is going on.

None of the radio reports speculates on our possible release. In fact, they mention a statement Islamic Jihad apparently released about a month ago with my picture saying specifically neither Tom nor I will be released soon, and containing new demands, for Israeli withdrawal from southern Lebanon. Can't take that seriously—they must know it's just bullshit, and the Israelis aren't going to do anything of the kind, even for their own missing soldiers, let alone for us.

As always, we discussed it up, down, sideways, and endlessly. Every time there is a mention of the hostages, a statement by our hosts, a comment by a government official, no matter how small or slight, it provides fuel for hours of pointless verbal game playing and scenario sketching. Problem is, any scenario—optimistic, pessimistic, or apocalyptic—can be built around the kinds of things that get said publicly. In the end, we come back to the same stone wall—we don't know. In fact, most likely, nobody who makes any public statements knows, and those who do know aren't going to say anything.

All such discussions end the same way, with the weak joke: "Give it a Ben." Ben Weir would always say about any new development: "Give it a month, and we'll see." We've given a lot of things a lot of Bens. Forty-one of them, for me. The only thing we've seen from all of them is another day chained to the wall.

John and I nearly got ourselves in deep trouble. One of the surlier guards suddenly decided he wanted to learn English. It occurs to all of them from time to time, lasts a couple of lessons, and fades away from terminal laziness. Anyway, this one speaks no English at all. He sat down in our cell, and after explaining in Arabic what he wanted, picked up John's plastic cup and held it under McCarthy's nose, where he could see it under the blindfold. *"Shu Eglisi?"* he asked. What English?

"Cup," John replied soberly.

Then the guard picked up a plastic spoon. *"Shu?"*

"Cup," John said. I sat up straighter, surprised. I couldn't see what he was holding, but guessed he hadn't picked up the same object twice.

"Cup?" the hamster asked.

"No, cup," John said, giving it a slightly different pronunciation.

The guard reached over to my mattress and picked up my Bible.

"Shu?"

Trying to appear serious, I leaned forward and peered under my blindfold. "Cup," I said.

"Cup?"

"No, cu-u-u-p," I replied.

After one or two more tries, he suddenly twigged to what

we were doing, said something rapid and low in Arabic, got up, and left. We started giggling, and couldn't stop for ten minutes. It may not have been smart, but it was fun.

It's amazing sometimes how much laughing we do. John's imitations, Brian's terrible shaggy-dog stories, Tom's awful puns and drinking songs, Frank's tales of Boston. Even the idiotic and frustrating things the guards do set us off in giggles. There's often a bitter touch to it. But not always. Just as often, it's just a relief to be able to laugh at something.

Four weeks since Cordes was released, and nothing has happened. Some optimistic news for John, and maybe Brian, on the radio. Britain and Iran have agreed to reopen relations. That's got to help. Britain could hardly do that without some kind of understanding about British hostages. But nothing concrete was reported.

No further mention of the Americans, no speculation about more releases. Nothing. The days go so slowly, yet pile up so quickly. It's hard to conceive of forty-two months just gone, evaporated. It's October 6, 1988. Just over 1,300 days. 1,302 to be exact. Three and a half years. I can't even remember all the places I've been kept.

I can't allow myself to think of that time wasted, that huge chunk of my life gone. It's frightening, especially when there's no hint, no indication how much longer it might be. Tom has reminded me (several times) of the stupid comment I made two years ago, while we were in southern Lebanon. "Well, Tom," I said. "It has to be all downhill from here."

Tom and I figured the other day we've had more than fifty guards, with about a dozen that stayed for long periods. In that time, between the five of us, at least a couple of hundred people have seen us, and knew who we were. Militiamen involved in the various moves, family members of our guards, others. Hard to believe that none of them has blown the secret, that U.S. or Israeli intelligence hasn't picked up enough information to know exactly where we are. Of course, even if they do, chances of making a successful raid are slim. More likely, one or more of us would get killed, which kind of defeats the purpose. And we know there are a number of other hostages, held elsewhere. If we're rescued, what happens to them?

Probably, though, the intelligence people just can't keep up with the moves we've made, which is obviously the purpose of moving so often. No Delta Force coming through the wall, folks. This ain't the movies. Makes a nice fantasy, though.

Frank has been taken away—allegedly to go home, though none of us believed it, and now it's obviously not true. They have played this cruel hoax before on all of us, but to do it to Frank is especially vicious. Abu Ali came in with a couple of other guards. "You go home now, Abu Tarek," he said, using Frank's nickname. They unchained Frank and took him out, without giving him a chance to say more than good-bye to the rest of us.

Why were we all so sure he wasn't going home? It was just wrong. There was something in the way Abu Ali spoke that said it was a lie. And then there had been nothing on the radio about an impending release. Islamic Jihad almost always announces a day in advance when they let someone go. It has now been two days, and there's still nothing on the radio. Frank is certainly in another prison, perhaps alone. Why do they have to do it like this? He has never fully recovered from his last stint in isolation. There is something in his attitude or posture or something that seems to invite abuse from the guards. When he's alone, there's no one to check it. At least with us, he's less of a target, and we can shelter him a bit. No way to know how long this will last. I fear for his sanity if it's more than a few weeks. But then, I fear for my own sanity if it goes on too much longer.

Finally, an American's out! Not one of us. In fact, not actually an American. But an Indian with a green card who has always been listed among American hostages—Professor Singh, according to the radio. He's one of the four professors from Beirut University College kidnapped more than a year and a half ago. Islamic Jihad made no reference to any kind of a deal involving all the hostages, but something must be happening.

Once again, the event sparks hours, even days, of speculation among us. Has a deal been made? Is it part of a series of releases? What happens now?

What happens now is we lost the radio, and stupidly. Whatever deal was going on, if there was one, Islamic Jihad doesn't seem to be playing the game. It released a statement in Beirut, accompanied by my picture (I seem to have become the official press release hostage) and threatening to off Tom and me and maybe others if the Israelis don't stop bombing southern Lebanon. Right. I'm sure that brought shudders to Tel Aviv.

Anyway, half an hour after we heard the report, the guards rushed in and snatched the radio away. We tried to tell them that we already knew about the death threats, and weren't particularly upset, since we doubted very much if they really would shoot us. But as usual, our protests meant nothing. "We have the order," Mahmoud said. That's that. We can try to protest to the Hajj or "Trust Me" Ali, if either ever shows up. But if experience means anything, it will be a while before we get it back.

That's terribly depressing. The radio at least kept us linked to the world, kept us from just sinking into depression and lethargy. The hamsters just can't understand that any kind of bad news is better than knowing absolutely nothing.

Week after week the same. Talk. Cards. Talk. Bad food. Talk. And all the while, running through all our heads are the numbers. 1,300. 1,310. 1,320. Tom keeps track religiously, and lets us know the exact figure often. I keep telling him I don't want to know, that it's too depressing. Truth is, I can't keep myself from counting. December 16 today, by our figuring. Nine days until another Christmas. My fourth.

Christmas, and things have suddenly turned horrible again. One of the surlier guards went berserk last night when Brian made an aggressive gesture. It seems the guard yanked on Brian's chain when he was locking him up after the toilet trip. Brian yanked back, and made some sort of move as if he were going to take a swing at the hamster. We other three heard the guard curse, jump up, and run out the door. He was back in a few seconds with tape and another guard, and they proceeded to tape Brian up completely, then beat him severely with a stick and a rifle. In the end, when the one guard was repeatedly cocking the AK-47 and threatening to kill Brian, screaming curses at him, the other guard stopped him. They left Brian taped and went out.

All through it, as I lay there in my blindfold, I said nothing. Tom and John did the same. Brian is maybe six feet away from me. I could hear the blows as if they were hitting me, could hear Brian grunt and finally, involuntarily, give cries of pain. I feel sick and weak and violated. I know I couldn't have done anything. With both guards in a mindless rage, shouting and screaming, if I had tried to interfere, it would simply have made it worse. I wouldn't mind if they had beaten me. In fact, I'd probably feel less soiled. It just wouldn't have stopped them from beating Brian, and probably would have prolonged it. As always, the only thing to do is curl up, not resist, and wait for them to calm down. But to lie here and make that judgment and know it's the proper thing does not take away the disgust at myself, the feeling that I've behaved weakly.

Brian was badly bruised, but not seriously injured. At least nothing was broken.

When they brought in food perhaps an hour or so later, I pushed it aside. "No. I do not eat," I said. One of the guards kicked at my dish and started shouting in Arabic.

Then Tom and John refused their food, as well. Brian was offered none. The guards were extremely angry, but left.

Today, Christmas Day, we refused breakfast and lunch. In the afternoon, Mahmoud came in with the other guards. We told him about the beating (of course, he already knew), and Brian displayed his back, legs, chest, and shoulders, all turning black and purple in great swaths. We said that they had to take the guard who did it away. He had no reason to do such a thing, and we couldn't accept it.

Mahmoud argued with us, and told us we had to eat or there would be big trouble. A short time after he left, a new man who the other two guards said was some kind of chief came into the cell. They taped me up and carried me upstairs, propped me in a kneeling position in the kitchen, and asked me about the hunger strike. I repeated what we had said earlier—the bad guard would have to go. We couldn't live with him. Obviously, from his inability to decide anything, the new man was not a boss.

They made some mild threats, then launched a ridiculous charade. Taking an air gun they used on the rats occasionally, they fired it next to my head, then gave out theatrical groans, apparently for the benefit of the other three hostages downstairs. I nearly laughed out loud. After a few minutes of that silliness, they told me that I was to persuade the others to eat or there would be serious trouble, and we would be separated and put in isolation again. Then they carried me down into the basement cell again, carefully placed plates of cookies in the center of the room, and left.

I explained to John, Tom, and Brian. After some giggles about the "mock execution," we sobered. The threats seemed real this time, at least the one about isolation. It was a serious one. None of us thought we could take that again easily. At the same time, we had gotten no concession on the guard. If we gave in this time, the usefulness of hunger strikes was at an end forever.

Brian took little part in the discussion. We agreed that each of us had to decide for himself, without pressure. I told the others I thought we had better not push it this time, that there weren't any chiefs around to stop them, and things would likely get rough. I would eat. Tom and John decided the same. Brian indicated he probably would, but not right now.

I picked up a cookie and ate it, facing the camera they had installed some weeks earlier in a corner of the room, near the ceiling. That was it. The "Great Protest" was over. Happy Christmas, 1988.

28

MADELEINE

NICOSIA, CYPRUS.
DECEMBER 1988.

As 1988 ended with more kidnappings in Lebanon, my life had become a routine of ups and downs. But with my family, friends, and the God I had come to know again helping me, I felt stronger after each disappointment. I was trying my best simply to make a good home for Sulome and to prepare her for whatever the future had in store for us.

In a resurgence of my womanhood, I was many times tempted to find a boyfriend. I also knew that my daughter needed a man around her, someone to treat her as a daughter. It scared me to feel this way. I knew that it would hurt Terry, but I still wanted to know I could feel like a woman, and be wanted like one. That all the sorrow and pain, and the guilt, had not destroyed my ability to appeal to a man.

I thought of an excuse—if Terry were in my place and I had been taken away, he would not wait for me this long. After all, we had been together only a year or so.

Every time I was depressed, I attributed it to loneliness and need. And I found quickly, to my surprise, that there were many men willing to approach me. Whenever I accepted a friendly invitation for dinner or a drink, I discovered again that my situation was of my own creation. The world was not closed. I didn't have to be lonely.

But my problem was not just needing a man. I didn't want just any man. I wanted the man I had said yes to when he asked me to spend the rest of my life with him. I wanted Sulome's father. Terry.

I felt shame and guilt, knowing that Terry was in Lebanon, in pain, chained and blindfolded, while I was here in freedom, fantasizing about my needs.

The year 1989 was one of silence. Silence from both the captors and the United States. It also began as a year of sickness for us. In early February, Sulome had a severe case of pneumonia. It started as a mild cough, and I treated her with cough syrup. A few days later, I had a couple of friends for dinner. Sulome was in bed when I heard her moaning and choking. I went quickly into the bedroom, and heard her say, "Mommy, I can't breathe."

She was hot and sweating, and her heartbeat was so fast, I thought she was having a heart attack. My friends helped me rush her to the emergency ward of the local hospital, where the nurses stripped off her clothes and worked to bring her temperature down.

At the X-ray station, surrounded by sick people, I broke down and cried, sobbing so loudly, everybody was staring at me. The fear of losing Sulome that night frightened me so badly. But my tears were for Terry's absence, as well. All the smaller illnesses over the years—colds, fevers, measles—that we had gone through alone. Missing the closeness that a family gains in sharing such times. I needed Terry very much now, and so did Sulome.

Sulome was in the hospital a week, and I almost lived there with her. Friends would bring me food they had cooked, and stay an hour or so with her while I went home to change clothes and freshen up. Sulome was home for two weeks after that before she could go back to school. Within days, I was in bed with a throat infection and high fever. I had overexhausted myself. The AP sent two doctors to see me at my home, and Cassandra was always there.

After I was on my feet again, I decided to go once again to see a psychiatrist. I was out of patience with myself, and unable to take more depressions and sicknesses and frustration at not being able to lead a normal life. My desires and *beliefs and ideals, my wish to remain decent and honest, were all confusing. By then, I wasn't even sure I loved Terry. I felt something that had gone beyond love, to a place that I could not understand and yet never wanted to let go of.*

I had been to see a psychiatrist in 1986. After an hour of talk, and much crying by me, he had told me: "You should leave your daughter with a nanny, or someone, and go out to work. Find yourself something to do, or you will end up finding a man because you are young and need someone to take care of you."

I thought he was crazy. How could I leave my daughter with someone else? Was she supposed to miss both her father and her mother? And I couldn't understand his linking working and finding a man. Terry had been gone only a year. The last thing I wanted was another man. I never went back to the psychiatrist.

This second psychiatrist was more diplomatic. "You are a woman. Why are you denying it?" He wanted to explore my childhood, and why I was fighting my natural needs.

But after a few sessions, I realized I was not being open with him, as I knew I should. I did not want to be faced with what he thought was right for me. He could not convince me that Terry would not mind if I had relations with another man. And I could not make him understand that I was thinking not just of Terry, but of my daughter, as well. I could not be with anyone other than her father, unless I knew our relationship was over, completely.

Again, I decided not to see the psychiatrist anymore, and put that part of my life back in limbo.

ELEVEN

STIGMATA VIII

As in all prisons, information
is both punishment and weapon.
All news is censored; none allowed
at all for weeks, then glimpses
granted of family, friends' concern.
Finally the game apparently
grows tiresome. Without a word,
a radio appears, magazines, even
television, and the world crashes in.
Not the one abandoned—
this is a frantic, changing place.
Wars, disasters, famines are
different, but the same.
What startles are the images
of empty-handed people defying tanks;
of nations by the score
reclaiming freedom; the abrupt
irrelevance of long-held enmities,
old alliances, and once-feared weapons;
of history resuming its
awkward, stumbling climb.

29

Back to the Big City again. On January 27, Mahmoud and another guard came into the cell with some sandwiches, then said, "Terry, eat quickly." I put the sandwich down and said, "What, Mahmoud? I'm ready." They took me upstairs and began wrapping me in the familiar plastic shipping tape. No chance for good-byes. "Am I going in the truck again?" I asked Mahmoud.

"I don't know," he said, giving his usual response to indiscreet questions.

"Well, don't wrap me so tight this time. Last time, I nearly got sick. It's not necessary. I'm not going to get away."

"Okay," he said. In fact, they barely wrapped up my arms and legs, with a couple of halfhearted turns around my blindfold. Then it was into the secret compartment in the truck and off for the three- or four-hour ride to Beirut.

I spent a week in the same apartment we had been in before, but alone this time. The brown stain where I had bashed my head a year or so ago was still there. It was almost a relief being by myself after so long with several other people. I had a few books, and the Bible. No radio, though. Then I was taken out again, without being taped, and dumped into the trunk of a car. I felt a second body being dumped on top of me, and was immediately sure it was Tom. Don't know why. We didn't exchange a word or sig-

303

nal. But I was certain, and correct, as I found out after a short ride.

The two of us were escorted blindfolded into an elevator and up to an apartment, where we were chained side by side to a filing cabinet. The chains were very short—there were only about six inches between our ankles—and one chain ran from my wrist to his ankle and my ankle to his wrist. Seemed a bit excessive, but no point in arguing.

Tom and I spent eight days like that, without magazines or books or anything, barely able to move and unable to turn over, until finally we were moved into a bedroom at the other end of the apartment. The room had been fixed up with steel plates over the windows and iron straps bolted into the walls for our chains.

At least now they've given us some books—a box of paperbacks apparently chosen randomly from a used bookstore. Most were published in the 1950s and early 1960s. They ranged from political textbooks to trashy thrillers. Even a couple of pornographic novels. Worse than that, several are Barbara Cartland romances.

This place is reasonably clean, and the guards seem to be going to some effort not to be offensive or nasty. Maybe they think we'll be going home "soon, and very soon," as Ali puts it. No way to know. Just have to keep on keepin' on, and give it a Ben.

The place isn't too bad, as prisons go. It's a large room, maybe fifteen feet by twenty. Tom and I are chained to opposite sides of the room, just close enough to be able to hand things to each other. The chain arrangement isn't too comfortable—we are each fastened by one wrist to a chain just long enough to allow us to stand up, if we crouch slightly. The room is clean, with one ceiling light, and the guards don't bother us much. They've brought us another box of books, with a promise of more when these are done. Another assortment of used paperbacks, anything from history to the worst kind of pulp fiction.

Still no radio, and no news. There seems to be a lot of shelling going on between East and West Beirut. We're somewhere near the Corniche Mazra, which separates Beirut proper from the southern suburbs, and apparently only a few blocks west of the Green Line, so we get shells quite near fairly frequently. Shakes the walls and knocks dust off the ceiling. Sometimes bits of shrapnel rattle off the steel plates covering the windows.

Had a visit from the subchief we call "Abu Jenzir" (Father of the Chain). He's apparently the man in charge of security, and is really paranoid. Decided we weren't fastened securely enough, and had the guards put another heavy metal staple in the floor between our mattresses, then wound a heavy logging chain through it and fastened each end to our ankles. They put it on only at night, but the damn thing has three-inch links and is just too short to allow us to turn over. That lasted a week or so before even they decided it was ridiculous and took it away.

Tom and I occasionally discuss the books we're reading, but otherwise stay mostly quiet. After several years together, we don't really have much to say anymore, I guess. We seem to be almost in suspended animation, just hanging on, waiting for something, anything, to happen.

We've been here three months now. It's about the middle of April—14 or 15, we think. I'm now well into my fifth year. Still no news. The guards brought in an Arabic newspaper on March 15, my fifth anniversary, with a message from Madeleine in it. Mahmoud translated it for me. "Trust Me" Ali has shown up a couple of times, but says nothing important. The usual crap about "good negotiations," and "something will happen soon." Last time, a few days ago, he said they had decided to end the "hostage problem" before the end of the year. Right.

We're mostly just floating along, trying not to notice the days passing. Had a couple of unpleasant spats with the guards that cost us our books for a few days each time. The first one involved Abu Ali, the one we call "the Mother Hen" because he loves to fuss about, arranging this and that. On our morning toilet trip, he kept the door open while I was trying to take a dump, squatting over the hole in the floor that passes for a toilet in the Middle East. He just lounged in the doorway, chatting with one of the other guards. I got really pissed, and when I'd finished, I began ranting at him. "Do you do this with your father, watch him shit? Would you do this with any man? It's forbidden."

As usual, my anger just sparked his. Only his meant punishment. He cleaned out the room, taking away the books and the small black-and-white TV we were given a while ago (just to watch entertainment shows—news is still forbidden). Also as usual, he calmed down and brought everything back after two days, and now they're all careful to close the door of the bathroom while we're in it. Small victory?

The other problem was more serious. The guards are occasionally careless with the chains, and Tom and I have discovered that quite often, we can slip them off our wrists. Not much point in it—the windows are sealed, and the door is heavily locked. But we still do it from time to time. Unfortunately, one of the guards was apparently peeking through the keyhole in the door the last time I pulled the chain off. Of course, they went bonkers. Came storming in and refastened both our chains even tighter, so they're sometimes painful. Strangely, though, there wasn't any other punishment. I guess they figure we're bound to try to escape.

We both sink into depressions that last for days. I still have to fight not to think about the months and years lost, about Madeleine and Sulome and Gabrielle and the rest of my family. I've become more practiced at pushing such things away, more accepting of the idea that it may still be a long time before this ends. But the fifteen-hundred-plus days are just a massive, horrible weight sitting in my chest. They're always there, and every month, every week, every day adds to the despair trying to overwhelm me.

In the night, when the blackness in my head grows, the only thing that will push it away is prayer. I still have the red Bible, and now we have a French Ecumenical Bible to go with it (as well as an English copy of the Koran). I read Paul frequently. I identify more readily with him now than I did before, when his chauvinism and dictatorial style put me off. He struggles so hard with his weaknesses and pride, as I do. Unlike me, though, he so often reaches into the real nature of Christ, so often and so eloquently expresses his love of God. He has helped me learn to accept, to stop struggling and just wait for whatever God chooses to do with me.

We have a book on prayer written by an English evangelist that is very good. He says that prayer is always answered, that the stricture "Ask and ye shall receive" is meant literally. I don't know about that. I'm not sure anymore that it is even right to ask for anything, except patience and strength to endure whatever comes, and help in understanding.

Sometimes I feel a real joy in prayer, a real understanding of what it means to be loved by God as I am, as I know myself to be—faulted, proud, self-indulgent. Those times ease the pain of this existence so much, give me hope that I can not only stick this out, but perhaps emerge whole and live a better life when it's over.

Prayer doesn't seem to do much for a toothache, though. My teeth have gone bad, and I'm eating Panadol like candy. The guards supply it whenever I ask, but they don't want me keeping any for later. I have to take it when they give it, which means long hours at night or during the day when my teeth start hurting, and before the next guard comes in. Amazing how much misery a simple toothache can bring.

I try to keep my mind occupied. The books are a blessing, even the bad ones. I read each one through quickly twice, then put it aside to reread when I've finished the lot. The guards have been pretty good about keeping us supplied, but since Tom reads much more slowly than I, and we still can't get a new box until the previous one is finished, I end up with days or sometimes a couple of weeks when I've read everything to the point of total boredom.

We have a chess set, but it just sits at the end of my mattress. Tom can't play, and isn't really interested in learning. The television takes up a couple of hours a day, but we have to get the guards to turn it on, and they turn it off again when it's news time in the evening and don't come back in after supper.

Both of us are getting fat. We can't exercise with the short chains, and the food is plentiful, if not often good. Every once in a while they bring in a "broasted" chicken, a specialty of Lebanon that is delicious. Usually, though, it's the old standby—Arabic-bread-and-cheese sandwiches in the morning and evening, rice and garbage for lunch. We fantasize cooking great meals. Actually, all I really long for is a thick, medium-rare steak and a bottle of really good wine. No alcohol for four years! At least I know my liver is pure as snow.

Had a couple of long sessions with "Trust Me" Ali, who has been showing up occasionally lately, trying to persuade him to let us have a radio. Wonder of wonders, finally won! We now have a reasonably new Sony transistor radio, and have been catching up on the world's disasters.

After considerable argument along the old lines of "If you're worried about our mental state, and our hearing bad news, don't. We're big boys. It's worse not knowing what's going on and imagining the worst than it would be to hear any conceivable bad news," Ali said he would go take a *fatwa*. Apparently, he means the same sort of thing Sayeed did with Tom a couple of years ago—choosing a Koranic verse at random, then interpreting it as a yes or no.

Anyway, he came back the next day to say the *fatwa* was negative. I was a bit short with him, saying more or less, "Well, go do it again." Surprisingly, he agreed, then came in with a radio. This time, the Koran said we could have it. Amazing.

First obvious news is that Beirut has gone to shit again. President Amin Gemayel appointed his Army commander, Gen. Michel Aoun (a Christian), acting prime minister when his term ended in 1988. The Muslims in West Beirut refused to accept it because the prime minister is supposed to be a Sunni Muslim. The country has had two governments ever since, neither of them effective. Aoun, in a fit of egomania, has announced he's going to drive Syria out of Lebanon. He's instituted a blockade of West Beirut, and there is all kinds of fighting between the two sides. That's what all the shelling we've been hearing is about. There's been a cease-fire, but like all cease-fires in Lebanon, it's frequently broken.

Nothing on about the hostages. We seem to be in limbo again as far as the world is concerned.

At least we know the date: April 1, 1989. 1,477 days.

30

Larry Heinzerling had been summoned without explanation. From the large corner office of Lou Boccardi, president of The Associated Press, you could see ice skaters seven floors below, bobbing, weaving, and dancing to music you could not hear. The soundless winter scene in Rockefeller Center made Heinzerling smile.

Boccardi, a small, neat man with a friendly manner and a touch, efficient mind, waved Heinzerling to a chair. As always, he was direct. "I want you to take over the Terry Anderson case starting today. Go to Washington next week for the anniversary ceremonies, and then let's see where we go from there."

The AP, and Boccardi, had come under considerable criticism from colleagues and even those within the company—the world's largest news organization—for its efforts on Anderson's behalf. Since those efforts had been made without fanfare or publicity, many thought The AP had not done enough.

Boccardi and other AP executives had over the past four years met with countless American and foreign officials, including Lt. Col. Oliver North and Anglican church envoy Terry Waite, now a hostage himself. It had fully financed and supported the varied activities of Peggy Say. It had supported and watched over both Anderson families—in Japan and Cyprus.

Now the fourth anniversary of Anderson's kidnapping

310

was upon them, each passing day an agony to family, friends, and colleagues. And he was no closer to freedom than he was the Saturday he was seized in Beirut.

It was now more than two years after North's 1986 arms-for-hostages debacle, about which The AP was kept in the dark, and all government attempts at finding a solution remained frozen. In Washington, you could not even discuss hostages or Iran and use the word *negotiation* in the same breath. The subject had been banned by the incoming Bush administration, still groping to find its way through the corridors of power.

Boccardi, in one of his frequent reports on the situation to The AP's board of directors, wrote: "Policy seems locked in the we-don't-negotiate-with-terrorists mode and, so far as we can see, little distinction is made between contact and concession. . . . We will press forward, as we must, but this is a grim situation."

Heinzerling's new assignment was a tough one, even for the former foreign correspondent and top executive. It was full-time and open-ended: he was to pursue every avenue, public and private, official and unofficial, at home and abroad in pursuit of Anderson's freedom. He had carte blanche. There were only three rules: First, he would be officially cut off from all AP editorial staffers, and could not discuss his work with anyone but Boccardi. Second, the AP would offer no ransom, and he should never leave the impression it would. Third, he could meet anyone, anywhere, at any time, but would keep forever every confidence he agreed to.

Boccardi did not discuss either the pressures he was under or the personal pain he felt over Anderson. Both he and Heinzerling had talked with him at the bureau chiefs meeting in 1985 in Cairo, just days before Anderson was snatched. Anderson had, in fact, pushed strongly for Heinzerling to go back to Beirut with him. Boccardi had vetoed it.

The AP president was adamant that The AP avoid any action that could endanger Anderson or prolong his captivity. But The AP also had to keep its most precious asset: its reputation for covering the news fully and objectively. There could be not the slightest indication that The AP could be manipulated or influenced by the fact that one of its men was held hostage.

Nor could the agency take a position, pro or con, on any government policy or lack of it. The AP had never in 140 years taken an editorial position on anything.

"We cannot let this destroy The AP's institutional value," Boccardi told Heinzerling. "As terrible as his suffering is, Terry would not want that."

As Heinzerling walked out of the corner office, he thought of the price The AP had often paid for its coverage: John Mulroy, blown up with 258 others, including his son, sister, and three other family members, aboard Pan Am 103; Natasha Simpson, eleven-year-old daughter of Rome News Editor Victor Simpson, murdered at Rome's airport by Abu Nidal's gunmen just a year after Anderson was taken; Mike Goldsmith, beaten unconscious by the self-proclaimed emperor of the Central African Empire, Jean Bedel Bokassa; Aly Mahmoud, who had worked for Terry in Bahrain, and who had spent years in prison under Nasser on spurious charges of spying for Israel. Even back to Bill Oatis, imprisoned in communist Czechoslovakia in 1951 after a show trial for espionage.

Heinzerling's father, Lynn, also an AP correspondent, had been assigned to track down another missing AP man, Joe Morton, in Slovakia during World War II. Morton, it was learned, had been tortured and shot in the head by the Germans.

"Lord, please," Heinzerling thought. "Don't give me a corpse to bring home."

Within The AP, Anderson's suffering cast shadows everywhere. His closest friends and colleagues were fully aware that Anderson's fate could have been their own. Some lashed out. Don Mell, deeply troubled and still suffering from the shock of having his friend and boss taken before his eyes, complained bitterly in an op-ed article in

The New York Times that "Terry Anderson has been forgotten by his country and abandoned by his profession." It must have seemed so to Mell.

"We take some shots about what has or hasn't been done on [Terry's] behalf, and there is not much that we can do about that," Boccardi reported to The AP board of directors. "The frustration that Terry's family and friends and colleagues feel is understandable. We all feel it. But we continue to pursue contacts of all sorts, some savory and some less so, and we do all that while wary that some efforts, however well intentioned, might backfire."

Everyone felt it. There was an uncontrollable need to do something, do anything, which fed itself, gnawed at you, even if the evidence showed there was nothing to be done now, in this set of circumstances, in this political framework, under these prevailing conditions. Conditions needed to be changed.

As Heinzerling went about his part of the crusade, clocking tens of thousands of miles on airplanes, meeting in bizarre places with mysterious and sometimes scary people, he would cross paths often with another man on a very similar mission—changing the conditions.

Giandomenico Picco, the six-foot-six, suave, and handsome Italian deputy to UN Secretary-General Javier Pérez du Cuéllar, was personally responsible for saving more lives than could be counted. He had managed to negotiate a lasting cease-fire in the seemingly endless war in Afghanistan, then immediately moved on to one even more intractable: Iran-Iraq. There also, he was finally successful, almost single-handedly working out the terms of the cease-fire that ended the eight-year-old conflict. A million Iranians and Iraqis had died already. How many more would have if the fighting had continued?

Picco had watched from afar the mess that was Iran-Contra. He had raised the subject of the Western hostages several times during his trips to Tehran in connection with the Iran-Iraq war. Always, he had been rebuffed. It was not yet time.

He did not give up, asking again and again, as his work built up a store of goodwill and respect in the Iranian capital. Finally, the break came.

In Washington, President Bush had publicly indicated his willingness to come to some accommodation with Tehran. "Goodwill begets goodwill," he said in his January 1989 inauguration speech. It was a clear call for the Iranians to offer something.

In yet another meeting in Tehran, Picco found a high official who was willing to discuss the question of the hostages. Officially, the position was unchanged: "This is not our responsibility. We have nothing to do with it." But the very fact that someone so high was even willing to dedicate an official meeting to the subject was enough for the veteran diplomat. The Iranians were ready to play.

Picco began his odyssey. He had nothing to offer anyone, other than his reputation, his skill, and his patience. He knew there would be no deal, as such, because the Americans would in no way make any kind of payoff. He also knew the process would be difficult, painstaking, and dangerous. But he was absolutely determined that it would succeed.

"There was never, ever a moment when I was prepared to fail," Picco said in 1993. "I said to myself, whatever happens, this thing has got to work. Even if everybody in the world betrays you, if everybody double-crosses you. And I mean everybody.

"So when difficulties came, I kept going like a train."

31

GENEVA. MARCH 1989.

Heinzerling's first foray into the real world of secrets took place on familiar territory. He had been raised in Geneva as a child, spending ten years there while his father was the AP chief of bureau. But the atmosphere was something else. A contact in the United States, a familiar figure in intelligence circles with influential links in Iran and Lebanon, had set up a meeting. The contact had given Heinzerling his picture as a "passport," telling him to present the wallet-size photo to a man who would contact him at a hotel in Geneva.

Tired and bleary-eyed from the transatlantic flight, mouth dry from tension and too many cigarettes, Heinzerling checked in and unpacked in his fifth-floor room. At the appointed time, he phoned his contact in the United States to report his arrival, using, as instructed, no names.

Five minutes later, the phone rang. A guttural voice with a heavy Middle Eastern accent said, "Can I come?"

Heinzerling left the room door ajar and waited. His visitor knocked, pushed the door open, entered, closed and locked the door and put the chain on, then walked toward him with an outstretched hand.

He resembled many of the young Lebanese gunmen in the TV news reports out of Beirut—designer jeans, a zipper jacket of dark brown leather, and a gaudy gold necklace. Below a mop of windblown black hair, his young but lined face showed both hardship and competence. But in his eyes, amazingly, was fear.

Heinzerling realized the young man was as nervous as he was. Both men sat.

"How can I help you? You want contact in Lebanon?" the visitor asked without further preliminaries.

"I think I should show you this first," Heinzerling ventured, taking the photo from his wallet.

"Ah, yes," the young man said, smiling. He recognized the face, and knew he had slipped. "You are welcome."

For two hours, they discussed in French the hostages, the demands of the kidnappers, the political and diplomatic deadlock between the United States and Iran, the role of Syria in Lebanon. Ransom, of course, came up, and Heinzerling expressed The AP's refusal to pay. Despite explanations, the young Lebanese believed the wire service to be some kind of intelligence arm of the U.S. government.

In the end, he proposed an intriguing idea. "You know Imam Moussa Sadr?" he asked, referring to the supreme and charismatic leader of Lebanon's Shiites, who had mysteriously disappeared without trace during a visit to Libya in 1978. It was assumed he had been assassinated on orders of Moammar Kadafy. "If your government can provide a report proving his death, it would be very powerful. Such an influence can be used to help Mr. Terry. It would have great impact in Lebanon."

And, Heinzerling thought, in Iran, which had been accused by some Shiites of failing to take the disappearance as seriously as it should.

The young man wanted travel money for a trip to Beirut and Tehran, as well as support from The AP to renew his Swiss work permit. Heinzerling had been drilled by experts: accept no claim by anyone who could not first prove access to the hostages with some sort of "sign of life." He asked the man first to deliver a letter to Terry and get a response. If it was forthcoming, they could talk further.

Two days later, intelligence sources in two European capitals confirmed that the man did indeed have high-level contacts in Tehran and "worked in Hezbollah circles." He had, in fact, contributed to providing a "sign of life" from one of the German hostages held in Lebanon. But others warned Heinzerling the man had a reputation as an intelligence peddler, who obtained information from one source and exchanged it for other information from another source, extracting payment each step of the way.

In this case, it didn't work. Heinzerling never heard of him again, and Anderson never received the letter. It was far from the last time such a contact, potentially promising, would evaporate into thin air.

Others were having more success, if sporadically. The Swiss government and the International Red Cross in Geneva were deeply involved in a highly secret initiative that apparently had been the key to the release of Polhill and Reed. No one knew exactly what the arrangements were, but both releases were "one-offs," with no real process established toward ending the whole problem. It was believed Reed and Polhill were chosen because both were sick. Polhill was diagnosed with throat cancer after his release, lost his voice, and had to have an electronic "voice box" installed in his throat. Reed's mental condition had worsened, until he believed he was having conversations with U.S. embassy officials in Beirut via a radio in his head.

The two releases involved more-or-less straight swaps of hostages for Lebanese held in the Israeli-controlled Khiam prison in southern Lebanon. At the same time, the process of negotiations over Iranian money held by the United States continued at The Hague. Neither party would admit any connection between those talks and the hostages. Certainly success, and the release of large sums by the Americans to the Iranians, helped the atmosphere a great deal.

At the United Nations, Picco was still involved in trying to put together a package that would provide the "global solution" everyone was looking for—release of *all* the hostages. The Swiss process was not good enough. "That was not a solution," Picco insisted later. "At that pace, it could have gone on for ten years." He wanted everyone out in months.

The aim was ambitious to the point of ridiculousness. He still had nothing much to give anyone. The Americans were now interested, but completely unwilling to consider any deal and still scared to death of any breath of the word *negotiation*.

"You have to understand, if you are in the decision making of the American government, and you touch this issue, the first thing you think as a politician is, I can get hurt right, left, and center if I don't play it right," Picco pointed out. "So the best approach is to do as little as possible, to say almost nothing, and to leave no trace of anything, even a conversation."

The Iranian government apparently wanted to end the whole episode, but did not have complete control over its own radicals, let alone the fundamentalists in Lebanon.

What Picco did have that no one else had was his reputation for total honesty; complete stubbornness; a negotiating ability honed in Cyprus, Afghanistan, and the Middle East; and a boss who was willing to take his lead on this subject. Secretary-General Pérez de Cuéllar allowed Picco to go where and when he needed to, and questioned him little, waiting patiently for briefings. He made the phone calls or initiated the conversations Picco suggested, and kept the sprawling UN bureaucracy off his assistant's back.

It would be more than a year after that first, faint indication of interest in Tehran before this most discreet and anonymous of UN officials was ready to take his plan where it would finally have to be presented—an anonymous apartment in the southern suburbs of Beirut.

MADELEINE

LARNACA, CYPRUS. MAY 1989.

Terry's fifth year in captivity began without any news from the captors or the U.S. government. Nor from any of the private initiatives I knew about that were at work for Terry and the other hostages.

Ray Barnett, the clergyman from Vancouver who headed Friends in the West, had been working on projects to aid the poor Shiites in Lebanon. He was in contact with several leaders in Hezbollah, believed to be the real parent of Islamic Jihad.

Ray came to Cyprus several times while on his way to and from Lebanon. Each time, he told me whatever he could about what his contacts were saying. His sources seemed to be good, close to the people who held the Western hostages.

Ray's work in helping the poor, especially the orphans and children of Lebanon, gave me hope and helped me to put my anger aside, to appreciate the price some of my own people were paying for the crimes of others, especially the crime of hostage taking.

But during this period, even Ray had nothing to tell me. Although he never stopped trying, he could get nowhere.

During the summer, Ray called from Seattle and asked me to call his contact in Beirut to pass on a message. It was difficult for him to get through to Lebanon then.

I was to ask the contact for any news, and also about a shipment of powdered milk Ray had sent to an orphanage in southern Lebanon.

I never questioned Ray about his actions or requests. But I was frightened. As the phone rang and a man's voice answered, I thought my heart would stop.

"Hello," I managed, knowing I sounded scared. "Is Dr.

Fadlallah there, please?" I didn't know if it was a code name or not.

"Speaking," the man answered with a very soft voice in a southern Lebanese accent. I gave my first name, and said I was calling on behalf of Ray Barnett.

He paused for a second. "Where are you calling from, miss?"

"Cyprus." Then I relayed the message. He hesitated at my request for news for Ray. His caution indicated to me that he had something to conceal, and that meant he was in some way connected with the hostages.

"Mr. Ray will be welcome anytime he comes," he said. "The milk shipment has arrived, and we are very grateful to him. Only, for his information, and I repeat we are very grateful for his efforts in helping our orphans, but the powdered milk was the wrong kind and cannot be consumed by the children."

I don't know why his statement frightened me. I felt I should make excuses for Ray. My main thought was, How is this going to affect Terry?

He continued in his soft voice. "The news is good, tell Mr. Ray. And I will be waiting for him here."

Is the good news about Terry? I wondered as the conversation came to a polite end. I waited for Ray's arrival, but he didn't show up. Plans had changed. Just another false hope, another plan unfulfilled. I was used to it by now.

It was early May when the news came of Ayatollah Khomeini's deteriorating health. I remembered that someone had said a long time ago that Khomeini was still young in his family, whose members often lived to 110 or 115. Still hating and blaming him for our suffering, I couldn't believe he would ever die. Cassandra asked once if I would ever forgive him for what he did to us. "Never," I replied.

As I was going to bed on June 1, something prompted me to pray for Khomeini. I was feeling sad, and yet my heart was open to forgiveness. Two days later, he died, and his legacy died with him. Watching the chaotic burial march, how the millions of people tried to touch his body and even take a piece of his burial robe, almost pulling the body from the coffin, I was glad I had prayed for him. The disrespect his people showed him in the name of love at his death was enough revenge for his cruelty in life.

32

BEIRUT. JUNE 1989.

Whatever progress is being made in the negotiations, as Ali insists there is, it hasn't stopped these people from adding to their stock. Another Briton, an old man named Jackie Mann, has been kidnapped on the street in Beirut. Not a good sign for us (and, of course, not good for Mr. Mann, either).

Khomeini has died in Iran. Saw incredible scenes on the television of huge mobs weeping and wailing and beating their heads. Our guards haven't reacted much at all.

Never have really understood how this old man was able to keep such a complete grip on Iran. I've read quite a bit about him, and know he is rated as a brilliant Islamic scholar. To me, he's just full of hatred and venom. Well, we've already spent several hours speculating on whether his death will mean any major changes in Iran, and any hope for us. Probably not. But we can hope.

We're getting lots of books these days—boxes full. It's still a pretty mixed bag, trash and good stuff. The list we gave them of books we'd like has evaporated into thin air. But at least we have plenty to read. And plenty of time to do it.

We've gone into a long spell of hardly saying a word all day. Every once in a while, Tom or I (usually I) read aloud something from one of the paperbacks.

I watch television quite a bit. Tom's eyes are too bad to

see very well, and he doesn't like TV, anyway. Neither do I, but there isn't much else.

Hard to keep cheerful as the weeks pile up.

Bad few days. Lost the radio for about four days after Colonel Higgins, an American member of the UN observer force, was hung. That came in retaliation, the killers said, for the kidnapping by Israel of Sheikh Abdul-Karim Obeid, a Hezbollah leader in southern Lebanon.

Tom and I were watching TV when a news clip came on reporting Higgins's murder. It showed what appeared to be his body hanging with a rope around the neck. A few minutes later, the guards rushed in and disconnected the TV, taking both it and the radio. We tried to tell them it was too late, that we'd already seen the part that they were trying to hide. No dice.

Four days later, and after much argument, they brought the radio and TV back in, without comment. That's when we learned that Higgins's killers, something called the Organization for the Oppressed on Earth, had also threatened to murder Joe Cicippio, and possibly others, but had decided not to after a storm of international protest.

Israel has openly said it kidnapped Obeid from his home in southern Lebanon in an effort to get back its own men, held in Lebanon by Hezbollah or missing.

I'm not at all sure Higgins was actually hung. I remember that our hosts had claimed to have executed William Buckley after he died of illness. Just trying to make use of the death. Suspect the same may be true this time. Such hostages are just too valuable to execute. There have been some newspaper reports speculating that Higgins may have died, then been hung for propaganda.

Our hosts have issued another statement demanding the release of their friends in Kuwaiti jails. As usual, this one was accompanied by a photograph of me. Looked like one taken last year. The usual response from Washington: "We will not negotiate with kidnappers."

* * *

Three months with little news, then an avalanche of messages. It's my birthday, October 27, and I've watched tapes of messages from my family on five channels, at least twice each. Saw Sulome, but not Madeleine, though her voice was there with a beautiful message of love. Heard Peg, and people in New York and Washington, telling me of their support. An incredible day!

SIS

Sister mine, you mock me,
jumping from your ordered place
in my mind's gallery.
It was a good place,
honored, near the door:
Big Sister, cherished,
no longer young and flighty
but mature, reliable—Good Old Sis.
Now this metamorphosis.
I watch your grave gavotte
across the world's stage,
at ease among the mighty.
This sudden weight, this *gravitas*
should not so much surprise—
your mind and heart were always there.
But love's assumptions, carelessness,
and distance blurred my eyes.
Now what do I do?
Where can I place this larger you
among the niches in my mind?
I'm middle-aged, there's no more room;
my head's already overcrowded
and I find myself less comfortable
with much that's new.
Perhaps instead I'll leave you free,
try keeping up with all your changes.

It's harder, but anyway I know
you'll not be caught and framed again.

Heard on the radio that the United States has agreed to release over half a billion dollars in Iranian money. Can't help going at least some way toward persuading the Iranians to get us released. Though it may not be enough. I don't think Iran has total control over this. Sure, they pay Hezbollah militiamen, and have influence. But probably not control.

Christmas Day again. My fifth in captivity. Both Tom and I heard brief messages from our families and friends on the radio and television. There are, it appears, committees of people working for both of us—Friends of Tom Sutherland in Iowa and Colorado, and the Journalists' Committee to Free Terry Anderson in New York and Washington. That cheered Tom up a bit, to hear how many people are trying to do something for him.

So much for the promises by Islamic Jihad, which our guards echoed, that we would be out of here by the end of the year. Hard to swallow, even though we tried hard not to get our hopes up.

Got another message. Ali brought in an *As-Safir* with a copy of a letter in both Arabic and English from Peg and Bill Foley, the former AP photographer who worked with me in Beirut. It was on behalf of the journalists' committee. No hard news, just hopes for an end to all this.

There's been a flurry of hostage stuff on the radio and television over the past two months, all hopeful again. For the first time, the Tehran *Times*, an English-language newspaper said to be a mouthpiece for Iranian President Rafsanjani, called for the unconditional release of all hostages in Beirut. "Maybe 1990 will be the year for the release of all the hostages," the paper said. Good development, except for the *maybe*, though once again Tom is dismayed by the mention of 1990. To tell the truth, it shakes me to think it may be the end of this year before we're out.

Even Sheikh Fadlallah, the one identified commonly as "spiritual leader of Hezbollah," is calling again for our release. The news said he just got back from a visit to Tehran. Maybe he got his marching orders?

Another month of near-constant hints and signals, but no real action. An emotional rush at each new report: Rafsanjani saying the "hostage problem" is nearly solved (I remember the Hajj said in June 1985, "Your situation is nearly cooked"); his brother meeting in Damascus with the Syrian foreign minister to "coordinate efforts to gain the release of all hostages"; Hussein Mussawi hoping for an "early release"; Fadlallah noting "encouraging signs"; many others. Back down on the roller coaster at the countering signals from hard-liners: Mohtashemi, leading opponent of Rafsanjani, in Tehran saying we are all spies and will not be released; a statement from the Revolutionary Justice Organization, which holds Cicippio and Edward Tracy, saying they had no intention of releasing anyone; Islamic Jihad for the Liberation of Palestine issuing another threat to kill Polhill, Alan Steen, and Jesse Turner if four hundred Arabs are not released from Israeli jails; Iran's Parliament voting that the Iranian government should not get involved in negotiations about hostages, since it was up to the Lebanese.

How are we supposed to sort all this crap out? Obviously something is going on, but equally obviously there are a lot of factions here and in Iran that do not want us released. I remember Gary Sick's book about the Iran embassy hostages in 1979. The former adviser to Jimmy Carter said the 444-day captivity of American diplomats was a result more of Iranian domestic politics than of any international conflict. Sounds as if that's a major factor here. If so, God help us.

At least, we know where we are now. Woke up to a hail of AK-47 fire outside the building this morning. Bullets were even dinging off the metal plate that covers the window on the west side. It lasted only a few minutes, but we heard just an hour later on the radio that Syrian soldiers had gotten into a gunfight with the bodyguards of Sheikh Subhi Tewfali, secretary-general of Hezbollah, just outside Tewfali's headquarters in the southern suburbs of Beirut. Since that was the only gunfight reported today, we are quite obviously being held by Tewfali. So much for Hezbollah's denial that they have anything to do with Islamic Jihad. Of course, we never believed the denials, and I don't think anyone else did, either.

Ali came by again for a rather peculiar visit. He had with him an Arabic translation of part of Robert Fisk's new book about Lebanon, *Pity the Nation*. It's being serialized in one of Beirut's newspapers. Ali said it was a good book, but the strange thing was he read a portion that had to do with me. Fisk related an incident in 1983 when we met the commander of the small British contingent in the Multinational Force at the Commodore Hotel. This guy, a brigadier, was a nut case. Went on and on about charging up into the hills around Beirut to teach them a lesson up there. Then he started talking about them as "niggers." I interrupted, saying, "We don't use words like that." He just looked at me, then spat. "They're black and have curly hair. I call 'em niggers." I got pissed off and walked out.

Ali interpreted that as testimony to my character in some way. "Maybe you are a good man, after all, Mr. Terry," he told me. Thanks. However, he said he couldn't get an English copy of Fisk's book for me to read. Too bad. It's bound to be excellent. Fisk is brilliant, probably the best foreign correspondent I've ever come across. I remember arguing with him about this book on several occasions as we sat on my balcony. He didn't want to start another so soon after finishing his opus on Ireland in World War II. I insisted he had to write it, that he knew Lebanon better than any other correspondent, and had a better, more vivid, and different view than anyone else.

* * *

More insanity among the Lebanese. General Aoun, in the midst of his "War of Liberation" against the Syrians and the rival Muslim government of Lebanon, has suddenly launched into a vicious war against his erstwhile allies, the Lebanese Forces Christian militia. Aoun's regular Army forces and the militiamen, who are organized and armed as well as the Army, have been bashing each other all over East Beirut, and destroying much of the city along the way. I think Aoun has gone completely off his rocker.

Still a lot of hints and rumors on the hostages. Ali keeps telling us that "the negotiate is good, and very good," and maybe it's not entirely lies.

It's all very confusing, but it seems obvious something is stirring, and Tom and I can't help feeling hopeful, though Tom is depressed at the idea it might take until the end of the year. I don't know what to think. I'm still just trying to chug along, keep things even, and not get on the roller coaster again.

It's April 1, 1990. I just finished my fifth year. 1,841 days.

33

BEIRUT. APRIL 1990.

Islamic Jihad for the Liberation of Palestine says it will free one hostage within forty-eight hours. The statement just came on the radio. IJ-for-LP is the group that has claimed to hold the Beirut University College professors. Four were taken originally, but the Indian with a U.S. green card was released last year. That leaves Jesse Turner, Robert Polhill, and Alan Steen. No indication who it might be. We've never come across any of them in our various prisons, at least not knowingly. The group says it is bowing to the wishes of the Iranians and Syrians, and making a "humanitarian gesture."

Cheerful news, even though it doesn't involve us. Every release brings us one closer to our own. Can't suppress the jealousy, though. I lie here imagining what it will be like for the one released. What does it feel like? What emotions take hold of you when they lift the blindfold, when you see your loved ones for the first time in years, and can actually touch and hold and kiss them? What will it be like to lie down next to Madeleine, and hold her, and be held?

I've heard several statements from Peg, even seen her at news conferences a couple of times. Nothing from Madeleine. And Tom has not seen or heard anything from Jean. Worries him sometimes. I know he's still sensitive about the fact that in most reports, my name is mentioned most prominently, and his seldom. I've tried to tell him it doesn't mean anything, but I understand why he feels slighted.

329

* * *

It was Polhill, and before he even finished his statement on arrival at the White House, Frank Reed was on his way to Damascus, and freedom! Things are definitely cooking. Looks like the various factions are taking turns.

Polhill has cancer of the throat, according to the news from his first medical. But he looked very cheerful on the television. Good coverage on the Lebanese channels, mostly from CNN.

Reed looked much worse at his press conference in Damascus. Hung his head and mumbled, didn't ever look anyone in the eye. The man must have had another breakdown. He's been alone for the past year, and if the past is any indication, he was probably badly treated by the guards.

Can't get too buoyed up, though. Don't dare. Past releases have been followed by months and years of nothing. But with these releases, and Iran saying publicly it will be all over by the end of the year, it looks very, very good!

Lots of news, but no action for a month now. Bush has promised to help find out what happened to four Iranians who disappeared in Beirut in 1982—one of the demands Tehran has been making. I could tell him. I was in Beirut when they got picked up by the Phalangists at the Green Line. All information then was that they were immediately shot and buried. Anyway, it's a gesture.

There have also been reports that Iran and the United States are making progress in talks over the return of more than ten billion dollars Iran claims the U.S. government has been holding.

All good, but we're still chained to the wall in this damned room. Tom and I just get through the days, reading and occasionally talking. I watch television a lot— American movies and situation comedies, French entertainment programs. There are now only three channels still on the air, instead of the six we could watch a few months ago. Obviously, the continued fighting between Aoun and the Lebanese Force has taken its toll. The destruction we see in news reports is enormous, and this time almost totally in East Beirut. The Christian side of the city got through the 1982 invasion and the subsequent fighting with very little damage. Now the Christians are doing it to themselves.

I pray a great deal, mostly at night, and read the Bible, in English or French. It helps keep me calm, and able to accept whatever happens. We've also collected another translation of the Koran. It isn't very good. Tom is quite disdainful, even bitingly sarcastic, about it. Can't make his way past the verbiage and unfamiliar style to the real content. I've got a better translation at home, and know how poetic and beautiful the words can be made, and how very similar to Christianity the themes and moral lessons are.

I still don't know how I'm going to straighten my life out when this ends, how I can bring myself more into harmony with my Christianity. I only know I have to, and somehow will. I don't expect to suddenly become an angel. I'm too old and stubborn and proud for that. But I do want to be a better man, and have come to feel strongly that the only way I can do that is with God's help. I am a Catholic. I know that. And I know there is a great conflict between what I have to do and the teachings of the church. I have to complete my divorce, if it isn't done, and I don't think it is. I have to marry Madeleine. No, not have to. Need to. Absolutely. I know it's possible that she won't want to marry me. Five and a half years is so long. She may have met someone else. If so, I don't know what will happen to me. Of course, I'll bow out. But she's so much at the center of me, so basic a part the world for me, I can't really think of not being with her.

Tom and I talk sometimes about what we're going to do when this is over. Take a long vacation, certainly. Maybe in the Caribbean, or somewhere else warm and sunny. I dream of taking a canoe and paddling up the east side of Lake Champlain, camping with Madeleine and Sulome each night. I remember how beautiful it was.

Tom worries constantly about getting a job, saying he's

too old for anyone to want him. I argue that he'll have more offers than he can handle and that, anyway, he has his retirement from Colorado State and doesn't have to work at anything he doesn't want to.

As for me, it's likely I'll be broke, but that doesn't worry me. Madeleine and I are both intelligent, competent, and willing to work hard. We'll get along. Money has never been important to me. Nice, but not important. Undoubtedly why I handle it so badly. Don't know what I'll do for a living, though. I alternate between thinking of working out possible posts with The AP, and thinking of dumping journalism altogether. Though I've enjoyed it very much, and it's been exciting, somehow it doesn't seem like enough anymore. I think I'd like to be something more than just a watcher.

SKIMMING

We skim the world, alighting
here and there to taste a war,
disaster, famine; sip at people's pain,
or all too seldom, happiness,
looking for rare vintages,
then resume erratic flight,
like careless bees, or some would say
a swarm of banded, garish wasps.
Unlike those insects, though,
we're aware at least in theory
that the aim of our flirtation
with the flowers of good and evil
is not our satisfaction,
or the sting we carry,
but the pollen that we spread.
Often we forget, become intoxicated
with our venom, hypnotized by flight itself.
It isn't all our fault—
even fine wine palls

with too much drinking,
and rather than the inoffensive dust
that sticks to bees,
our burdens sometimes scar our souls.
What stings us more, though,
than accumulated pain of others' wounds
is we know that we're just watching,
while it's they who live.

I know now that I'm likely to be the last one released, or next to last if Islamic Jihad thinks Terry Waite is more important. Don't like it, but can't do anything about it. Somebody has to be last, and I got the short straw, it looks like. Asked Ali about it, and the way he hemmed and hawed only confirmed my belief. Whether that's a result of the campaign on my behalf, or because I'm a journalist, or because I have managed to stay healthy physically and mentally so they think I can last longer, or some other reason, there's no way to tell, and it doesn't matter, anyway. It's just the way it is.

Just keep plugging along, until The Day.

TWELVE

STIGMATA IX

Companions leave; new friends
arrive only to go home in turn,
stirring hope, envy, and frustration.
Negotiations start, stumble,
stop, and start again
as each participant gropes
and grasps for small advantages.
But slowly, it becomes apparent
that the roller coaster ride
has neared its end.
Soon it will be time to
leave this unamusement park.
What of the man who will emerge,
pale, shocked by the images
cast from distorted mirrors?
Better, or worse?
Or like the world
that greets him,
unchanged in essence,
but shaken into new relations
with himself, and others?

34

MADELEINE

**NICOSIA, CYPRUS.
JUNE 1989–JUNE 1990.**

*Sulome turned four years old on June 7, 1989. As usual, we
made a videotape to send to Beirut television stations in the
hope they would broadcast it and Terry might see it. She
seemed to change from day to day—so small, always bringing happiness to my heart, but making me feel a hundred
years older. At school, her nickname was "Fidget-bottom."
My mother said she was "like a bird in heaven," because
she never just walked, but seemed to hop everywhere, like
a bird. Now that she could talk and understand so much
more than when she was smaller, our relations were more
interesting. Her questions about her daddy were more penetrating, and I could only answer with the truth. She often
cried after I talked about him, but the tears were always
followed by smiles and hugs, as if she was thanking me for
making her understand. She gave me strength, and the assurance that at least with her, I had not failed.*

*With my family visiting from Lebanon for another sum-
mer, life became a routine—and, strangely, a happy one. It
had taken much time to build the shell around us, and we
had become accustomed to the way we were living. It was
a prison of my own making, and it also gave me strength.
I occupied myself with trying to analyze over and over the
situation we were all in. I had started a diary when Terry
was first kidnapped, but stopped writing in it. The longer
he was gone, the less need I had for it. I was going to*

337

church regularly now, and joined several women's groups and a Bible study class.

I knew from the released hostages and from other sources in Lebanon that Terry was doing well. I would sit for hours and analyze him and what he could be going through. I hoped he was also drawing strength from his experience, and hoped he had become a "professional" hostage. I believed that if you have to do something, you had better do it well, or you will always be the loser. Terry had to be there, and I had to be here. We could grow only by being strong.

October 27, 1989. Terry's forty-second birthday, and another year gone from his life. The only news we had had was a year-old picture sent by his captors, along with a demand for the release of their comrades jailed in Kuwait.

As we had done the year before, Sulome and I went to the mountains for a picnic alone, to celebrate Terry's birthday under the same tree, and carve the date in its trunk. Again we taped a happy birthday message for him before we left and sent it to the Lebanese TV stations.

The year ended for us with nothing but silence, fear of the unknown, hope that 1990 would end our imprisonment, and more violence in Lebanon. The newly elected president, Rene Muawad, was murdered just days after he was elected. Another president was chosen immediately, as the country fought to find its way to a semblance of normality.

In February 1990, the first positive news in a long time began coming out of Iran. Clergymen there and in Lebanon were saying that the hostage problem would be solved before the end of the year. Radical fundamentalist leaders who before had opposed releasing the hostages began saying the same thing. For me, the rumors had ceased to raise my hopes or cause me to change my daily routine. They were a nuisance, a source of depression. I convinced myself I would react only when I saw Terry face-to-face. My family also tried to tell me that the word in Beirut, among the Shiites who claimed to have contacts inside Hezbollah, was that the end was nearing. I asked them not to mention the subject to me because it just made me feel worse.

Sulome fell sick with pneumonia again, just as she had at the same time last year, and just as seriously. This time, I was more experienced, but it was still frightening to see her like this. Again, like last year, as she got better, I fell very sick and was in bed for nearly a week. Those were very hard times, which I don't want to remember.

Larry Heinzerling was also encouraged by the information he was receiving. Larry helped me keep my sanity with his persistent kindness. By now, I learned later, he had full knowledge of the negotiations and arrangements for release of all the hostages. But he called me only when he was absolutely sure of what he was telling me. I was very grateful to him, and to Carolyn Turolla, the other AP executive concerned with Terry. She also never stopped calling to keep me up to date with Terry's family and with all the efforts going on for him in the States.

Many, many people whom we did not know took us into their hearts and sent us letters. Many also sent Sulome presents each Christmas and on her birthdays. When executives of the Mattel Company saw Sulome on television saying she was hoping for a Barbie house for her birthday, they called The AP, got our address, and sent her a Barbie van. These people touched my heart and made me feel that we were not alone in this.

The support the American people were giving the hostages in prayer and in public events was sowing seeds of change. The hostage saga was beginning to turn against those who caused it. The radical fundamentalists in Iran who sponsored and encouraged the kidnappers were in trouble with the new regime of President Rafsanjani and were losing their power. The president's brother, Mahmoud Rafsanjani, was shuttling from Iran to Lebanon to Syria almost every week in an effort to get the hostages released, and to exert control over the Shiite community in Lebanon. The Lebanese civil war was ending, and the government was regaining some small measure of sovereignty.

In March of 1990, as Terry entered his sixth year in captivity, I was for the first time holding high hopes that the year would be the last. The dream was finally coming true. I started speculating on possible dates for his release. I knew, as everyone did, that the kidnappers would have to find some way to save face.

I also began taking care of myself a little. Although I knew Terry liked my hair long, I decided to cut it, to look fresh and new and young when he came home. I bought some new clothes, and started going again to an aerobics class.

Although the fear of disappointment haunted me, I had to do these things for my own sanity. I had neglected myself. When I thought now of some of the things I had done, I realized I was on the edge of losing my mind. One summer, I had decided I would only wash my hair, but never comb it. I just left it tangled for five months. The need to run away from reality was enormous. Several times, I had thought of just leaving, going somewhere no one could find us and starting a new life. I was trying to convince myself that if I went away, the problem would go away, too. Sometimes I believed I was crazy to wait for Terry, that he might not even want to continue his life with me. After all, he had never really mentioned me in any of the videotapes they had let him make. He mentioned only his daughters. I had heard from the men who were with him about his love for me and his desire to continue what we had started. What if they were wrong? Or did not want to hurt me by telling me something else?

At the bottom, I just was determined to look my best when he came home. I had learned that what was not mine I did not need. All I wanted was for him to come home. Let what happens happen.

On April 22, 1990, Robert Polhill was released. Eight days later, it was Frank Reed who went free. It felt for everyone like the beginning of the end, a happy ending. Journalists converged on Larnaca and Nicosia, filling the hotels. They gave the impression of knowledge, of expecta-

tion. I planned with Larry Heinzerling and Carolyn Turolla to find a place in Switzerland for Terry and Sulome and me to go to, because it was close to Wiesbaden, Germany, where he would go first after his release. AP President Lou Boccardi was willing to send us anywhere. The plan was to have Terry's sisters and brother Jack come, as well, and stay nearby. We hoped his daughter Gabrielle would also come, though it was doubtful. She was a young lady of fifteen now who loved her father but wasn't sure that he loved her. I sent several messages through Carolyn to tell her how much Terry loved her, and how many times I saw him crying over her when he and her mother were divorcing, before he was taken.

I tried to tell her how painful it had been for him, and how concerned he was for her. I hoped Gabrielle would come to see her half-sister. Sulome knew about Gabrielle and was telling everyone about her, how she lived in Japan and they had never met but looked alike. Maybe our wish to meet Terry's other daughter would come true at last.

35

MADELEINE

LARNACA, CYPRUS. JUNE 1990.

*There was a series of goodwill gestures from both sides, the
United States and Iran, throughout the first half of 1990,
but no sign of releases. The climax came when America offered to send humanitarian aid to Iran after the big earthquake in the Caspian Sea region. More than a hundred
villages and towns were destroyed, thirty-five thousand people died, and over four hundred thousand were left home-
less.*

*On June 7, Sulome's fifth birthday, we made another tape
for the Lebanese TV stations. For her birthday party, I
asked all the guests to bring no presents, but to give a do-
nation to a charity, or put it in an envelope that I would
give to our pastor to help in the many charities he worked
with in Lebanon. Fighting in and around Beirut had esca-
lated since Gen. Michel Aoun took over from Amin
Gemayel, whose term as president had run out. There were
thousands of refugees from Lebanon in Cyprus already.*

*While we waited for someone to take the money to Leb-
anon, the earthquake occurred in Iran. I contacted an Iranian woman whose daughter went to ballet class with
Sulome to ask if there was anything I could do. With her
help, I sent the money to Iran, instead of Lebanon.*

*Her husband was a wealthy merchant who had left Iran
early in the revolution and settled in Cyprus. He still had
contacts in Iran, including the president's brother,
Mahmoud Rafsanjani. I asked if he could find out anything*

about Terry's condition. About a month later, he called to say hurriedly, "The people in Beirut have decided to let Terry Waite go tonight. I don't know what is happening, but I think it is the beginning of the end for everybody." He hung up abruptly.

I knew if Terry Waite was coming home, my Terry would very soon follow. I went to The AP and called Larry Heinzerling. I had put him in contact with the Iranian merchant months earlier. "Larry, I just spoke to our friend here, and he said Big Terry is going out tonight." He calmly assured me he would check it out. When he called back a few hours later, he said his sources indicated something was indeed going on.

I spent the night listening to the BBC on the radio, full of hope. But nothing happened then, or the next night. I learned later from both Larry and the merchant that the kidnappers were unhappy about something in the arrangement, and changed the plan. Another hope had vanished into thin air. I put another stone in the wall I was trying to build against the pain.

The merchant was rarely available to me after that, and when he would talk to me, he had little to say. I knew as a Lebanese that he had been embarrassed when his information did not prove to be true. His ego was damaged. I stopped contacting him, knowing it would be useless.

NICOSIA, CYPRUS. JUNE 1990.

Heinzerling had become obsessed with the campaign to free Anderson ever since he had been assigned to it full-time by The AP. His travels never seemed to cease, and when he did make it home, he took the obsession with him, brooding over the latest development, weighing the most recent "signal" from Tehran or the latest statement by Hezbollah. And he was not the only one. Anderson's plight intruded on everything, touching children, spouses, even former spouses and acquaintances and their families.

His wife, Sig, had to bear the obsession, as well, and ended up adopting the cause as her own. The two spent hours on their back porch in Princeton, New Jersey, trying to unravel the mysteries of diplomacy and the Middle East.

Heinzerling had become an expert, devouring shelves full of books on the region, on Shiites, terrorism, Lebanon, Syria, and so on during the hourlong train rides to and from work. He would leave for Washington or Bonn, Geneva or Jerusalem, Tehran or Damascus on almost no notice.

On a sticky July night in 1990, he found himself in Nicosia, Cyprus, en route from Jerusalem to Damascus. He was making a brief stop to update Anderson's fiancée, Madeleine, on his so-far fruitless efforts. The AP bureau chief, Nick Ludington, and his wife, Cass, already the closest of Madeleine's friends, invited him to an office party for another staffer. Madeleine was routinely invited to such affairs, but almost never came. This time she did, a visibly lonely and depressed woman.

An hour into the party, Heinzerling looked around for her, but couldn't find her. Cass pointed to the front door. There, alone on the steps, sat Madeleine playing with a cat. He sat beside her.

"What are you doing out here by yourself?"

"Oh, I just wanted some time alone," she said gently. "It's okay."

The scene somehow summed up the entire tragedy for Heinzerling. The lovely young woman could not enjoy a party because it would be a betrayal of Terry. But sitting alone at home with Sulome and the demons of despair would bring on deeper depression. So she had come, but remained alone in a tortured compromise for a tortured soul. Madeleine, like Terry, was caught up in suspended time. He had no choices; she had many, and they were all difficult. Whose experience was worse?

Madeleine was obviously so deeply in love, but surely inwardly terrified by the uncertainty. What would follow so many years of rage, separation, and pain, the lonely experience of raising a child without a father for so long? What would emerge from Lebanon when the hostages were finally released? How could she survive, wondering each day, Does Terry still love me? How would she cope with a possibly psychologically broken man, a stranger?

He could only admire the balance and devotion she exhibited. She was an extremely private person and expressed her sorrows mostly to close friends like Cass. Heinzerling had once asked her how she would feel about making a public plea to the kidnappers for Terry's release. "I would not give them the pleasure of seeing my face," she snapped.

"I guess it's impossible to enjoy yourself with so many people here to remind you of Terry," Heinzerling said to her as they sat on the steps. He touched her arm gently. "It's going to be okay."

"Do you really believe it?" she asked.

"Yes," he said firmly, though he knew the solution was still not in sight. Then he rose and left her with the cat, the sound of crickets in the July night, and the pain etched on her face.

36

Once again, we seem to have been swallowed up by greater events. For two months, absolutely nothing has happened. Each day has been exactly the same—wake up, eat whatever the guards bring (invariably a sandwich and a cup of bad tea); toilet run; listen to the radio and read whatever's handy; usual lunch of garbage and rice; read and talk; turn on the television in the afternoon for whatever senseless American or French show Lebanese TV may be carrying; supper, and the return of the eternal sandwich; TV and reading; lights out and a night of dozing and dreaming and praying. Our mood swings have been less violent simply because there's been nothing to swing on.

Now the Middle East has gone into another convulsion with the invasion of Kuwait by Iraq, and the U.S. leading a *jihad* against Saddam Hussein. As usual, our analysis focuses almost wholly on what this will mean for us.

There's one bit of good news that has leaked out almost unnoticed in the general avalanche: the seventeen Shia radicals held in Kuwaiti jails have disappeared, apparently freed during the invasion. If Hussein has them, it's likely he'll turn them over to Iran just to try to keep on the Iranians' good side; if he doesn't, then they were probably sent straight back to Iran by the Kuwaitis. The news reports are vague, but there's no suggestion that the Kuwaitis simply took them out and shot them. The few reports all definitely say they've been freed, but their whereabouts are unknown.

Unfortunately, I have to conclude that whatever was going on toward our release before this war is very likely to be put on hold. None of the parties that would have to be involved—the U.S. government, the Iranian government, maybe the UN—will have any time for such a minor issue for the next few months.

A couple of Swiss men, International Red Cross workers, were freed yesterday. But they were apparently taken and held in southern Lebanon, and have nothing to do with us.

Brian's gone home! And we're back with John. No warning, no indication that something was going to happen. The guards just came in, ordered us to stand up, taped our arms and around our eyes, then dumped us in a car trunk for a ten-minute ride, apparently just a few blocks.

When we were unwrapped in our new abode, another apartment in the southern suburbs of Beirut, John was sitting against the wall, bearded and grinning with relief.

It seems Brian and he had been together, along with Frank Reed, for more than a year. Suddenly, Reed was taken out nearly four months ago; then two days ago, they came for Brian. John said that when Brian realized he was being freed, he actually fought with the guards, shouting he would not go without John.

John said he was frightened at being left alone again, afraid he couldn't take it.

They've had absolutely no news. No radio, no TV, nothing. He was amazed when we asked the guards for our radio, and they brought it in immediately! Many, many reports on Brian. We even heard his incredibly powerful and emotional statement at his press conference, and his tribute to John.*

---

* "Hostage is a crucifying aloneness," Brian told the hushed group of journalists at his news conference. "There's a silent, screaming slide into the

We spent the first couple of days together listening to the news about Brian, and bringing John up to date on the Iraqi invasion of Kuwait and dozens of other things we've heard over the past year. Once again, the roller coaster is on the rise. We're all almost euphoric, convinced that something is really happening, that we might actually be free soon. Not tomorrow, but not next year, either.

The apartment is the same one I was kept in with Fontaine, and again later. The blood mark from beating my head on the wall is still there, a little faded but obvious.

John says Reed was in very bad shape when they were put together with him, and didn't get much better. He had been abused badly, and was being treated with contempt by the guards until John and Brian protested. They said he had gone off his head—believed he had a radio in his head and could talk with the U.S. embassy in East Beirut.

John also said there was another prisoner in the apartment, in the next room, and both he and Brian believed it was Terry Waite. They had communicated sporadically and vaguely with knocks on the wall, but couldn't really exchange any information. Both he and Brian were chained on the opposite side of the room from the wall between the two rooms, and could tap on it only during exercise periods. But the door was always open then, with guards outside, and it was too dangerous to continue.

Sent John into gales of laughter when we demanded our

bowels of ultimate despair. Hostage is a man hanging by his fingernails over the edge of chaos and feeling his fingers slowly straightening.

"Hostage is the humiliating stripping away of every sense and fiber of body and mind and spirit that make you what you are. Hostage is a mutant creation, full of self-loathing, guilt, and death-wishing. But he's a man, a rare, unique, and beautiful creation of which these things are no part."

Brian appealed to the press to be restrained in their coverage. "All of us are but teeth on a comb, and if one of us is snapped off in a sudden rage it cannot, cannot be put back."

Of John he said: "My soulmate and cellmate: John Boy, I called him. How can I put across his abundant love of life, which so many times seemed to menace almost to extinction those grinding moments of hopelessness which we all faced?"

bicycle. Just a couple of weeks ago, the guards in the other apartment brought in a stationary exercise cycle and allowed us to use it for a few minutes occasionally. "A bicycle!" he shouted. "Do you know Brian has been telling them for years he wanted a bicycle, and you actually got one! Fucking Americans."

"Yeah," I told him. "Next week we get a grand piano."

There isn't any explanation for why we have been allowed to have a radio and TV, and books. These three, held by the same people only a few blocks away, have had nothing. Only thing we can figure out is that we kept asking, kept insisting, while after a while they gave up.

The routine has improved here again. The food is getting better, with more fruit and fresh vegetables and meat, and the guards are more accommodating. We even get half an hour each off the chain after the morning toilet run to exercise. Tom and I are amazingly fat after nearly eighteen months without even standing up more than ten minutes a day. Have to work it all off.

It's great to have John with us again, and incredible how he's kept his sense of humor and cheerful nature. Like suddenly walking outside and into a fresh breeze.

MADELEINE

NICOSIA, CYPRUS. AUGUST 1990.

Cyprus is a quiet place, especially in August, when everyone leaves for summer vacation. But the city was startled and shaken by Iraq's invasion of Kuwait. The press once again converged on the island, the closest reasonable capital outside the war zone.

In the midst of the war, reports came that a hostage was to be released from Lebanon. Everyone thought it a little strange, but understandable from the viewpoint that Iran wanted to make some propaganda points while Iraq, once a Western ally, was looking bad.

Brian Keenan was released on August 24. It was very encouraging when he reported that he had been with Terry and Tom Sutherland less than a year ago, and was with John McCarthy up until the day of his release. It was the first news of Terry for two years.

I flew with Sulome to England, met with Larry there, and we all went on to Dublin. We telephoned Brian, and in a whispering voice, he said he would very much like to meet me, and that he had a message from Terry. They had all arranged messages for the loved ones in case anyone went home. Brian sounded affectionate and warm.

He met me at the small airport at Galway, on the west coast of Ireland, where he was staying in a friend's cottage. The first thing that struck me was that his eyes were red and he had difficulty looking straight at anything. He told me he had not seen strong light since the day he was kidnapped. His voice was still a whisper, and his hands were shaking. We sat and talked for hours. I was shocked at his condition, a result of so many years in the hands of merciless thugs.

Brian had a lot of stories about Terry to tell me. How he was maintaining himself, what kept him going. First, he relieved me of any doubt that Terry might be angry at all Lebanese, and might not want me. "Terry loves you so much, you will never know," he said.

He told me about the places they had been held in, sometimes in conditions not fit for animals. I could have stayed forever listening to him talk, feeling close to Terry, imagining the conditions he was still in. When the day ended, I felt as if I were leaving my heart with Brian.

I didn't realize what the meeting was doing to Sulome until much later, when she seemed very nervous and began behaving badly. At the hotel, while Larry and I were discussing the meeting, she began acting strangely, and I had to leave the table and take her upstairs. In the bedroom, she started asking me about Brian.

"Is Mr. Keenan sick, Mummy?" she asked.

"No, he isn't," I said. "Why are you asking that?"

"I think he is very sick," she answered. "He is shaking all the time, and he has no voice."

Before I could say anything, she continued. "Is Daddy very sick, Mummy?" Her eyes were wide, and there were tears in them. I suddenly saw what she had been going through as I talked to Brian. I didn't know what to say. I didn't think Terry was in such bad shape, but I had no real idea how he would be when he was freed. I held her tight, and we both started crying.

"I am afraid, Mummy," Sulome said. "When is Daddy coming home? Will I ever see him?"

It was hard to hide my emotions and fears from her.

"If Daddy comes home sick and shaking like Mr. Keenan, we will have to help him get better, and give him lots of love, because Mr. Keenan said Daddy misses us a lot and is always thinking of us," I told her.

I think the magic words were "help him." Sulome began telling me how she would read for him, because she is a good reader and Daddy will be proud of her. And she will make him tea every day, and take him out for walks and hold his hand. Her ideas went on for a long time. Still, we were depressed for many weeks.

Terry was forty-three years old on October 27, 1990—his sixth birthday in captivity. Again Sulome and I went into the mountains, to the same tree and carved another date on it, wondering if we would be back next year. The Iraqi invasion had taken up all the interest of the world, especially the United States, with hundreds of foreigners held by the Iraqi regime and many others in hiding in Iraq and Kuwait. The issue of the Lebanon hostages was dead again.

Still hoping this would be our last Christmas without Terry, I decided to take Sulome to Lebanon to spend Christmas with my family. This was her first trip to Lebanon, a chance to meet the rest of her family and see the country that was once the most beautiful I knew. It was also my first time back since Terry was kidnapped in 1985.

Peace seemed to be blooming in Lebanon, especially Beirut. I had not known how much I missed it until my sister and her husband and three children met us at the airport. It looked gloomy and smaller than when I had seen it last, but more peaceful, at least on the surface. I saw the Lebanese soldiers seemingly in control, but also noticed the Syrian officers standing nearby.

We drove immediately into the mountains above Beirut, where I had planned to stay. On the way, we passed through the southern slums, where the hostages were believed to be held. Signs carried slogans: "Death to America" and "The Struggle against Satan America Starts Here."

"We will pass by a place in the next street where you will see young men standing around," my brother-in-law, a former police lieutenant, told me as we drove through the slum of Hay El-sellum. "It is known to be a place where they kept some of the hostages. We don't know which ones, or if Terry was among them."

The half dozen young men standing outside the two-story cement-block building, pocked with bullet holes, were chatting and laughing innocently.

"Don't look directly at them, Madeleine," my brother-in-law cautioned. "They are very suspicious, and their guns are just inside the door. If there are hostages there now, there will be dozens of these men inside the building."

My heart was pounding with fear, and with the thought that Terry, or some other poor man, might be in there. There was nothing we or anyone else could do.

"You will find many people who will tell you they know where the hostages are, but nobody will take the chance of getting himself or someone else killed," my brother-in-law continued.

That Christmas, I wrote a letter to Terry trying to tell him how close we were to him, and yet so far from him.

37

September 5, 1990. My two thousandth day.

I've established contact with Terry Waite. He is next door, as John and Brian thought. I began by tapping on the wall and, when he tapped back, painstakingly tapped out the series 1-2-3-4 . . . to 26. Then, using numbers for the alphabet (1 = *a*, 2 = *b*, and so on), I tapped out our names. It took a while, but he caught on. I spent all one night tapping out a summary of all the news: Brian's release; Frank's release; the comments and promises of Iran, Syria, and others on hostages over the past year. Then the world news: the Berlin Wall's falling, communism's demise in eastern Europe, free elections in the Soviet Union, work toward a multiracial government in South Africa. All the incredible things that have happened since he was taken nearly three years ago. He thought I was crazy.

He's been in isolation all that time, without even a scrap of news. I knew he was brave, risking his life for us. But he must also be an incredibly tough man. Sounds sane and rational. When I apologized for dragging him into this with the letters we sent so long ago, there was no bitterness in his gracious reply.

It takes an agonizingly long time to exchange any message, what with stops and starts, misspellings and miscountings. My knuckles are already scraped raw from the concrete wall. But he obviously needs this contact so badly, I can't stop. I have had to tell him not to knock so loudly, and not to do it when the apartment is very quiet, late at night. The sound carries through the walls, and God only knows what they'll do if they catch us.

Asked guards about Waite again today, or at least about "the other hostage in the apartment." Got short shrift, and lies. "He is a bad man, a Lebanese," Abu Ali told me. It was the second time, and he ended by saying, "Do not ask about this again." Guess that's that. Waite has been asking why we have a radio and he doesn't. Suggested he just ask for one, and keep asking until he gets it.

My knees have swollen like footballs. Apparently pushing the exercise too much. I run back and forth across the room almost constantly during my half hour off the chain. Then I do some sit-ups and use the dozen volumes of the *Encyclopedia Americana* we have as weights, doing sets of presses and curls. It's awkward, but it serves the purpose. I'm appallingly weak, but at least I'm losing some of the gut.

Tom spends all night every night with the radio on his ear, listening to the news. Don't know how he can stand it. An hour or two is all I can take. Funny. I used to be the news junkie. Now, most of it doesn't seem to mean much. Once I get the main report, I lose interest.

Tom told me while John was in the bathroom that he had heard John's mother had died some time ago. Didn't know whether to tell him or not. I advised him to do so. "It's his right to know. I would want to know something like that." When John returned, Tom tried to tell him, but stumbled and hesitated so much that I finally broke in to say it gently as I could, but directly.

Of course, John took it well, but it was obviously a great blow. He was very quiet all day, trying to absorb it.

John has never talked much about himself, or those close to him. But we've begun talking a bit more, especially late at night when we both smoke the last cigarette we've been saving all day, and Tom is dozing or listening to the radio.

I was surprised to discover John's diffidence is not just politeness, but a reflection of the fairly low esteem he has for himself. Thinks he wasted his university career and doesn't have a deep mind. I've always found him intelligent and knowledgeable, as well as extremely civilized. Are all the jokes, the ready wit, partially defensive?

He doesn't say much about his fiancée, Jill, though we've all heard several times of the incredible campaign she's waging on his behalf. Perhaps too painful. I know I have difficulty talking about Madeleine, or even thinking about her too much.

There have been good reports on the outside: Israel's proxy militia, the South Lebanese Army, released forty of the Lebanese they've been holding in Khiam prison on the Prophet Mohammed's birthday, October 1, "to encourage the release of Western hostages in Lebanon." Part of a deal? No way to tell. A Beirut paper also quoted diplomatic sources as saying Iran and Syria have agreed on a plan to gain our release. And another one says the remaining three British hostages, Waite, McCarthy, and Jackie Mann, will be released soon. On the other hand (there's always another hand), there are reports saying that Syria is holding up the release of the Brits until Britain agrees to restore diplomatic relations.

So many of these reports, and so many turn out to be false. But enough have been true to make us greet each one with hope. More endless analysis by all three of us, until we're all too tired of it to think of any more scenarios.

At least part of Lebanon's seemingly unending civil war is over. The Syrians have stormed the presidential palace, killing 750 of General Aoun's followers. Aoun's days as acting prime minister of a rump government are over, and he's hiding in the French embassy. All the bombast, and he fled at the first push. The now totally legitimized President Elias Hrawi says nearly all the various militia groups in the country have agreed to withdraw from the capital and eventually be disarmed. Once again, it all sounds good. But so many past failures make it hard for anyone to believe in anything.

Had a chance to learn personally whether my advice to Tom about breaking bad news quickly was right. When I woke up this morning, he told me quietly but straight—both Dad and Rich are dead. At least, I'm sure it's Rich. The radio report said only that my father and brother had died during my captivity. It has to be Rich.

I had tried not to think about Dad too much. I hadn't seen or heard anything about him since that first tape four years ago, and I knew that with his emphysema and other problems, he was unlikely to have lasted this long. But Rich. I feared for him, but couldn't think about it. He was so fat on that tape, and has had cancer all his life, since he was sixteen. I guess it was his heart. Wouldn't give up smoking or eating and drinking too much.

There isn't any deep grief in my heart. Just sadness. It's as if it happened so long ago, and I'd already done the mourning, even though I just heard about it.

I can't imagine what the remainder of our family is like, what the relationships are, what kind of wholeness there is. We had a structure, each in a place. With Mom gone more than a dozen years, there were Dad and Rich and Peg, seemingly permanent, like a tripod. Feuding and fighting and always in crisis, but there. Bruce was written off long ago. He's been gone so long, in and out of jail, on the carnival trail, wherever. Not really a part. Strange how when he divorced Penny, he left and we kept her in the family. Still very much our sister. Jack and Judy, the twins, were too young for me to really know. And the various wives, husbands, grandkids—must be nearly twenty of them now.

Not an original marriage left among the six of us. All on second or third mates. Why? For all their fighting, Mom and Dad never divorced. Dad loved her too much, I guess.

We're a strange family. What they would probably call dysfunctional now. Always fighting. But with so strong a sense of family. I haven't really been a part of it, either.

Left when I was seventeen, and just kept moving. The Marines, Japan, Vietnam. Iowa, college, Detroit. Louisville. New York. Japan again, and South Africa, and finally Beirut. Brief visits. Rarely a letter—we're all lousy correspondents, except Peg.

At least I got to know Dad, when he came to Japan, then Beirut. Nearly got him killed there, during the fighting. But I did finally know him as an adult, and liked him. He was a good man, charming and friendly. Weak in some ways, but not completely. There had to be strength and stubbornness to keep working so hard, for so long, to keep us fed and clothed. Six kids in a poor family doesn't make for an easy life.

But Rich. It's wrong, incomplete. He was always my big brother, always there when I had to get out of the house, always just down the road, with a home full of books and tolerance. Argumentative, stubborn. Interested in everything, passionate about all sorts of injustice and stupidity.

Once again, I have to retreat into prayer. Find acceptance, comfort. It will be there, I know. It always is.

> You always were a stubborn,
> independent cuss, determined
> to do exactly as you chose.
> I'm surprised, and disappointed,
> though, that you agreed
> to go before we met again.
> Our father's death I more
> or less expected. Worn out
> by work, his great, arthritic hands
> and lungs three-quarters filled
> with dust gave him little peace.
> Stubborner than you,
> he would not give up
> until he got his promised span.
> But I think he must
> have gone quite readily.
> He saw us all become adults,

watched our children grow,
even held another generation.
He was pleased with what he'd done.
His life was hard, but somehow whole.
You had so many miles to go,
so many battles left.
All our life I watched you
don your rusty armor,
hoist a battered shield
and break a lance with anyone
who offered, for principle,
or pride, or just for fun.
You were an eager veteran of
a thousand battles lost,
and as many won. Even that
most dreaded horseman,
whose very name is Fear,
could not defeat you.
Some thought you argumentative,
and they were right.
You'd debate the wind,
and use each shift
to prove your point.
They couldn't see
it was the joy of using
all you'd learned from
ten thousand books, and life;
the pleasure of a self-taught man,
no harm intended, no grudges held.
It was your pride and stubbornness
that killed you, like so many heroes;
and indulgence. Too many cigarettes,
good food, alcohol, and independence.
You never would accept
the wisdom of the crowd,
even when the crowd was right.
I wonder if, at the end,
you still maintained

your pleasures had been
worth the time they cost you?
Probably. I can't see you cowed,
repentant, even at the Throne.
"So you do exist," you likely said.
"That's good. I wanted to speak
with someone about the way
that things are run down there."
I know He laughed, and certainly forgave.
He'd see all that compassion,
and love of justice
that fueled your indignation.
I wish you'd waited
just a little, though.
He has eternity to embrace you.
I had so short a while,
and needed more.

Now what? We've all been packed up and hauled back to the Bekaa Valley! Another terrible move, with us taped up like mummies and transported in the hidden compartments under trucks, the "coffins." This time, there was a guard in the compartment with me, and his AK-47 kept digging into my side. I became ill at one point, and was struggling with the tape over my mouth, trying to rub it off against the top of the compartment. At first, the guard tried to stop me, but then realized I couldn't breathe and ripped the tape partly off. When they finally pulled me out and stood me up to unwrap me, I just fell over on my back. Couldn't move for about ten minutes. God, I hope this was the last time.

We're now in an unfinished half-basement of what seems to be a villa. John, Tom, and I are chained to the wall in a kind of hallway, three in a row. Waite is in the next room.

No word on what all this means. Just another move, or a staging point for release? Are things moving forward or backward? No mention of any hostage news on the radio. What the hell is going on?

* * *

Finally met Terry Waite. He was allowed to talk with us for
about fifteen minutes today. Very emotional. The man has
been held in total isolation for nearly four years! We've
whispered to him in the next room several times since we
moved here a little over a week ago—even got caught
twice, but the guards didn't seem outraged. Just told us to
stop.

I heard the Hajj's voice in the hallway this morning, and
told Mahmouds to ask him to come speak with us. He did,
and assured us things were going very well. "Our friends
are home," he said, confirming the vague news reports that
the Shiite prisoners in Kuwait were set free when Iraq invaded.

"*Mabrouk,*" I said. Congratulations. "Now can we go
home?"

"Soon," he said. But he was vague about what remained
to be done. New demands? New problems? Anyway, that's
one obstacle out of the way.

"Look, Hajj," I said at the end. "We know that's Terry
Waite next door. He knows we're here. You know that we
know. We know that you know that we know. The whole
world knows. Why don't you let the poor man come in
here with us?"

He laughed, and patted my hand. Then he gave some orders in Arabic, and a few minutes later, they brought Waite
in.

They sat him down on Tom's bed, then allowed us to
talk quietly. When I touched his arm, he was trembling. We
hugged each other, then Tom and John did the same. He's
so big! Six feet seven inches. But skinny. He's not well.
We've heard him coughing and gasping for breath for hours
in the next room. Asthma, apparently. He says it was
brought on by the insect spray they used in the last place.
Also emotional strain, I think. God knows, what he's gone
through is enough to strain even the strongest constitution.
It's a wonder any of us are healthy.

They've given him some medicine—several kinds of

pills. But it doesn't seem to help much. The best thing they can do is let him go. But that doesn't seem likely in the near future. I didn't like the Hajj's evasiveness. If the seventeen are really free and home, what more is it they want? There've been some reports linking Sheikh Obeid, the Shiite cleric the Israels kidnapped, to us. That would be a tough one, because the Israelis aren't going to let him go unless they get their own missing soldiers back.

Lord, don't let it get complicated again. Eight weeks till Christmas—my sixth in here.

They've moved us all upstairs, into a bedroom of this villa. It's fixed up just like all the other prisons we've been in: steel plates over the windows, door handle removed and covered with a small piece of steel, and—most important—heavy steel staples sunk into the concrete-block walls. Terry Waite is with us. The four of us are lined up along one wall of the room on mattresses, with a chain around the ankle fastened to the staple. At least, they gave us a choice this time—ankle or wrist. We're all pros by now—we know that the ankle is better, if the chain is long enough to allow you to sit with your back to the wall. These are, just.

We've got a small black-and-white TV and now two radios. TW (his new nickname, to distinguish the two Terrys) brought the small one they finally gave him in the last place. Nothing much on the TV. We can't get the Beirut channels, which occasionally carry English news clips from CNN, or French ones from Antenne 2. Two of the channels here are run by Shiites, one by the Iranian Revolutionary guards, and one by the Christians in Zahle, just down the road. All are in Arabic, with only the occasional bad American movies.

We are obviously in Baalbek—all the channels carry it on their logos. Our best guess is we're somewhere near the Sheikh Abdullah barracks—the old Lebanese army barracks the Rev guards took over when they arrived here in 1982.

The conditions aren't bad—they've given us two plastic chess sets and a couple of decks of cards, so we play chess and bridge all the time. I've taught John how to play chess, and he's picked it up amazingly quickly. His mind seems peculiarly suited to the game, and we enjoy it. Tom and TW have also learned, but both are still beginners. Tom taught us three bridge, although he couldn't recall any of the more sophisticated bidding systems, so we use a very simple one. TW is nearly hopeless—no card sense at all. But at least he makes a fourth, and we switch partners every day.

Books are a disappointment. We got a few—every one by Barbara Cartland! Even I can't read them, and I'll read anything. We keep asking, but no luck and no explanation why. Tom and I got boxes of books for eighteen months— probably five or six hundred—in Beirut. Now nothing. The guards promise magazines "soon, and very soon."

Our biggest problem is TW. He's very sick. Spends hours, usually late at night, gasping and wheezing until it seems he'll collapse. The medicine doesn't do much good. None of us know very much about asthma. The only thing I can recall is that emotional or psychological stress often brings on an attack. We've got plenty of both. I think TW gets into that cycle where his breathing becomes difficult, he gets scared and starts hyperventilating, the stress makes it worse, and on and on.

I usually end up sitting up with him, talking to him until three or four o'clock, trying to keep him calm—almost hypnotizing him. "Breathe slowly, TW. Don't hyperventilate. Slowly and deeply. Slowly and deeply. Calm." For hours, until the attack passes. He's becoming enormously dependent on me, and it scares me, because I have no idea if I'm doing anything right. I even gave him my rosary and helped him use it, hoping the soothing effect of repetitive, formulaic prayers would calm him. He's desperate.

The sad thing is the attacks and the strain are affecting the relationships among us. Tom and John, and to some extent I, find it extremely wearing to listen to the loud gasps and whistling wheezes for hours. We're sympathetic. We know he's sick. Nonetheless, it is a strain. We're not all that stable psychologically ourselves, after all these years. Tom especially tends to take it as a personal, almost deliberate affront, to turn it into a grievance. He doesn't like TW, anyway—which is surprising, since for the first few days he took to him enormously, and would talk to him for hours. Don't know what made him turn. We're all peculiar, anyway, I think. Surprise, surprise.

TW conducts church services every Sunday, now. Even that posed a bit of a problem. He's not a clergyman, but a lay preacher. We appreciate the services, but after a while of listening to him, we tried to gently tell him we would like to pass leadership of the services around. He still leads, but we each take turns choosing verses and themes, except for Tom. He maintains he's an agnostic now, and while he takes part in the services, he won't lead. Somehow, though, the services don't have the spirit they once did. I doubt if they will last very long.

I still pray the rosary at night. Neither John nor I sleep very well. Late at night, there are periods of such sadness, even despair. November 22, 1990. 2,077 days. Five and a half years. How can I believe it's ever going to end, despite the rumors we've been hearing all year? Dear God.

A quiet Christmas. We're all fighting hard to maintain an even keel through the incredible mix of optimistic and pessimistic signs we hear on the radio. Our hosts' promises that we would all be home by the end of the year, despite their confirmation by Iranian President Rafsanjani, are obviously not going to be kept. At the same time, it's equally obvious that a great deal of activity is going on, and some progress is being made toward our release.

38

Giandomenico Picco thought he had it all set up. After more than a year of meticulous work involving repeated trips to Tehran, Geneva, Washington, and elsewhere, all the parties had agreed it was time to end the hostage problem.

The UN diplomat had not been involved in the last few hostage releases: Keenan, Reed, and Polhill. Those had been negotiated one by one—Keenan by the Irish, the others by the Swiss government with the help of the International Red Cross. While the details were still not known, each apparently involved winning some concession from Israel, such as the release of some Shiites from Khiam prison in southern Lebanon, run by Israel's proxy militia, the South Lebanese Army. But these one-offs got more and more difficult each time.

Having other people working on the same problem he was made it more complicated. But Picco was interested only in a complete solution, one that would lead to all the hostages' being released within a relatively brief period. It was a complicated deal—in fact, more an assemblage of understandings than a deal. To be truthful, the understandings were almost totally between Picco and the Iranians right up until the end, when the diplomat had to bring in the United States and Israel to iron out the last details.

To put it plainly, Picco was winging it. He had a plan, and he thought he understood what everyone wanted and what they would absolutely have to have. But he was telling the Iranians, and through them the kidnappers, that he had agreement from Israel and the United States on things he hadn't even asked them about just yet.

"When you do these things, you are like a vicious circle," Picco said in an interview in 1993. "One side says, 'I agree if they agree,' and the other says 'I agree if they agree.' So what do you do?"

Apparently, act as if you've got an agreement that you haven't.

"I had the belief that I knew what they wanted. And I also knew, you see, there is a moment in the making of this agreement when you have got to say more than you have got, because otherwise you cannot make another person say more than they want to say." Picco smiled. "You tell me, 'I give you the agreement that the highway is fine as far as the right side of the pavement is concerned [if] you can tell me that it's fine on the left side.' I say, 'Fine.' At that point, I can go to the left side, which in fact has not told me yes, and say I have an agreement there is a right side of the road."

So far, Picco has been able to offer the Iranians and their protégés a considerable amount in the field of public relations—or, more pertinently, "face." Still the discreet diplomat, he would not say in the 1993 interview what exactly he had promised. But it certainly involved a UN finding that Iraq was primarily to blame for the incredibly bloody Iran-Iraq war. That was important to Tehran both for reasons of principle and because it held out the hope, however faint, of eventual reparations.

That report by Pérez de Cuéllar was issued on December 10, 1991, formally blaming Iraq for starting the war by attacking Iran.

Pérez de Cuéllar, ever ready to help his assistant, also agreed to travel to Tehran to discuss war damage and the fulfillment of UN resolutions concerning it. While the question of the billions of dollars of Iranian money Washington had impounded was not directly or overtly involved, it didn't hurt that those negotiations, conducted at The Hague, were proceeding smoothly, and several large payments were made to Iran during the period of Picco's negotiations.

That left mainly the problem of satisfying the Lebanese kidnappers themselves. Subject to Iranian influence and funded by Iranian money, they were by no means Iranian puppets. In fact, there had been a breach growing between Hezbollah and Tehran for some time. The seventeen fundamentalists who had been jailed in Kuwait in 1984, and whose release was demanded by Islamic Jihad—the faction holding Anderson, Sutherland, and several others—were already home. They had been freed when their Kuwaiti jailers opened the prison doors on August 2, 1990, the day Iraq invaded Kuwait. Nonetheless, other factions demanded some sort of satisfaction before an overall agreement to release all the hostages had been concluded.

Picco was confident the Israelis would go along with the idea of releasing Lebanese prisoners from the prison at Khiam, and would probably even agree to let go some prisoners from Israel itself. They would, of course, have to receive something concerning their own soldiers who were missing or being held in Lebanon. That also could be arranged.

Then came the first major hitch.

Picco was in Beirut, meeting with an "intermediary" to discuss, he thought, details of what had already been agreed in principle. But his interlocutor suddenly told him, "There are problems. We need some time."

"When you start hearing that in Beirut, it's bad news. I didn't like it," Picco said later. "Things were unraveling. . . . I really made the decision that I have to play everything I've got. And the only thing I've got is me."

The diplomat demanded an immediate meeting directly with the kidnappers. The intermediary agreed to do his best.

As Picco waited at the apartment he was using in Beirut, the folly of his proposal struck him. "I really began to think, my God, what have you said? I thought I had overplayed my hand. But I was also convinced that there was no other choice. Things were going very badly. Even badly physically in Beirut [where heavy fighting had started again]."

Picco didn't even tell his boss, Pérez de Cuéllar, what he was going to do, because he knew the secretary-general would forbid him. Within hours, he had his answer—the meeting was on. Following instructions, Picco left his apartment and walked down a Beirut street. A car pulled up beside him, the door opened, and he got in. He was immediately blindfolded.

The trip took some time, driving seemingly at random through the streets of the city. Picco thought of his teenage son, and of Terry Waite, who had also counted on the immunity of a negotiator.

When they finally arrived at their destination, after having changed cars, Picco was gently helped out and into another apartment. He was searched, but politely. When he was finally allowed to sit down, he guessed there were perhaps a dozen people there with him.

"Mr. Picco, why should we trust you?" one of the unseen men asked him abruptly.

"There is a very good reason," Picco answered quietly. "I have made a great act of faith coming to see you, totally alone. This was not a political calculation. The only thing in this situation that works is the reasoning of two people, two men, human beings. I put my life in your hands to come here and talk to you. If you have half the guts I have shown, the least you can do is trust me. I don't ask you to put your life in my hands. I ask much less. That is why you should trust me."

With the challenge out of the way, the discussion continued. It quickly became apparent that the "problems" were simply a lack of resolve or ability on the part of the kidnappers to end the hostage problem. There seemed to be a disagreement among the factions or subgroups involved.

"I tried to explain to them that by not going ahead, there would be more difficulties, not less," Picco recalled. He knew he had to get the problem settled immediately—or, at the very least, get them to agree to another meeting within hours to continue the discussion. He could not allow the process he had set up so carefully to bog down.

The first meeting lasted several hours. A second was set for the next right. Picco was scared but determined. And his pushing worked. "At the second meeting, I met a hostage," he said. He would not say which one, and none of the hostages has publicly revealed such a meeting. "I think what I told him helped him," was Picco's only comment. More important, he won agreement from the kidnappers to go ahead with the plan. All the hostages would be out by the end of 1991, they promised, if all went well. Then it was time to begin settling the details. How many prisoners from Khiam for how many hostages and exactly what information about the missing Israelis? Who would move first? What was the schedule?

First, Picco went to the Americans. He wanted Washington to be "in the loop," even if the U.S. government wouldn't agree to take part in the deal itself. He asked the Bush administration to provide an "introduction" to the Israelis—really, an endorsement of what he was doing. He got it. Then he added Tel Aviv to his shuttle schedule, already frenetic. There would be more meetings in Lebanon with the kidnappers, always frightening. By now, Picco was not afraid of being harmed by the men he was talking to. But he knew there were others in the radical fundamentalist assemblage called Hezbollah that did not want him succeeding, and would try to stop him.

"It was an absorbing affair because I'm alone," Picco said later. "I have to do everything myself. I have to do the planning, I have to do the discussions. As we discuss, I have to take my own notes, I have to take notes on what they say. I have to take care of my own security, to make my own plans. To this day, some of my notes are still untyped because I didn't have time to do it then."

Picco was growing ever more confident that it could be pulled off. But as always, the devil would be in the details.

39

I've finally managed to get the guards to understand that Terry Waite needs something more for his asthma. They kept saying their doctor told them asthma is not fatal, but his severe attacks finally scared them, and one night, they took him out and to a doctor down the road in Baalbek. Must have been one of their own. TW said they took him into some kind of clinic, where the doctor examined him and gave the guards some prescriptions for pills. They brought him back early the next morning. Unfortunately, the new pills haven't helped that much. He still has attacks, and is growing exhausted. The other night, he passed out briefly in the middle of one attack. I think he's near collapse.

It's frightening to guess when I have so little knowledge, but finally I suggested they get more of the same medicine he's taking, except in an inhaler rather than as pills. Dad used one for his severe emphysema, and it worked very well. After I kept insisting, they got one, and it was almost like magic. The asthma attacks immediately became less frequent and less severe.

Now, though, with TW more active and alert, tension in the room has increased. Tom's dislike for Terry has deepened into outright antagonism. We've tried to have a couple of "encounter sessions," to talk quietly and calmly about the problem, but they haven't worked very well. Terry cannot seem to understand that there are things he does that

369

drive the rest of us crazy, especially Tom, whose mattress is right next to him, just inches away. TW is not very observant, or very good at reading moods. Often, each of us just wants to be alone and undisturbed with our thoughts. Maybe read one of the magazines the guards bring in every couple of weeks. Tom and John and I have learned to read those signs in each other, and heed them. TW wants to talk all the time, no matter what we want.

When he does engage in conversation, he has the large man's habit of moving in close, until he looms over you. I tried the other day to ask him not to do that, to tell him that it is disconcerting and disturbing. In here, we've grown jealous of our personal space, and even outside, I don't like people that close to me. He just couldn't understand.

Tom poses a bigger problem for me. We've grown close over the years, and know each other very well. But that makes it harder, rather than easier, for me to tell him when he's being a jerk. He can't seem to accept the idea that in this place, in these circumstances, we can't afford to display our anger with each other. We have to get along. He's blown up at TW a couple of times, and refuses to speak to him at all. That's silly—four men in a room twenty-four hours a day, and one won't speak to another!

I know things I do also bother them. I still, despite so many efforts to change, dominate conversations too often. I also know TW often feels excluded. Tom and John and I have been together for a long time. We've learned each others' peculiarities. TW is the new boy, moving into this three-way relationship. And, frankly, none of us has that much reserve energy left to make new adjustments.

Thankfully, we have more to do now besides talk. While we can't seem to get books, for some reason the guards bring in a stack of magazines every two weeks: *Time, Newsweek, Business Week,* even *Fortune.* Best of all, *The Economist* of London, probably the best weekly published anywhere. Tom and I spend hours trying to figure out the principles of the markets the magazine talks about so confidently—bonds, stocks, foreign exchange, and so forth.

Even the weekly lessons in "basic" economics it carries are sophisticated and difficult, which makes trying to understand them fun.

We play both chess and bridge a lot. TW still has very little card sense. He's never played such games. I've taken him on as a permanent partner simply because it's impossible for Tom and him to play together.

Chess has been very good for Terry, and he's gotten quite enthusiastic. When he first joined us, after more than three years in solitary confinement, his mind was almost like a butterfly. He couldn't hold a thought for more than one or two sentences, skipping on to something else. The mental discipline of chess has helped him to concentrate.

Surprisingly, the quiet and diffident John immediately grasped the game, learned the basics, most of the main openings, and moved within months to begin to feel the elegance and beauty of tactics and strategy that I love. He's now within a pawn of my level—I'm an average but enthusiastic club player. We play so closely that we can manage only two games in a day. If we try a third, we both begin to get tired and sloppy. It uses up hours and refreshes our minds.

I've grown to like John very much in these past months. He has acted with dignity and integrity through all this, and kept his brilliant sense of humor. He has been a great help to all of us. I can't understand his diffidence, though. He seems to think of himself as an intellectual lightweight. In fact, he has an excellent mind, and one peculiarly suited to chess. I've never seen anyone absorb the game so quickly.

We've also got the radios to listen to, and we do so constantly. TW spends hours with one balanced on his ear as he lies on his mattress. The guards make no objection to the speed with which we use up batteries, and always supply new ones when they're needed.

In fact, the attitude of our guards has changed dramatically. They make an effort to be friendly most of the time, and even try to bring us the food we ask for. We still have occasional clashes, but they are very restrained when they get upset. The violent outbursts are completely gone. One of them said to me the other day after one such argument, "I have been told I cannot get angry at you." Obviously, the chiefs have warned them against giving us a hard time.

Well, that sure was a short war. Our guards seem kind of stunned by the display the United States put on in Kuwait. They had maintained for the past few months that it would be very bloody, with thousands of Americans killed. They despise the Iraqis. But Arab pride and wishful thinking made them sure Saddam Hussein would fight well.

It's going to take some time for things to settle down. But we're all very hopeful that with the war over so quickly, whatever negotiations were going on to free us will resume.

TW had his fifth anniversary in captivity the other day, January 20, 1990. There was a great deal about him on the BBC, especially on the *Outlook* program. One of the three cohosts of *Outlook* happens to be his cousin, John Waite.

TW was especially affected by a church service he listened to that was dedicated to him. John, Tom, and I also have heard reports of activities held by our families and friends.

The analyses and summaries about the hostage problem that have been carried in association with TW's anniversary all seem to be relatively optimistic. The Lebanese and Syrian governments have both made strong promises of action.

It even looks as if Syria and Britain are going to exchange ambassadors, four years after relations were broken off because of accusations Syria was involved in an attempt to put a bomb on an El Al plane at Heathrow. That's got to be good for John. We all believe that Syria cannot order our release, but is capable of disrupting negotiations if it wishes to.

Up and down, up and down. The roller coaster rolls on. First, Israel released twelve Arabs from its prisons, including three leaders of Hezbollah. No mention of an exchange, but the Israelis don't generally give something for nothing.

Then, Hezbollah chief Subhi Tewfali announced that the group "will not help" in ending the hostage crisis. Since everyone more or less knows Hezbollah is Islamic Jihad, what is that supposed to mean?

Then there were reports of quiet messages from Washington to Tehran that the United States wanted to reopen some sort of talks with Iran, and Secretary of State James Baker discussed the hostage problem on a visit to Damascus.

Once again, all kinds of contradictory noises and no way to interpret them. We talk among ourselves about each new "development," dissect it, construct scenarios, and in the end know nothing. But we still feel something is going to happen soon. Please.

March 16, 1991. My sixth anniversary. No message from Sulome and Madeleine on the television, probably because we're in the Bekaa and the Shiite stations just didn't carry it. They did have some brief news clips mentioning my name, but nothing in English.

Peg was on the radio saying she was "very optimistic" that we would all be released. She made the same analysis a lot of others have: Syria and Iran have both changed their attitude, and conditions in the Middle East have changed with the Gulf War. Hope she's right.

The weather is getting much warmer. Even though Terry Waite's asthma is easing considerably, the guards came in the other day and knocked a hole high up in the wall to install an air conditioner. Guess they want to make sure he stays alive. They certainly aren't short of money. One of the guards said it cost two thousand American dollars.

Lots of comments in the news about us—Bush, Rafsanjani, Hussein Mussawi of Islamic Amal and Hezbollah, others. Seems to boil down to: Bush is offering only "enormous goodwill" if Iran gets us out. Iran and Mussawi say that's not enough, that the United States should get Israel to release Sheikh Obeid and the other Lebanese it holds. The makings of a deal? Problem is, the Israelis still have soldiers missing in Lebanon, at least one believed still alive and in the hands of Hezbollah. Surely they'll want them? Everybody in the Middle East wants his price.

We're just trying to coast along, still. I spend much of my time trying to keep Tom calmed down. He has really built up a head of steam against TW. John and I agree we don't need this right now. The strain is already too much.

Tom's sixtieth birthday—May 2, 1991. Wonderful message for him from his wife, Jean, that really set him up. Also heard one of his daughters on the radio. Jean has stayed in Beirut for the past six years, teaching at the American University.

As usual, though, Tom's thoughts quickly turned to his age. He feels strongly that he won't be able to get a job when he does get out. "Nobody wants a sixty-year-old," he keeps saying. I can't convince him differently, though I keep trying.

More good news on the radio—I think. The Iranians have said definitely they'll help with the hostages, but there are more and more stories saying they don't have control anymore, that there's been a rift between them and Hezbollah. Don't know if it's true, or just a way to allow them to back away from responsibility.

The deal seems to be falling into place. Hezbollah is saying it's willing to swap Israel's missing soldiers for the Lebanese held in Khiam prison and Sheikh Obeid. The Israelis have made it plain they will go along eagerly. There have even been stories saying there's a new leader of Hezbollah, Abbas Mussawi, replacing our former host, Subhi Tewfali. The stories all say Mussawi is more pro-Iranian than Tewfali was, and more willing to go along with what Iran wants. And that seems to be an end to the hostage problem, which is keeping it from improving economic relations with other countries.

There have been lots of fits and stumbles, with other radical leaders and even one of the groups claiming to hold hostages denying there will be any deal. But it seems very likely that it's going to end in the not too distant future. Maybe this time, they'll make the end-of-the-year deadline they announced.

We spend a good deal more of our time talking about our futures now. What we'd like to do when we get out, where we'll go for a vacation. The Caribbean, Hawaii, California. It seems so unreal, and still feels dangerous to give full rein to optimism. Something can still go wrong. It has so many times before.

Tom still wants to go back to the American University in Beirut. He even talks about trying to become president. He certainly has the ability, and I've stopped trying to make him understand that no one is ever going to let him stay in Beirut.

John thinks he'd like to try writing, maybe as a print journalist, instead of the television he's been doing. TW doesn't seem sure what he would like to do. We all agree a long vacation is our first priority.

I still have no idea if my divorce has been completed or not. I suspect not, that my kidnapping halted the procedure completely. If so, I'll have to get that straightened out. Then marry Madeleine, if she'll still have me. As for work, I don't know. I could certainly stay with The AP, go overseas again, maybe to Moscow, which would be interesting. I don't think I'd want to be a bureau chief in the United States. Too much selling and traveling, and not enough news.

More and more, though, I think about what I'd do other than journalism. Write a couple of books maybe, about the Middle East, or the PLO. Maybe a biography of Arafat, if someone hasn't done one. Tom thinks I should go into politics. He says with my skill at debating and intelligence, I'd do well. Maybe. Can't pretend it's not an attractive idea. I even seriously considered it years ago, when I was working in Iowa for a TV station there, but decided to stay in journalism. If I did try politics, the way I've screwed up my personal life would probably hurt. People, or at least journalists, seem so tied up in politicians' private lives these days—at least their sex lives. It's the old Calvinist equation—morality equals sex. It's a fair question to ask only of those who pretend to be better than others, like evangelists, or politicians who think they have the right to regulate the sex lives of other people. Well, like a lot of others, I've done some things I'm ashamed of, and some things others might criticize. I've also paid for them, and learned from them. I told Father Martin once, "I think I've paid by now for all the sins I ever committed, with enough left over for maybe a peccadillo or two to come."

We've had a visit from a couple of new chiefs, with "Trust Me" Ali tagging along. Both of the new guys spoke fair English. They said again that the negotiations are going well, and that more releases are likely sometime soon. Wouldn't say whether they would be from our little group, or what exactly the negotiations involve. Seems things have focused on Sheikh Obeid and the other Lebanese held by the Israelis. They implied, though, that their people might be willing to give some information to Israel about the missing Israeli soldiers. It seems so optimistic now that it's hard to keep from getting too hopeful again. None of us wants to get on that roller coaster again.

There was a report on the radio that one American and one Briton would be released very soon. That, of course, set off all kinds of speculation among us on combinations. TW and me? John and Tom? John and me? Then there are the others, held apart from us, allegedly by other groups: the Beirut University College professors, and Jackie Mann. Any number of combinations are possible. But for sure, something is going on.

* * *

John's gone home. There was no ceremony and no notice. The guards just came in and told John to stand up, then unlocked his chains and took him out. I had time only for a quick "Good luck, John."

Within hours, we were watching him on television. Even the local Shiite stations in the Bekaa Valley carried the live CNN coverage. He looked so incredibly cheerful and young stepping out the door of the military airplane in Britain, smiling and waving. The radio, of course, has been full of the celebration in Britain. The news that he's carrying a message for UN Secretary-General Pérez de Cuéllar has been greeted with enthusiasm and hope that an end is in sight for all the hostages. I hope they're right. I believe they're right. I told Tom, "This has to be part of the ritual dance. They've already made a deal. This has all been agreed to beforehand." I sounded a great deal more confident than I felt.

MADELEINE

NICOSIA, CYPRUS. AUGUST 1991.

We stayed in Lebanon a week, over Christmas, and I took Sulome to the AP office. I wanted her to see where her father had worked, and the people he worked with, to help her see him as a real man and not just a phantom.

We then went back to Cyprus and resumed our lives, no different from the years before. There were a few sicknesses and some false hopes. Mostly, I just kept trying to believe that this was the work not of God, but perhaps of another power, an evil power.

As always, Larry Heinzerling kept in close contact, and for the first time began telling me that his contacts were giving him hope that things were moving. I had been skeptical when I first heard in 1990 that a UN official was taking up the negotiations for the hostages as a "humanita-

rian" matter. I thought how little humanity my people had shown themselves to have. But Larry gave me encouraging reports of UN Assistant Secretary-General Giandomenico Picco's work.

It was about then that we learned the fifteen "Dawa" prisoners—those jailed in Kuwait, whose freedom Islamic Jihad had always demanded as the price for releasing Terry and the others—had been let out of jail when Iraq invaded Kuwait in August 1990. Apparently, their Kuwaiti jailers had released them. "Dawa" (The Call) was originally formed in opposition to the regime of Iraqi President Saddam Hussein. Two of the original seventeen had already served their prison sentences and been released by the Kuwaitis.

Some of the freed prisoners were reported to have fled to Iran, while others returned to Beirut.* The reports were very encouraging, because they meant a greater possibility that some of the hostages, including Terry and Tom Sutherland, might be released.

When Iraq freed all the Americans it had held hostage for a time at the beginning of the Gulf War, it was a big victory for America. But it meant both joy and pain for me. More hostages freed, just like the Reverend Ben Weir, Father Martin Jenco, David Jacobsen, the French captives. All rejoining their families while Terry was still in his cell. I knew by now he would be the last to come home.

I had been happy for each captive freed and restored to a normal life. But each release also knocked me from the emotional equilibrium I had worked so hard to achieve over the years. It always took a big effort to get back to that balance.

By the middle of 1991, there were so many stories about possible pending deals and releases that it was impossible

---

* Among those who returned to Lebanon was Imad Mugniyeh's brother-in-law, Mustapha Badreddine, who immediately took over the hostage operation from Mugniyeh. He chaired the next meeting with Giandomenico Picco.

to keep track of them. Some involved the Western hostages and Shiites held in prison in southern Lebanon by the Israelis, others brought in Israeli soldiers captured or missing in the fighting in Lebanon. Many mentioned Sheikh Abdul-Karim Obeid, the Shiite clergyman kidnapped by the Israelis in 1989. The Hamadi brothers, two Lebanese convicted of hijacking in Germany and sentenced to prison terms there, were connected to the Western hostages by some reports.

Despite the flood of reports, Sulome's sixth birthday came and went on June 7, 1991, with our most important wish still ungranted.

But on August 6, Islamic Jihad issued a statement, accompanied by Terry's picture, as so many of their earlier statements had been. They said they were sending a "special envoy" to UN Secretary-General Javier Pérez de Cuéllar, in a bid to end the hostage affair. Many of us thought that the envoy might be Terry.

It was not. Two days later, John McCarthy was released after five years as a hostage. I watched his arrival in England, when he stepped out of the airplane looking healthy, full of life, and calm. It was the first real indication that maybe the hostage affair was really, finally coming to an end.

A few days later, John called from the hospital where he stayed for the first few days of his freedom. "If you think I look well, you should see how Terry looks," he told me. "He looks ten times better than me. He has even put some weight on lately." He laughed and added, "He is trying to lose it before he comes home."

As he spoke, tears were running down my face. Listening to John talk of Terry, make jokes about him as if he were sitting next to him, I could not control them. Sulome was sitting next to me as I talked on the telephone and without understanding began crying, as well. I gave her the phone, and John told her, "Do you know your daddy has your picture hanging over his bed, and it is his best companion when he is away from you and your mummy?"

Her face went red, and she didn't know what to say. She looked at me happily and told me what John had said. They talked for over fifteen minutes, with John asking her questions and she giving him an account of her two cats, their colors and how playful and naughty they were.

When I took the phone back, John's voice was choked up. "This is the first child I have spoken with for over five years," he said. After talking for what seemed forever, we arranged to meet in England a week later.

We flew from Cyprus to London, then met Larry Heinzerling and took a car to a secret location to meet John. The limousine driver turned out to be a member of a private security team hired by the World Television News, John's employers, to protect his privacy.

As we drove, I began recalling the past six and a half years, and all the things that had happened. I knew that with John's release, the end was near. I remembered Terry Waite's telling me on the phone, just before his last trip to Lebanon in 1987, "When the British hostages are freed, your Terry and the other Americans will be freed immediately after." Waite was now the only British hostage left.

The peaceful, green countryside we were passing through seemed to encourage the memories. I thought of the many, many lonely nights, going to bed after long, tiring days when I needed someone to talk to, dreaming of Terry beside me listening to my complaints about the day with a smile, then making love with me. It is actually coming to an end. Loneliness will no longer be part of my daily routine. I won't have to do the crazy things I found myself doing, like talking to myself, crying or screaming at myself. I won't have to be both man and woman, father and mother. I looked at Sulome, grabbing Larry's attention from the driver. I didn't know how this was affecting her, if she also could feel that this was the beginning of the end, or if it was just another trip to see some man we said was Daddy's friend in captivity.

John had made a big impression on her in the telephone call, and she had ever since asked repeatedly about him.

"When are we going to see Mr. McCarthy, Mummy?" she kept saying.

I couldn't wait to get to him myself, to embrace him, and to see Terry in his eyes. As the car approached the "safe house" where John was staying, I felt my heart coming out of my chest.

The country home we were approaching appeared so peaceful, even in the pouring rain, with horses in the back, and a setting that looked like Robin Hood's woods. As the car stopped, John came walking out, ignoring the rain, a big, bright smile on his face. His father and brother followed him.

"I can't believe how well you look," John kept saying.

"I wonder how Terry described me to you," I said when we embraced. We were crying, while at the same time I had a huge grin on my face.

John took Sulome in his arms and told her about Terry's love for her, and how many times he saw him talk to her picture, and how she was his best companion in his captivity. She hugged John, then turned to me, a shy smile on her face. Like all of us, she was overwhelmed with emotion.

Inside the friendly, warm home, we talked for nearly two hours, with Larry listening and Sulome playing nearby. She kept demanding that John take her to the horse.

John told us how the hostages' treatment had improved in the last eighteen months. They had books most of the time, and the food was getting better, at least no longer garbage. John told us Terry Waite had been moved into the same room with him and Tom Sutherland and Terry a year ago. He added Terry Waite was sick with asthma and needed attention. My Terry was nursing the big man almost every night, all night, during his asthma attacks, John said.

After lunch, John and I went for a walk around the house. John told me how Terry loved me, and what Sulome and I meant to him. "He knows why you only show Sulome on the videotapes, and not yourself. He is very happy to have been able to see his daughter, as she is growing. He *agrees with every decision you make concerning the child and yourself.*

"He often told us, 'Madeleine is a very independent person and knows what she wants. She will not make hasty decisions.' "

His words made me feel strong. I knew I had made the right decision in not going public, exposing my life and Sulome's to the press to become some sort of target every time there was a story from or about the hostages.

When I asked if Terry knew I was still waiting for him, John had no answer. "We both really understood if you and Jill could not wait for us that long," he said, referring to his fiancée. Then he added with a great smile, "But you did wait, and it is wonderful."

When we asked about the psychiatric help John got on his release, he said it had helped greatly both with his family and with Jill, in starting their relationships again. He gave us the names and numbers of the psychiatrists who had worked with him.

We called them immediately, then met in Cambridge the next day with Dr. Keron Fletcher, the Royal Air Force psychiatrist who had treated the British kidnap victims.

Dr. Fletcher spent five hours with us, even bringing his father along to baby-sit with Sulome while we talked. The success of my reunion with Terry later was due in large part to the advice he gave me in those talks. Dr. Fletcher explained what steps to take to make Terry's return to the free world easier, what was important now, and what could wait. Many of the things I had been thinking he advised against, and he prevented me from making many mistakes.

Larry and I both asked AP President Lou Boccardi if he could get Dr. Fletcher and his supervisor, Dr. Ken Craig, to work with us on Terry's release. Boccardi agreed, and made the arrangements.

John had said one of his captors had told him all the hostages would be released within two months. We went home with our hopes high. I believed strongly Terry would be home by Christmas.

The weeks passed as in a dream. Sulome was trying to decide which of her friends should get her birds, her cats and tortoises, while I was giving away our plants and other things we would not need when we left Cyprus.

Although the fear of something's going wrong was always there, this time preparation was like food for my soul. I needed the time to get ready.

John had also said he and Terry and the others always listened to the radio, especially the BBC. A friend of mine, BBC correspondent Keith Graves, told me some of the other families were using the network to send messages to their hostage relatives. I knew now if I did the same, Terry would certainly hear it. He had said in a videotape released just after John went home that he had gotten Sulome's message that Jim Muir of the BBC had broadcast just a little while before. For the first time, I spoke on the radio myself, along with my daughter, in an interview Keith did for the BBC's *Outlook* program.

On November 16, 1991, Larry Heinzerling called from the States to tell me that Tom Sutherland and Terry Waite were about to be released. "Your Terry will be the last one [freed], but it won't be very long before he's home," he said.

Two days later, both men were released, carrying a message that Terry would be freed in five days. The joy that engulfed our house cannot be described. My mother, a woman in her early seventies, was dancing like a teenage girl with tears in her eyes. My aunt and my sister, who were also staying with me, could not sleep that night. But I slept as I never had before.

I can't explain my feelings. I can say only that the days that followed were days of extreme happiness and a mountain of joy. For Sulome, the dream was finally becoming a reality. "Am I really going to see my daddy?" she asked. "What will he do when he sees me?"

On November 20, Tom Sutherland called from Wiesbaden, the U.S. military base in Germany where the hostages *were taken after their release. He sounded so happy, and I felt very close to him, knowing he was the one who had spent the most time with Terry. Tom carried eleven poems and a letter from Terry. He told me many stories, and said how happy I had made Terry with the message on the BBC.*

"You cannot imagine how happy that message made Terry feel," he said. "You have a special man in Terry, and he loves you now as much as he loved you before." Tom again reassured me that "although Terry would have always liked to hear your voice or see your face on TV with Sulome, he at the same time understands and respects the fact that you chose not to." When Tom repeated almost the same words as John McCarthy had told me, I knew that somewhere in the long silence, I had put doubts in Terry's mind that I was waiting for him. But Tom Sutherland insisted that Terry was not hurt, especially not now, after the message.

Tom sent Terry's letter and the poems by mail, and I received them three days later. To me, the poems were the result of seven years of meditation, of Terry's Thousand and One Nights looking into himself. Digging deeper and deeper, unable to keep his mind from searching within even when he wanted to.

The letter, my first real, direct contact with Terry for years, was short but said everything. I saw in it a confident man, one who had crossed from heaven to hell and come back with knowledge and control. I also saw love in a man who was taken for years from every humane thing and yet kept love in his heart. I couldn't wait to see him, to feel a part of this wonderful man.

BEIRUT. AUGUST 8–9, 1991.

McCarthy's release had finally come off, just as Picco had planned it. It was the beginning of the end, the launching of the carefully worked out dance that involved the release of all the hostages and the release of hundreds of Israeli prisoners, and perhaps something on the missing Israeli soldiers, as well. Picco wasn't sure about that. In fact, he hadn't even worked out with the Israelis the formula of how-many-for-what.

"By the time John McCarthy comes out with the letter in that airplane, I still don't know if the Israelis are on board," Picco would recount later. "I'm [still] on my own. At that point, I'm flying so low that if somebody says, 'You have no plane,' I'm dead."

But he remained confident—until a French medical worker was kidnapped in Beirut a day after McCarthy's release. The anonymous kidnappers threatened to kill him if any more American hostages were freed. The unexpected move threw those Picco was negotiating with, and him, into a panic.

"They were absolutely unprepared to continue," Picco said. He demanded yet another meeting, immediately. The drill was the same—the anonymous men in a car, the blindfold, the complicated route.

Amazingly, although the Syrian Army had launched an intensive search throughout the Lebanese capital and its suburbs for the Frenchman, Picco's escort passed through the many checkpoints unhindered, "like a hot knife through butter."

By now, the fundamentalists are more comfortable with the Italian, and remove the blindfold when he arrives. He can see just the man sitting in front of him, not the dozen or so standing behind him.

The meeting is stormy and very long. "I feel in my bones the danger of things falling apart, or at the best being postponed to such an extent that I would lose the excitement, the momentum that is generated by McCarthy's letter, by the secretary-general going to Tehran, all this big affair [that Picco had stage-managed].

"I know at this moment, while I sit with them, it may just evaporate in thin air."

The Islamic Jihad official told Picco that they had not kidnapped the Frenchman. "You want us to give you another hostage?" he asked. "You want the Frenchman killed?"

Picco was not going to let it happen. He ignored his interlocutors' flat refusal to continue the releases. He demanded. He shouted. He insisted, over and over.

"Well, this is where the big boys come in," Picco recalled telling them. "You are the big boys. You have to do both things. You have to make sure that nothing happens to the French guy, and you've got to release another hostage."

"What if something goes wrong?" Picco was asked.

"I can't foresee that," he replied immediately. "Because if something goes wrong, then you and I are out of business. It's finished. End of story.

"If you stop it [the release process], it means you can't deliver. If you can't deliver ... whatever happens to me, you will have no others [to negotiate with] in the future. It's finished for you. For me, maybe, because you decide. But it's finished for you. You've lost your credibility."

The discussions and arguments went on for five hours. "It was tense, very tense. There was utter confusion" among the Lebanese fundamentalists in the room.

Picco finally clinched it when he said, "Whoever has taken the Frenchman is challenging you. Not only is he challenging, but he's winning if you don't release the next hostage. So, you want to lose, or you want to win? Who is in charge here?"

Edward Tracy was released on Saturday, August 11. The Frenchman was released by his unknown kidnappers at the same time.

BAALBEK, LEBANON. AUGUST 1991.

John has left an enormous hole in our little society. It's only now that I realize how much I'd come to depend on him, and to enjoy our chess games and the quiet talks we had late at night. I'm afraid I've withdrawn a bit from the other two. I can't seem to muster much energy for listening to

Tom's complaints about TW. I read the magazines and listen to the radio a lot, especially during the night.

We watched John arrive at Lyneham Air Force Base in England, clutching the envelope containing the message our captors gave him. He met UN Secretary-General Pérez de Cuéllar briefly and gave him the envelope. One of the news reports said he had refused to let go of it at all until then.

He looked very good on the TV. Still young and very confident. As though the past five years have hardly affected him. I wonder what his reunion with Jill was like. Restrained, English? John is very English, and Jill seems to be. Or full of passion? I know he loves her very much, though he never talked a great deal about her. She's quite beautiful. What will it be like when I hold Maddy again? Will I hold her? How has she changed in these years? It has been so hard on her, I know. Has she moved on in her life? Found someone? The few messages I've gotten seem full of love. But she wouldn't want to hurt me in these circumstances. I just have to believe our love has been strong enough to hold her. But we had so little time together, and that was so long ago.

It's obvious now there's an overall deal in place, and everyone is now just playing out the script. But it's not obvious it will succeed. So many things can go wrong, and there's no way to know if all the seemingly contradictory statements everybody is issuing are part of the script or attempts to mess up the whole thing.

They've had me make another videotape, and this one is pretty encouraging. I was free to say pretty much what I wanted to, and tried to reassure everyone that we're okay. I was able to say that our captors had told us there would be "good news" soon, but not to be specific. Actually, all we know is that they're saying the whole hostage issue is being wrapped up. I guess someone will be going home soon, but we don't know who. We speculate endlessly on the possibilities. TW thinks he'll be last. I still think it will be me.

* * *

Madeleine has finally broken her long silence, and gone on the BBC's *Outlook* program with the most beautiful message I could imagine. All those doubts and fears evaporated as I listened to her husky, warm voice tell me how much she loved me, how she and Sulome were waiting for my release, so we could all begin again.

"Terry, I'm amazed. You have given us great hope today about your health, the way you look, your expectations for the future, and the way you are. You have maintained the Terry that I know, that Sulome [knows], the image of you in Sulome's head and heart. You have been always in our hearts. There's never one day that we didn't talk to you, whether in prayers or alone. . . .

"I love you, Terry. I always did. I'll always love you. And I'm looking forward to a brighter future where we can pick up where we left behind. I miss you, and we are out here waiting."

Seven years, and she has never wavered, has never given up. A weight, a fear that I had always refused to think about, could not think about, is gone.

I'm writing poetry! That definitely deserves an exclamation mark. I never thought I was that imaginative. I spent another long white night the other night, just letting my mind drift, thinking nothing in particular. I remembered staring out the window of one of my classes in high school, so long ago, daydreaming about all the things I would do, while the teacher droned away in the front of the room. I spent a lot of time in school being somewhere else in my head. Then I thought about how much I did the same thing in here, over the years. Just going somewhere else, trying to make what was happening to me become unreal. I remembered some of the places I'd gone mentally: Vietnam and Japan and the war and the bar girls on R&R; back to Iowa, and skydiving; Japan and the many Buddhist temples in the little village of Kitakamakura; South Africa; and, of course, Lebanon, and the summer days on the beach with

Madeleine. Suddenly, it began to come together in a poem: "I'm not here most days."

I fiddled with the lines here and there, and the scansion. I recited it silently half a dozen or more times, getting more and more excited. It seemed to be good! I had to get another opinion, so I woke Tom up at dawn. "Tom. I wrote a poem."

"Hunhh?" Not exactly an enthusiastic response.

"Listen, I've never written a poem in my life. Not even 'Roses Are Red' stuff in school. But I think this one is pretty good."

When he sat up, I recited it to him. That woke TW, so I recited it again. They both seemed to think it was pretty good.

The next night, I wrote another. Then two more during the following day and night. Now I've got eleven of them. It's very strange. I thought I knew myself very well after this last six and a half years. Lord knows, I've spent plenty of time exploring the nooks and crannies of my mind. I know my strengths and weaknesses. But these poems surprise me, make me see that there are things in my mind I still haven't discovered.

Some of the poems are about what's happened to me in here. Others are about religion. A couple about journalism. It's as if all the time I spent poking around in my head this past six and a half years has suddenly crystallized; all my experiences, the things I've come to believe over the years, have been boiled down and now are coming out in their purest expression.

I don't know if these things would rate highly as poetry. I've always loved poetry, and read a great deal of it. Some of the things I'm composing are close to formal poetry. Others seem too loose. They're almost like miniessays, compressed meditations. I don't know. All I can say is they express very strongly what I feel.

I think I'll try a long poem, a ten- or twelve-part composition to sum up my experience in here. I've already thought of a title: "Stigmata." The reference to Jesus, the echoes of Paul, the allusion to scars that I know will never fade—that, in fact, should be borne proudly—it feels right.

I'm alone, as I began. It's very much a relief, instead of the incredible shock and strain it was nearly seven years ago.

The two new chiefs came in late in the afternoon to announce that Tom and TW were to be released. They added that I would be going home within days—five days, one of them said. The hostage problem is over.

They were in a fair hurry, and told Tom and TW that they had only twenty minutes or so to get ready. I asked them for three favors: that they take off my chains, since if I was going home in days, they weren't necessary; that they allow me to write a letter for Tom and TW to carry to Madeleine and my family; and that, since the Germans were still being held, they be brought to me, or I to them, so that we could spend the remaining days of our captivity together.

"It is very difficult for someone to go from solitary confinement back to the real world," I told them. "I hear from the radio that the Germans are being kept alone. They need to prepare for their release also. And I would not like to be alone."

The first request was granted as soon as I asked. Mahmoud and Khalil, two of the guards who have been with us for a long time, immediately unlocked my chains, then for good measure went out and got a large wrench, which they used to remove the bolts that had been sunk in the concrete walls of our room.

They also agreed to let me write a letter, and gave me a pen and some paper. "You must hurry," they said. "We are leaving soon."

The third request they could not grant, they said. They did not hold the Germans and had no influence over those who did. Surprisingly, they explained that a Lebanese Shiite clan called the Hamadi family held the two men, and were being very stubborn about trying to get two Hamadis out of jail in Germany. They sounded quite annoyed at the Hamadis, as if they were messing up the program.

I quickly wrote a two-page note to Maddy and my family, then set about copying out my poems. I just wanted them on paper in case something goes wrong. Especially the one for Maddy. I embraced both Tom and TW, and they were gone.

The place is quiet now. I have the two small radios, and heard the two of them in Damascus, and all the news reports of their release. Giandomenico Picco is getting the credit for negotiating their release. There's a great deal of speculation about when I might come out.

My guards are quite friendly now, and disturb me very little. I spend the day listening to the radio and exercising. I've taken the two plastic jugs that Tom and TW used for urine bottles, filled them with water, and use them for dumbbells. I jog around the room for thirty or forty-five minutes at a time, and do a lot of push-ups and sit-ups. And I think about what it will be like when I go free.

I haven't come to any decisions about what I want to do. I know that whatever it is, we will have to decide together—Madeleine and I. And we'll have to consider Sulome, as well.

I told Tom I want Madeleine to be there, with Sulome, when I go to Damascus. I'd like my older daughter, Gabrielle, to come, as well, if she will. I know it would be difficult for her, and don't really expect it. But I will never exclude her from anything in the future. I also asked if Robert Fisk, my best friend, would be able to come. He will be the best one to tell me all that's happened over the years, to bring me up to date.

It is very strange planning all this, after so long. I still have a strong reluctance to allow myself to be caught up in the expectation of a quick release. What happens if something goes wrong? How would I withstand disappointment this time? But everything seems to be so certain. It will probably take more time than they said it would. My hosts have never been very good at keeping to schedules. Two or three or four weeks is more likely than the few days they promised.

I'm still composing poetry. I go over all the things I've thought about during these years: my job, my family, my religion. And this imprisonment. Certain things, certain themes seem to jump out at me. I remember, for instance, that brief glimpse of my little sister, Judy, sitting in a church pew. Her face was serious, and I could see so clearly in those seconds the family traits that she had never shown.

JUDY

You were a clearer image of our mother once,
though slighter, spritelier—an almost-elf.
Now our father's stamp is showing through;
this legacy he sometimes carried poorly,
but passed so strong to all our milling crew.
It was always in you—we all have it;
some, like me, with jagged edges, others
smoother, more acceptable—a kind of charm,
a ready tongue, intelligence, covering
a steely, springy core that, battered,
sways and bends and stands up straighter
than before, less bruised than any batterer
and determined to show none.
With age, this toughness shows
its virtues and its faults:
firmness and rigidity, pride and egotism.
The charm may be smoother,
social graces better polished,
but all that is beside the point.
You show the world more clearly now
what we always knew—you're one of us.

I spent long hours in the night looking back, trying to crystallize what I thought about all the things I'd seen, the places I'd been, and what I really felt. I'd been so busy in my life, I never really took time to sum things up. My new-found faith, for instance. In dozens of conversations with Tom, I had tried to tell him what had brought me back to being a Christian. I hadn't convinced him—wasn't trying to, really. All those talks were just me groping to express myself, to myself. Now, it came together—the conviction, the questions. Half a dozen of the poems, or meditations, that came to me said virtually all I could say about it. Faith. The Prison Eucharist. Being Catholic. And the questions I still had.

About journalism, I could see now what it had done to me, and so many of my friends and colleagues. So much violence to take in as daily fare, so much of other people's pain, and nowhere to put it except in a few pages of copy, or a couple of minutes of film. No wonder I knew no more than two or three journalists still on their first marriage, and so many who were semialcoholic, or bitter and cynical, or just weird.

WHORES

We are peculiarly unchoosy whores.
We'll let ourselves be used
by anyone, deliver any message,
lie, boast, or threat;
be inspiring or wallow
in the gutter as you choose.
And through it all, we'll feel ourselves
untouched, above the fray.
Objectivity is our defense;
we're just reporters—
it isn't us who say and do
these things, it's you.
Between us, folks, of course
that's largely nonsense.
We have as many, maybe more,

opinions of the world as you.
We're outraged, bemused,
or angered by the things we see,
and in subtle ways
we let you know our views.
The best that we can do
is try to keep remembering
we're supposed to be just mirrors,
able only to produce reflections,
not reality. And even those reflect,
as much as anything, ourselves.

I know now I could never really go back to that. I couldn't stand any more violence, and I had never been interested in becoming an editor, or an administrator—the natural and inevitable progress for most reporters. It was only pride and ambition and the taste for power that brought me as far as becoming an AP bureau chief.

The days passed quickly. Five days, maybe a week, the two new chiefs had said. I never expected them to keep to that schedule—timing was never a major virtue of the hamsters. After the first week, I occasionally had the terrible thought that something had gone wrong, but Mahmoud and the other guards, in brief conversations, always assured me that everything was "good, and very good." "No problem, you go soon, and very soon." And there was so much on the radio about the end of the hostage problem, and my release.

Joe Cicippio is out. It took a little longer than the five days they had promised, but at least it's moving again. Israel is also back in the game, releasing twenty-five of the prisoners from Khiam. That leaves only Jesse Turner and me—and, of course, the two Germans, who my hosts keep saying are not part of this deal. Poor sods. I wonder what will happen to them.

And then there was one. Steen's gone. Just one day between Cicippio's release and his. I thought it would take longer, and was quite prepared for another couple of weeks in here. Now I don't know. Maybe it really will be "soon, and very soon."

MADELEINE

NICOSIA, CYPRUS. DECEMBER 1, 1991.

Early on Sunday morning, the phone rang again. It was Nick Ludington, AP bureau chief in Cyprus. Nick, like his wife, Cass, was a friend who for years had helped keep my mind straight with his honesty and knowledge of the Middle East, not to mention his big heart and the love for children he always showered on Sulome.

"Do you have your little bag ready to go, Madeleine?" Nick asked. The words I had waited for so long. I needed to wake up first; I wasn't sure it was not a dream. "Is Terry coming home?" were the only words I found to say.

"I don't know if it is today," he said. "But we must leave for Damascus today, and Larry [Heinzerling] will meet us there. He called me at three this morning on his way to a plane to Damascus."

As Nick told me he and Cass were getting ready, I found myself mumbling to him, not making any sense even to myself. An enormous feeling of unreality came over me, and I just stood there for what felt forever after Nick hung up, holding the telephone in my hand, afraid I might wake up from the dream if I put it down.

I ran to Sulome's room and held her in my arms while she was still asleep. The need to be with my daughter at that moment was all I felt.

Then, as I was packing the last few items before leaving, Terry Waite called from England for the first time since his release. We could talk only for a few minutes.

In Damascus, we all moved into a small hotel, trying to avoid the places journalists usually stayed. Cass and I went to the crowded soukh *(market)* to pick up a few things, and I remembered going there as a young teenager with my family. We used to visit relatives in Damascus. It was just as I remembered it, except there seemed to be more women than there had been twenty-five years ago.

It was difficult to sleep that night. Sulome prayed that her daddy would quickly be released, and asked to make sure he knew he must take her to the circus as soon as possible.

In the morning, Larry Heinzerling arrived to explain what was happening. He didn't know how long we would have to wait, but was taking all the necessary steps, such as getting the papers needed at the U.S. embassy for Sulome and me and himself to get on the military plane that would take Terry from here to Wiesbaden.

We were told that even the U.S. representatives waiting to receive Terry from the Syrians as soon as he was released didn't know what was happening and, like us; were waiting impatiently for news.

On Monday, we stayed at the hotel, waiting for a word or a phone call. The press had received the word that Terry was coming out, and newspeople were converging on Damascus. They were looking everywhere for us. I was still not ready to meet or talk to anybody, so we remained at the hotel all day.

It was, by coincidence, the day President Hafez el-Assad was being reelected president of Syria. Syrians crowded the streets holding giant "YES" signs, signaling their approval of the ritual vote. State-run restaurants were serving free meals all day, and hundreds of people waited in line for them. I watched it all from the hotel room window, even counting heads in the crowd below, just to keep my mind occupied.

Sulome, with little to play with, kept asking the same questions: "How long are we going to stay in the hotel, Mummy? When is Daddy coming home?" I was running out of patience, explaining it all to her for the tenth time. The wait was exhausting my spirit and my nerves.

There was still no word by Tuesday evening. Sulome for the first time began asking about our house on Cyprus and her friends. She wanted to know if we were ever going back, and wanted to see her animals. "We have been here for days, Mummy. Why isn't Daddy here yet?" As I put her to bed, crying and nervous, her uncertainty made me feel lost and doubtful, as well. What if they decided not to let him go? What shall we do after coming so far, physically and emotionally, tearing up our routine and our stability. Sulome and I were both so exhausted emotionally, we were crying together like two little girls lost in the wind.

At ten A.M. Wednesday, Nick came in to say that the Iranian News Agency had just announced that Terry had been freed and was on his way to Damascus. A bomb of emotions burst in me. Nick took me in his arms, saying "Mabrouk." Congratulations. "It's finally over." Larry and Cassandra did the same.

All I can remember is that I had a smile painted on my face for the longest time, but my feelings were in a place I could not reach. It was like watching a movie, which you hear and see, but are not a part of.

I asked Nick if The AP wanted some pictures, and he sent for a photographer. Then we found out that some press people had located us, so Larry called the U.S. embassy, and they sent a car to take us to the house of the deputy chief of mission, the ambassador's deputy. We would wait there for word of Terry's whereabouts.

That was definitely the longest day I have ever experienced—something that's easy to say but very difficult to live through. After just a couple of hours, I started feeling the urge to get out, to flee back to Cyprus and crawl back in my shell. Still no news of Terry.

The waiting and the strange surroundings were also a great strain for Sulome, who was on the verge of a tantrum. And Larry was chain-smoking, burning one cigarette after another. I had quit smoking when I first got pregnant, but right then, I could have smoked anything.

The worst part was thinking about Terry, about what he might be doing just then. I wondered if they would tell him in advance he was to be released, and what he would be thinking. What if they changed their minds for one reason or another? The thought of him getting ready to leave, then being told he wasn't going haunted me.

The ambassador, Christopher Ross, arrived about four P.M. He said he had no news so far, and no idea what was going on. He was still sure Terry would be released that day, but didn't know the reason for the delay. He was also going to wait with us.

We all waited in the Craigs' house until midnight, when the phone rang for Ross. He told us before leaving, "When I call you to get ready, a car will come and take you to my house."

Sulome had long since gone to sleep. I got her out of bed, and the call came half an hour later.

Those moments in the car on the way to the ambassador's house, the ending of almost seven years of broken hearts, misery, deprivation, were the most meaningful and happiest moments of my entire life. My body was in the car, but my soul was floating out in the night, trying to push time forward. I was numb, clinging to Sulome, who remained asleep. I felt God's blessing on us.

BAALBEK, LEBANON. DECEMBER 4, 1991.

The 2,454th day, and the last. The two new subchiefs came in this morning to say that I would be going home tonight. They talked with me awhile about various things. Strangely, they seemed mostly concerned with justifying themselves, and the last seven years. They said that their group now realized that this had all been a mistake, and they had gotten little out of it. They knew that the release last year of their brothers in Kuwait, the main goal they'd had in the beginning and for all those years, had nothing to do with the hostages they had held so long. "This tactic [kidnapping] is not useful. We will not do it again," one of them said. "We are not giving up. But we will use other means."

He did not explain what that meant, and I was not interested enough to pursue the subject.

"Trust Me" Ali was also there, and tried to start an argument about the same old subjects—the evil of the West, and how the Arabs, especially the Lebanese Shiites, had been oppressed. After a couple of minutes, I told him, "Ali, we've had this argument before. It doesn't settle anything."

One of the two subchiefs rebuked him in Arabic, and he went off to sit at the other side of the room. Then they asked me if I would make one last videotape, telling the world what they thought of the whole matter. I agreed, provided that I was allowed to say directly that this was their statement, which I was only reading and did not agree with. They had no objection. A man came in with a small video camera, and they gave me several pages, translated into English but in the usual florid Arab style. I read the statement, then added at the end, bluntly, that it was my captors' statement, not mine. But, I said, I thought it was important to hear what they had to say.

They gave me a new shirt, a pair of trousers, and some shoes, then left. I've been sitting here most of the day playing solitaire by candlelight—the electricity is out again—and listening to the radio. It's very strange—all the news reports say I've been turned over to the Syrians already, and am on my way to Damascus. They say there's a delay because of snow in the mountains between Beirut and Damascus. Of course, I'm in the Bekaa, and there's no snow.

It's been interesting, listening to the news analyses, and the recaps of the past seven years. The newscasts are full of praise for me—I don't know for what, except perhaps for surviving. It's like listening to your own obituary.

My mind is so full, spinning so fast, with so many things. Maddy— she's in Damascus, according to the radio, with Sulome. How is she feeling? What will we say to each other, after so much pain? What will I do? It is so good, with her last radio message, knowing she is waiting, and we can start again. What has it been like for her? How could she wait so long? I know the depth of my love. Hers must be so much greater, her strength so incredible.

I know the drill at Damascus. I've seen it so many times, as hostage after hostage has been released. The first ceremony at the Syrian Foreign Ministry. Thank everybody—the Syrians, the Israelis, the U.S. government, even the Iranians—ironic that, but necessary, I suppose.

I have less constraint than the others—I'm the last, except for the two Germans. I'd like to say something about the Lebanese held in Khiam prison by the Israelis, without trial, without a chance to defend themselves. But I'm not sure I should—Picco is working on that problem, and I would certainly not want to screw up any deal that my release is part of.

What do I say about my kidnappers? I have no love for them. The small kindnesses of a few guards over the years, the mostly decent treatment of the past few months, mean nothing compared to nearly seven years chained to a wall. But I don't hate them. I could, easily, but I cannot let myself. My life will begin again in a few hours. What am I going to make of it? Can I keep the faith and the determination of this time? Will I be able to keep from slipping back to the self-indulgence, the arrogance that I know I was full of then?

I am forty-four years old. I don't feel it. I still felt young when I was taken seven years ago. I feel young today. But I'm not.

All my thoughts are fleeting, drifting in and out of my mind. I can't concentrate on anything, except the cards. Game after game of solitaire, interrupted for moments as I tune one radio or the other to another newscast. Lunch comes, then dinner. Mahmoud asks me, as he brings the food: "Are you happy?"

"I'll be happy when I'm free, Mahmoud."

It's dark outside now. They always prefer to wait for

darkness to fall before making any move. The door opens. Several guards come in. I'm already dressed—I put on my new clothes two hours ago. Mahmoud says, as he has so many times, "Stand up."

No tape this time. Just the blindfold. The new subchiefs are there. One of them hands me a small bouquet. Half a dozen carnations. "Give this to your wife, and tell her we're sorry."

Someone takes my arm, guides me through the door, outside, and into a car. Another Mercedes, just like the one they forced me into so long ago. "Trust Me" Ali is in the backseat with me. He's ranting about Bush's ingratitude, his failure to mention the Khiam prisoners in his first statement about my release. I'm impatient. Shut up, man. I don't need any more of this shit.

The car stops. I'm pulled out. Someone puts his hand on my shoulder. "I'm a Syrian colonel. You're free."

MADELEINE

DAMASCUS. DECEMBER 4, 1991.

There were more than a dozen people in the hallway of the ambassador's house as we entered. They were all watching me, the look in their eyes approving. Larry took Sulome from me and put her down on a couch, still asleep and looking like an angel. Someone asked if I wanted a drink. I didn't, but said yes, anyway. My legs couldn't hold me up anymore, and I abruptly sat down on the nearest couch.

It was only a minute, but felt like forever, before the ambassador came in and said, "You can go in now, Madeleine. Terry wants to see you." I looked at him blankly, not sure he was speaking to me. He nodded and smiled at me. I tried to get up, but I couldn't. I felt glued to the seat, dozens of faces staring at me. I realized I was afraid to leave the room. I was afraid to see him. After all these years of imagining what it would be like, I was now afraid of it.

I stood up and walked in the direction the ambassador was pointing. I was looking for another room with a door, but as I turned the corner from the living room, I saw Terry standing right in front of me, his hands behind his back, looking at me and waiting. He looked just as well as when I last saw him, on that Saturday morning, March 16, 1985. His eyes were full of love. We walked into each other's arms, and in the warmth of his body, I found myself at last. His arms, as always, could wrap around my whole body. "Don't ever leave me again," I whispered, crying.

"It's over, it's over," his soft voice reassured me. Yes, it was over.

AFTERWORD

BRONXVILLE, NEW YORK.
APRIL 1993.

Madeleine and I were married on April 18, 1993, before a
few friends and family in the living room of the old home
we bought late last year.

We cannot say we have come "full circle," because we
are a long way from where and who we were when we first
planned to marry, nine years ago. Much of that distance we
traveled separately, enduring our own private trials and
pain. We had many close and dear friends to help us, and
we had the knowledge of each other's love to sustain us.
But we also had the terrible uncertainty of what those years
were doing to us, fearing that the changes we saw in ourselves, and knew were happening to the other, would somehow overwhelm that love. We were forced to look inside
ourselves, alone, to find the strength and faith we both
needed so desperately.

In the past seventeen months, we have traveled even further on our personal journey, but this time together. Again,
we had the aid of many dear friends, as well as the full support of our "family" at The Associated Press.

The AP arranged for us to fly straight from our incred-
ibly warm homecomings in New York and Washington
to the Caribbean island of Antigua. AP President Lou
Boccardi borrowed the two Royal Air Force psychiatrists
Maddy had talked to in England, Dr. Keron Fletcher and
Dr. Ken Craig. They charted for us the difficulties we faced

in renewing our life together, in knitting ourselves into a close family with our beautiful six-year-old daughter, Sulome, and in handling the pressures of being public people and the many demands of living in this so-busy world.

It has been at times difficult, but always fascinating. There has been far more joy than tears, and enormous happiness. The warmth and concern shown for us by everyone, everywhere we go, has helped greatly.

While no one chooses the kind of terrible events that engulfed us, we have much to be thankful for out of those years of testing. We know ourselves, and each other, much better than we might have. We know the depth and strength of our love. And we have a deeper, stronger faith in God.

"That which does not destroy me, makes me stronger," Nietzsche wrote. We are stronger, and our life is full of joy.

STIGMATA X

No man can ever start anew completely;
he's everything he's ever done
or said or failed to do.
Each bit is added on,
Altering the whole,
But covering, not replacing
what has gone before.
A piece of unfired clay,
he bears the marks
and scars of all his years.
Not just clay, though—
sculptor, too;
he helps to mold himself:
Object, artist, audience.
Sometimes, though, larger hands—
destiny, fate, karma, God—
take firmly hold and,
wielding fierce events,
risk fracture to hack

and carve away some
awkward, ugly bits.
The final work cannot be seen
until it's fired,
and all fires cooled.

Paul knew: suffering and pain
are the truest ways,
the only ways for some of us,
to draw out that within
which answers to
the purpose of it all.

INDEX